NEW FRONTIERS IN HIS

series editors

Mark Greengrass
Department of History, Sheffield University

John Stevenson
Worcester College, Oxford

This important series reflects the substantial expansion that has occurred in the scope of history syllabuses. As new subject areas have emerged and syllabuses have come to focus more upon methods of historical enquiry and knowledge of source materials, a growing need has arisen for correspondingly broad-ranging textbooks.

New Frontiers in History provides up-to-date overviews of key topics in British, European and world history, together with accompanying source material and appendices. Authors focus upon subjects where revisionist work is being undertaken, providing a fresh viewpoint welcomed by students and sixth-formers. The series also explores established topics which have attracted much conflicting analysis and require a synthesis of the state of the debate.

Published titles

C. J. Bartlett   Defence and diplomacy: Britain and the Great Powers, 1815–1914

Jeremy Black   The politics of Britain, 1688–1800

Paul Bookbinder   The Weimar Republic

Michael Broers   Europe after Napoleon: Revolution, reaction and romanticism, 1814–1848

David Brooks   The age of upheaval: Edwardian politics, 1899–1914

Conan Fischer   The rise of the Nazis

Keith Laybourn   The General Strike of 1926

Panikos Panayi   Immigration, ethnicity and racism in Britain, 1815–1945

Daniel Szechi   The Jacobites: Britain and Europe, 1688–1788

John Whittam   Fascist Italy

Carl Chinn   Poverty amidst prosperity: the urban poor in England, 1834–1914

T. A. Jenkins   Parliament, party and politics in Victorian Britain

Forthcoming titles

Joanna Bourke   Production and reproduction: working women in Britain, 1860–1960

Ciaran Brady   The unplanned conquest: social changes and political conflict in sixteenth-century Ireland

Susan-Mary Grant   The American Civil War and reconstruction

Evan Mawdsley   The Stalin years: the Soviet Union 1922–1956

Alan O'Day   Irish Home Rule

David Taylor   Crime, conflict and control: the advent and impact of the new police

The nerves of state

Frontispiece In 1621, Parliament ordered that Sir Francis Michell, a monopolist and associate of Sir Giles Mompesson, should be made to ride backwards on a horse through London. A similar punishment had been visited upon a purveyor by Star Chamber in 1605. This illustration, taken from a pamphlet of 1640, seems to recall such punishments, perhaps in anticipation of future actions against monopolists. This kind of shaming punishment ('riding') provides a point of contact between official and 'popular' rituals of justice. In these official cases, it was used against people suspected of self-interest and profiteering under cover of government activity. It was used unofficially to shame husbands beaten or cuckolded by their wives.

Source: M. Ingram, 'Ridings, rough music and mocking rhymes in early modern England', in B. Reay (ed.) *Popular culture in seventeenth-century England*, London, 1988, pp. 166–97 (p. 173). For hostility to Mompesson and others in 1621, see R. Lockyer, *The early Stuarts: a political history of England, 1603–42*, London, 1989, pp. 192–5. I am grateful to Helen Weinstein for drawing my attention to this woodcut and to Dr Martin Ingram for discussing its significance with me.

The nerves of state

Taxation and the financing
of the English state, 1558–1714

Michael J. Braddick

Manchester University Press

Manchester and New York

Distributed exclusively in the USA and Canada by St. Martin's Press

Published by Manchester University Press
Oxford Road, Manchester M13 9NR, UK
and Room 400, 175 Fifth Avenue, New York, NY 10010, USA

Distributed exclusively in the USA and Canada
by St. Martin's Press, Inc., 175 Fifth Avenue, New York,
NY 10010, USA

British Library Cataloguing-in-Publication Data
A catalogue record for this book is available from the British Library

Library of Congress Cataloging-in-Publication Data
    Braddick, M. J. (Michael J.), 1962–
        The nerves of state : taxation and the financing of the English
    state, 1558–1714 / Michael J. Braddick.
            p.   cm. — (New frontiers in history)
        Includes bibliographical references.
        ISBN 0–7190–3871–5.—ISBN 0–7190–3872–3 (alk. paper : pbk.)
        1. Taxation—England—History—17th century.   2. Finance, Public—
    England—History—17th century.   3. Great Britain—History—Tudors,
    1485–1603.   4. Great Britain—History—Stuarts, 1603–1714.
    I. Title.   II. Series.
    HJ612.B729   1996
    336.2'00942—dc20   95–33392
                                                                      CIP

ISBN 0 7190 3871 5 hardback
     0 7190 3872 3 paperback

First published 1996

00 99 98 97 96   10 9 8 7 6 5 4 3 2 1

Typeset in Great Britain
by Northern Phototypesetting Co. Ltd, Bolton
Printed in Great Britain
by Bell & Bain Ltd, Glasgow

Contents

Contents

Figures

Contents

Tables

Acknowledgements

In writing this book I have benefited from the help and advice of a number of people. Mark Greengrass first suggested that I write it and has been an encouraging and thoughtful editor throughout. A number of people (knowingly or unknowingly) helped me to refine my ideas or to become better informed, in particular Simon Walker, John Walter and John Watts. Joan Kent, Mark Ormrod and Tim Wales all offered important advice on particular points. Mark Greengrass and John Morrill each read a draft of the whole book and it has benefited greatly from their comments. Emma Davies read drafts of some of the chapters and they have gained considerably in coherence and clarity as a result. I am also particularly grateful to Ian Archer, Patrick O'Brien, Phillip Hunt and Trevor Griffiths for allowing me to cite unpublished data and to Martyn Bennett who first drew my attention to the Gell MS, an extract of which is reproduced here as document 26. My principal intellectual debt, of course, is to the historians whose work I have drawn upon, a debt which is inadequately reflected in the footnotes and bibliographical essay. I have an on-going debt to the Department of History at the University of Sheffield which provides a stimulating intellectual environment and a supportive atmosphere for research.

The research on which this book is based was supported by a Small Personal Research Grant from the British Academy and by the University of Sheffield. I am grateful to the staffs of the British Library, Chester City Record Office, Derbyshire Record Office, the Institute of Historical Research and the Public

Acknowledgements

Record Office, Chancery Lane for their help and for permission to reproduce extracts from documents in their care. Katherine Braddick typed a substantial part of the first draft for me, greatly facilitating its progress. Finally, Manchester University Press has been an exemplary publisher. I am very grateful to (in chronological order) Jane Carpenter, Jane Thorniley-Walker, Michelle O'Connell, Vanessa Graham and Pauline Leng for their help.

1

Taxation and national finances in England, 1558–1714

Students of this period will come across taxation at many points and yet there is no brief introduction to its history or that of national finances as a whole. Another problem for those new to the subject arises from differences between historiographical traditions. Economic historians not only have different concerns from political or legal historians, but they use a different terminology in describing taxation. This book seeks to examine the politics of taxation in the broadest sense, in the villages, courts and parliament of England. These politics, however, changed according to the quantity of taxation being demanded and the way in which the burden fell. They also varied according to the authority by which it was being demanded and the means by which it was collected. None of these things was constant; indeed, there were significant changes in all these respects between 1558 and 1714. In order fully to understand the politics of taxation in this period, then, it is necessary to understand the broad outlines of the changing structure of public finance. Having done this it is possible to consider how political reactions to taxation were prompted by this transformation and also to begin to consider the ways in which this transformation was itself moulded by political opinion. Before attempting a general account of the history of taxation and its role in public finances, however, it is necessary to review the ways in which taxation has been examined and the terms that have been used in studies of this period.

Approaches to the history of finance and taxation

One common approach to the history of taxation is, of course, economic. However, this is only part of a broader concern with the history of finances, to which there are three components. The management of government finances entails balancing revenue and expenditure. This might mean maximising revenue, minimising expenditure or, most likely, applying pressure in both directions. In order to cover temporary imbalances governments borrow and this is the third important part of the economics of government finances. Because the economic activities of governments are usually on a large scale relative to the economies in which they are located, the way that they earn, spend and borrow has important implications for the economy at large. This period is well served by studies of this kind and most students need to become familiar with the terminology of economic historians. The overall structure of finances is considered in this chapter, and the following chapter is concerned with spending and borrowing. However, this study is mainly concerned with revenue raising, not finances as a whole, and among the various means of raising revenue it is particularly concerned with taxation. It is the terms used by economic historians of taxation that need to be introduced here.

The general concern of economic historians of taxation is to examine the burden of taxation and the way that it fell: on which items tax was payable and with what economic consequences. In seeking to examine the economics of revenue raising historians distinguish between direct and indirect taxation. Direct taxation is levied directly from taxpayers and usually falls on their wealth or income. A contemporary example would be income tax. Indirect taxation is levied on expenditure, for example VAT (Value Added Tax). In general, direct taxation is 'progressive' in that the amount of taxation paid by individuals is related to the amount of wealth or income that they have. Indirect taxation is sometimes 'regressive', however, because the amount paid by individuals is unrelated to the amount of wealth or income that they have. As a result the weight of taxation is relatively heavier for poorer taxpayers. This is the case when the tax is raised on items of consumption that everyone buys. For example, a purchase tax on bread raises a similar amount of money from everyone, no matter how wealthy they are. By contrast, a tax on a luxury item falls only on those rich enough to purchase such items. One important concern of economic histories of taxation is the balance between direct and indirect taxation, and the kinds of commodities on which indirect taxation falls. In this way historians can appraise the extent to which the tax regime is regressive or progressive. From this kind of analysis a more general account of the economic effects of taxation can be developed.

The effects of the financial system might be considerable. Taxation might reduce demand for certain types of commodity by raising prices. On the other hand, government spending might increase demand for other commodities. For example, after 1649 the largest industrial concerns in the country were the state naval dockyards funded, ultimately, by taxation. Tax regimes can affect the distribution of wealth by taxing particular groups relatively heavily or lightly. This, too, can have implications for the pattern of demand in an economy. In this sense the effects of taxation are not purely 'fiscal', they affect the operation of the economy more generally. Some modern governments deliberately use taxation for these non-fiscal purposes, to redistribute wealth or to create different patterns of demand. As we will see, some contemporaries began to demand that these broader economic effects of taxation be taken more seriously or even that they be consciously manipulated. There are, clearly, important questions arising from the economic history of taxation. This is particularly the case in the early modern period, when tax levels were increasing at the same time that the English economy was thriving.

Political and constitutional historians of this period have also paid considerable attention to financial matters, but the terminology that they employ is rather different. Raising taxation involves disposing of the private wealth or income of an individual for some public purpose. It is, inevitably, a very sensitive political issue as a result. Political, legal and constitutional historians tend to be interested in this dimension of government finance and tend to categorise types of revenue in political as well as economic terms. The concern is as much with who has the power to grant, collect, audit and spend revenues as with whether they are indirect or direct taxes or how regressive they are. These questions are of particular interest in our period because not all revenues were taxes. Some derived instead from the personal property of the monarch or the personal powers of the monarchy. Most accounts of the revenues of this period, therefore, employ this political and constitutional vocabulary and so we need to consider this terminology, too.

Most political histories of this period categorise revenues according to contemporary usage, that is as either ordinary or extra-ordinary. Ordinary revenues were the recurring revenues raised by the crown in order to cover the normal expenses of government. In addition, the government raised revenues for particular reasons beyond the ordinary, that is for extra-ordinary purposes. Of the ordinary revenues, a considerable part was supplied by the personal income due to the monarch from his or her own lands. These revenues are usually referred to as demesne revenues, and were clearly not taxes. In addition the crown could raise money from individuals by reason of some personal obligation. These obligations, for example to pay the king for the right to inherit a piece of land, are loosely termed feudal dues. They derive from a personal obligation to the monarch by an individual. Some economic historians regard these dues as forms of taxation, but to most political historians they are distinct because the relationship is personal and tenurial rather than public. On the whole they provided part of the ordinary revenue of the crown, although some such dues were raised for particular purposes, for example to pay for the marriage of the children of the monarch. Some duties were raised not from a particular personal, tenurial relationship but from a more generalised obligation to the monarch. These are referred to as prerogative revenues, because the authority by which they were raised was the personal prerogative of the monarch. Again some of these revenues appear to us to be very similar to taxes, but political historians distinguish them on the grounds of the authority by which they were collected. The best example of this is ship money which was raised in the 1630s in order to pay for the king's navy. Contribution was compulsory and followed ratings of an individual's wealth, but many contemporaries and many modern historians would hesitate to refer to it as a tax. In economic terms, of course, it is quite reasonable to refer to it as a form of direct taxation.

Direct taxation, to most political historians, refers to parliamentary taxation, and this was used, in theory at least, only for extra-ordinary purposes. Among direct taxes historians distin-

4

guish between assessed and quota taxes. In the case of the former the wealth of all taxpayers was assessed and a proportion of that amount demanded. Quota taxation, by contrast, set a target figure to be raised from particular localities without specifying the means by which this was to be achieved. The result was that taxpayers in different parts of the country might contribute towards quota taxation on different forms of wealth and in varying proportions. Confusingly, some authors use the term 'rate' in preference to quota taxation. Indirect taxation before 1640 consisted of the customs dues, raised by a mixture of parliamentary and prerogative authority. In the later seventeenth century there was a rapid expansion of indirect taxation on inland commodities, the excises. These were in any terminology taxes since they were granted by parliament.

These variations in terminology can be confusing to the lay person, but they also reflect differing priorities. To an economic historian the relationship between public finance and the national economy is of pre-eminent interest. In this the relative proportion of national wealth being commanded by the state, the sources of that revenue and the implications for demand and supply are the main concerns. All these things are political, in that they can cause argument, but the politics are different from those revealed by the terminology of the political, legal and constitutional histories. Here the principal concerns are with the relationship between the power of government and the property rights of the individual. In this context it is sometimes extremely significant that a particular exaction was a personal obligation to the monarch rather than a parliamentary tax. One concern of this book is to bring together these divergent preoccupations.

This does not exhaust the variety of contexts in which taxation is studied. Tax records are an important source for social historians interested in the distribution of wealth, for example. Recently, too, historians have tried to place resistance to taxation within the more general context of the social history of riot or rebellion. An important context for these issues of 'popular politics' is an overall sense of the structure and scale of public finances and of the political implications of the authority by which they were raised and audited. This book seeks to incorporate this dimension of the politics of taxation too.

The next section introduces this general context for the economic, social and political effects of taxation by seeking to outline a history of finances that is sensitive to the interests of all these historians.

National revenues, 1558–1714

The study of national finances in this period is fraught with difficulty. Aggregate figures for national revenues are not particularly trustworthy, especially down to 1640. National revenues were not accounted for in national balance sheets. Instead the historian must collate information from separate accounts for particular sources of revenue which may have been organised on different principles. For many sources of revenue there are no national accounts at all, or accounts only for particular periods. In some cases too, the amount paid to government was smaller than the sum raised, contractors of one kind or another having taken a profit between collection and account. The administrative machinery was, in total, formidably complex and interpreting the records that it has left often poses considerable technical difficulties. Even worse, some revenues raised for national purposes such as war were never accounted for with national government at all, but were raised and spent locally.

We know much more about the scale and composition of national government revenues, however, as a result of recent work by O'Brien and Hunt, drawing on the findings of a large number of specialised studies.[1] The difficulties with the data should caution us against placing too much weight on figures for revenues in particular years or for short periods of time. In general outline, however, the findings are unlikely to be fundamentally challenged. What O'Brien and Hunt have demonstrated is that there was a significant increase in the proportion of national wealth commanded by government in this period. In effect, the capacity of the government to tax was growing more quickly than the economy. We may assume that this phenomenon had important political implications and also that it is something that requires explanation. Given the prominence of tax resistance in most accounts of the political history of this period, it is certainly a striking fact.

Figure 1.1 gives an impression of the chronology of this development, distinguishing between revenues in peace- and war-

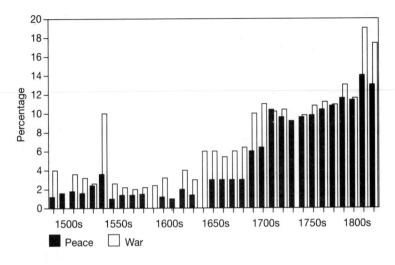

1.1 Total revenues as shares of conjectures of national income, 1485–1815
Source: P. K. O'Brien and P. A. Hunt, 'The rise of a fiscal state in England, 1485–1815', *Historical Research*, LXVI, 1993, p. 159.

time. In the 1640s the scale of war-time revenues increased dramatically and this increase was sustained until the 1680s. Peace-time revenues were also increasing, so that there was a long-term increase in the share of national wealth commanded by national government. In the 1690s further increases took government revenues to levels which were not exceeded for a further century. These increases are all the more striking because they followed centuries of rough stability. The reign of Henry VII saw the restoration of revenues to levels achieved in the mid fourteenth century, a peak which was considerably higher than levels of revenue achieved in the late thirteenth century.[2] Assuming that the nation was wealthier in 1500 than it had been in the mid fourteenth century, this fourteenth century peak represents an historic high in the proportion of national wealth that government was able to command. It was not exceeded for several centuries. The 1540s too, saw a large proportion of national wealth being spent by government, a proportion not exceeded until the 1690s. The 1640s and the 1690s therefore witnessed levels of extraction by government that were striking even in the context of this very long period of history. In these economic terms the seventeenth century was clearly an important period in the history of government revenue raising.

The seventeenth century was also a period of considerable importance in the history of, specifically, taxation. In order to understand this point it is necessary to look a little more closely at the data. Figure 1.2 gives an initial impression of why this is, in that it seems to show that taxation came to provide a steadily increasing proportion of total government revenue in our period. We should be wary of overstating the case, of course, since the crown had depended on non-landed revenue for some time. Moreover, the 1540s were something of a special case, as we will see, and the small proportion of total revenue deriving from taxation in that decade has a short-term explanation. It seems clear that the landed income of the crown had not supported it for much of the medieval period. English monarchs were land-poor, although the position improved under Henry VII and then at the dissolution of the monasteries. On the whole, however the crown lands were not sufficient to support the government (for reasons considered in chapter 4) which was, as a result, dependent on taxation.

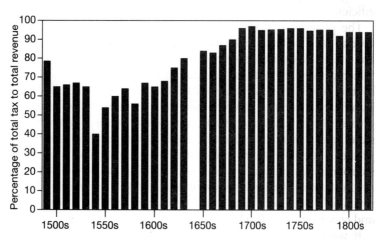

1.2 Share of total tax to total revenue by decade, 1485–1815
Source: P. K. O'Brien and P. A. Hunt, 'The rise of a fiscal state in England, 1485–1815', *Historical Research*, LXVI, 1993, p. 164.

If we adopt an economist's terminology then, we can say that as early as the 1490s taxation provided nearly 80 per cent of total revenue. The increase during our period to more than 90 per cent seems to be a matter of degree, not a change in kind. In the 1540s the proportion fell to 40 per cent, but this was due to the vast windfall of the dissolution which provided a volume of non-tax revenue which was unrepeatable. In subsequent years the proportion of revenue derived from taxation climbed again, reaching 80 per cent by the 1630s and mounting steadily to over 90 per cent by the 1680s and 1690s. In practice then, at no point in our period had the English crown lived off its land. In this respect the significance of taxation lies in its contribution to increases to total revenue. Measured in constant prices total revenue was constant from 1490 to 1640 and seems to have been of a similar magnitude since the peak of the mid fourteenth century. From 1650, however, and more particularly from 1690, the English state extracted much larger sums of money, and this extractive capacity grew faster than the economy. Total revenues, as a share of national income grew in the 1540s, the period from 1640 to 1680, and then from the 1690s onwards. In these latter decades taxation was of crucial significance and this might prompt us to ask what had changed in the tax system to enable this increased extractive efficiency.

The peak in total revenue levels achieved in the 1540s was a special case and was probably unrepeatable. Those of the 1640s and 1690s, however, depended on new tax and credit techniques which proved more durable. Innovations in these periods, driven by the need for heavy military expenditure, were of long-term significance for the development of the state. Moreover, the greater share of national wealth controlled and disposed of by the state was clearly of economic significance. It also involved a greater intervention by the state in everyday life, raising in sharper form questions about the limits of its power. On this account, then, of a state consistently dependent on taxation for its revenues, the history of taxation is of considerable political, social and economic significance.

If we introduce some of the concerns of political historians, however, we can unpick the data still further. Such an analysis reveals another important context for an understanding of taxation in this period. Table 1.1 breaks the data down in more detail

and it reveals some important changes in the nature of government revenues. Taking the period as a whole the most marked
changes are in the decline of crown income and the rise of indirect
taxation. In itself this suggests an erosion of the personal control
of the monarch. The point becomes clearer the more closely we
interrogate the material. Indirect taxation before 1640 consisted
primarily of various kinds of customs duties and the revenues
from monopolies (see chapters 3 and 4 for a description of these
revenues). Much of this revenue was, effectively, controlled by the
monarch and was raised as a matter of prerogative power. After
1660 all forms of indirect taxation were under parliamentary control. They were raised by parliamentary authority at rates and for
periods set in parliament. Table 1.2 gives a similar sense of these
changes in the complexion of direct taxes. Of these kinds of taxation sporadic levies and fines and purveyance were controlled by
monarchical authority, as was most of the quota taxation in the
period 1625–40. After 1640 all direct taxation was under parliamentary control.

Table 1.1   *Composition of national revenues, 1558–1714*

	Total (£000s)	Annual (£000s)	(a)	(b)	(c)	(d)	(e)
1558–1603	18,360	399.13	28.83	42.54	23.62	4.67	0.45
1604–1625	12,544	570.18	20.41	33.00	39.49	6.85	.26
1626–1640	11,996	799.73	12.24	34.34	44.60	8.72	0.10
1649–1659	18,919	1,719.91	3.16	55.22	29.38	12.24	0.00
1661–1685	41,066	1,642.64	5.41	33.59	56.66	4.33	0.02
1686–1688	5,925	1,975.00	6.97	11.80	80.10	0.96	0.17
1689–1714	119,607	4,600.27	1.98	39.98	56.91	1.09	0.04

Notes: (a) Crown income as percentage of total revenue
(b) Direct taxation as percentage of total revenue
(c) Indirect taxation as percentage of total revenue
(d) Sales of assets as percentage of total revenue
(e) Mint profits as percentage of total revenue
Source: European State Finance Database Project (ESFDB), obrien/engg001. Data
are not complete. 1561, 1574 and 1654 are years of incomplete data. This serves to
depress figures of total and annual revenues for the relevant periods. The years
1641-8 inclusive and 1660 have been excluded entirely. Otherwise presentation of
data follows, as closely as possible, regnal dates. The reigns of William, Mary and
Anne have been bracketed. Years in which the crown changed hands are assigned
to the previous monarch.

Taxation and national finances, 1558–1714

Table 1.2 *Composition of direct taxation, 1560–1659*

	(a)	(b)	(c)	(d)	(e)	(f)	Total (£000s)
1560–1602	25	21	23	14	6	11	192
1603–1625	18	30	26	11	6	9	193
1626–1640	11	38	22	14	8	7	276
1648–1653		10		90			1,431
1654–1659		2		98			563

Notes: (a) Lay subsidies as percentage of total direct taxation
(b) Sporadic levies and fines as percentage of total direct taxation
(c) Purveyance as percentage of total direct taxation
(d) Quotas: fifteenth and tenth, assessments as percentage of total direct taxation
(e) Clerical subsidies and fines as percentage of total direct taxation
(f) Clerical fruits and tenths as percentage of total direct taxation
Source: Provisional and unpublished data kindly supplied by Professor P. K. O'Brien and Dr. T. Griffiths; dates follow as closely as possible regnal years. I am very grateful for permission to cite this material prior to publication.

Putting all this together, we can produce a rough picture of the proportion of government revenue that was publicly controlled. Table 1.3 divides both direct and indirect taxation between parliamentary and non-parliamentary kinds, and expresses this as a proportion of total revenue.[3] The figures are by no means precise, but the general picture is clear (figure 1.3). About three-quarters of total revenue was controlled by the monarch before 1640, and this proportion was probably rising rather than falling. After 1660 all tax revenue was parliamentary and the degree of monarchical control over revenue was markedly reduced. Alongside the increasing effectiveness of national government in securing resources, then, there was a transformation in the authority behind these exactions. One concern of this book is to examine the relationship between these two phenomena.

Table 1.3 *Approximate proportions of 'parliamentary' and 'non-parliamentary'*
revenues, 1560–1640

	(a)	(b)	(c)	(d)	(e)	(f)	(g)	(h)	(i)
1560–1602	27.00	6.00	1.00	10.70	13.30	16.38	25.62	27.08	72.92
1603–1625	19.00	9.00	0.00	17.84	22.16	9.28	22.72	27.12	72.88
1626–1640	11.00	7.00	0.00	20.52	25.48	3.96	32.04	24.48	75.52

Notes: (a) Crown revenues as percentage of total revenue
      (b) Sales of assets as percentage of total revenue
      (c) Mint profits as percentage of total revenue
      (d) Parliamentary indirect taxation as percentage of total revenue
      (e) Non-parliamentary indirect taxation as percentage of total revenue
      (f) Parliamentary direct taxation as percentage of total revenue
      (g) Non-Parliamentary direct taxation as percentage of total revenue
      (h) Parliamentary revenue as percentage of total revenue
      (i) Non-parliamentary revenue as percentage of total revenue
Source: See table 1.2; dates follow as closely as possible regnal years. The basis for
these calculations is explained in note 3, chapter 1.

The rise of the tax state

One way of understanding this second change is in terms coined
by the economist and historian Joseph Schumpeter.[4] Schumpeter
argued that the early modern period saw the emergence of the
modern state and that an important part of this process was the
transformation of the basis of state finances. In the medieval
period politics were dominated by lord–vassal relations and revenues had derived from a variety of particular rights and privileges which rulers held personally. These he referred to as
'demesne revenues'. The term refers not simply to the lands of the
monarch, but to all revenues arising from a personal right belonging to the monarch. In the early modern period pressure for
spending increased considerably. Partly, he argued, this was due
to the extravagance of rulers and their courts, and to financial
mismanagement. However, the principal pressure, he argued,
came from the costs of waging war. In the face of these escalating
expenditures older sources of revenue proved inadequate. As a
result they were at first supplemented, and ultimately replaced,
by taxation and credit. This development he summarised as the
replacement of the demesne state by the tax state. Taxes were
granted by representative institutions and required the creation

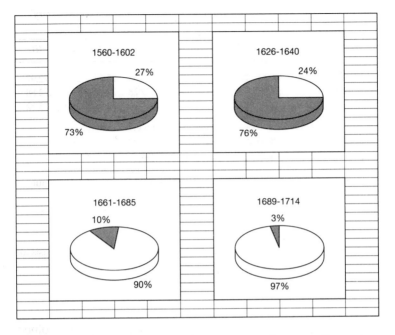

1.3 Relative importance of parliamentary and non-parliamentary revenues, 1560–1714
Sources: 1560–1602, 1626–1640: see table 1.3.
1661–1685, 1689–1714: see table 1.1 (parliamentary = columns (b) and (c); non-parliamentary = columns (a), (d) and (e)).

of bureaucratic apparatuses to collect and audit these moneys. Although Schumpeter was primarily concerned with the economic and social consequences of this transformation, his account is also, centrally, political. Demesne does not refer simply to crown lands but to dues raised by the personal authority of the prince – these dues may resemble taxes but they are demesne revenues in a political sense. By extension, then, the transformation of finances changed the nature of the authority of the state too. This model offers a way of describing the second transformation described in the previous section, that relating to the political authority by which revenues were raised.

This essentially political distinction offers another way of understanding the importance of taxation in this period. Not all taxes included in the totals for the period before 1640 were regarded as such by contemporaries. They may have been, in economic terms, taxes but they were raised instead as rights to revenue associated with the monarch personally. The best example, as we have seen, is ship money. In a sense it was a concealed or prerogative tax, an exaction that was *effectively* but not *explicitly* a tax. There are other examples of such concealed or prerogative taxes in the period 1558–1640. Purveyance, wardship, forest fines, monopolies, and perhaps even forced loans and benevolences, could all be described in these terms because none of them were raised as taxes in Schumpeter's sense. Instead they represented dues arising to the monarch as a personal prerogative – they were income associated with the demesne, broadly conceived, rather than taxation.

This may seem, from an economic point of view a rather artificial and arcane distinction, and many contemporaries seem to have thought so too. However, such distinctions were and are politically significant. Prerogative revenues caused considerable political debate in the earlier part of the period, and were all abolished or replaced by tax revenues in 1660. As we have seen, however, if they are removed from O'Brien and Hunt's tax category before 1640, the difference between the contribution to tax revenues before and after the civil war is more marked. Moreover, customs occupied an ambiguous position before 1640. The authority for collection of some duties was parliament, but for others was the royal prerogative. What the customs actually yielded was governed by the book of rates, which determined the levels of the duties on particular commodities. It was the crown which controlled the issue of books of rates and, therefore, the yield of the customs. There is an argument, therefore, for regarding the customs as non-tax revenues in political terms, before 1640, and as tax revenues thereafter (see chapter 3). This would further emphasise the difference in the composition of total revenues between the earlier and later parts of the period.

The quantitative data reveal, clearly, that this was a state that depended on what, in economist's terms, we must consider to be taxes. However, the political reality was rather different. One indication of this is provided by the terms in which contemporaries discussed the revenues. In the Tudor period 'the revenue of the Crown was treated almost exactly like that of a large estate, and in this connection the term – "the manor of England" – was sometimes used to describe the property and income of the sovereign'. The analogy is plain in the case of the crown lands, but it applied also to the 'feudal revenue', the customs and the revenue generated by the various functions of government. 'Just as the lord of a manor, instead of collecting certain dues himself, might let these at a fixed rent, so many branches of the Crown revenue were "farmed out".' The receipts from these sources, much of the ordinary revenue, were 'reducible to a rental'.[5] This is the language of estates rather than the state. The key to Elizabethan and early Stuart finance was the management of the ordinary revenue, hopefully with the effect of generating an accumulating surplus. Extra-ordinary expenditure would then be met from this surplus and supplementary grants, but all the revenue was controlled by the monarch. Even parliamentary grants, made with a specific purpose in mind, were not policed by parliament. Only for the subsidies of 1624 did parliament seek to ensure that the money was used for the stated purpose, and the necessary formal procedures of scrutiny which would allow parliament to do this on a regular basis were a product of the 1660s. A striking example of this discretion is in the disposal of the proceeds of tonnage and poundage: in 1625 £150,000 was raised, of which only £22,000 was paid to the navy.[6]

In this political sense the revenues before 1640s were inflated by additions to the demesne income, by claims to rights arising from the demesne that were effectively taxes but which were not granted as such. Hurstfield made the point rather pungently:

> [ship money, monopolies, exploitation of the forest laws, distraint of knighthood and other revenues] were the bastard revenues, neither medieval nor modern, neither legal nor illegal, unjustifiable in theory and indispensable in practice. Whatever might be said in their defence, they constituted an affront to the commonsense and the interests of the propertied classes. But the crown had no choice. Blocked in its efforts to tap effectively by direct or indirect taxation the national income from land and trade, it was driven to search for an income by applying and distorting its constitutional rights, where opportunity served.[7]

After 1640 they disappeared. Wardship, monopolies, purveyance, ship money, forest fines, distraint for knighthood, benevolences and forced loans were all political casualties of the long parliament. After 1641 customs were fully controlled by parliament, and can clearly be transferred to the tax side. During the 1640s and 1650s parliament had few alternatives to taxation. It had no demesne rights, but it could raise money through the sale of seized assets, and this explains the remaining gap between tax revenue and total revenue. After 1660 the demesne rights of the monarch in these respects were replaced by parliamentary taxation: demesne revenue was unequivocally marginal. In the terms used by Schumpeter then, in the period 1558–1640, the English state was effectively funded by taxation, but did not have the political arrangements to match. No such ambiguity or disjunction can be detected in the restoration period, and the politics of taxation were different.

The politics of taxation, 1558–1714

There are two important changes in public revenue in this period, then, in quantitative and political terms. Both the scale and the composition of total revenue changed dramatically, and taxation was central to both these processes. These changes had important political, legal, social and economic ramifications. By 1714 public revenue depended on taxation raised by parliamentary consent. It amounted to a larger proportion of national income, and involved the agencies of government in unprecedented intervention in social and economic life. Debate about many 'taxes' of the early seventeenth century centred on their legal or constitutional propriety, and economic arguments were restricted largely to assertions about the burden of taxation on the poor. In the later seventeenth and early eighteenth centuries debate about the economic effects of taxation was more broadly-based and concerned with the development of trade, the protection of domestic agriculture and manufactures. The tax state was not simply bigger in the sense that it controlled a greater proportion of national wealth either. It employed larger numbers of people recognisable as tax collectors. Tax collection became, in a sense, a more visible activity. In the earlier period inland taxation was raised almost exclusively by local officeholders – magistrates and constables. After 1640 it was increasingly the case that professional revenue agents appeared in the localities. This created hostilities, but also widened the social basis of participation in the activities of the state, offering new means of making a living. By the same token this added to the reservoir of crown patronage. In the 1690s a remarkable expansion of the basis of government borrowing was enabled by secure tax revenues and this borrowing broadened the range of participation in the activities of the state. The creation of a state explicitly based on taxation and credit obviously had political consequences, and these form one of the major concerns of this book.

This period saw the creation of a state based, unambiguously, on taxation. At the same time the tax state was also a more greedy state, commanding a greater share of national wealth. These related phenomena had a variety of legal, social, economic and political implications, and as a result references to taxation in the histories of the sixteenth and seventeenth centuries are frequent in a variety of contexts. In seeking to give a general account of the changing role of taxation in this period this book assumes a broad chronological distinction. The large increases in the revenue totals were a product first of the 1640s and then of the 1690s. The political status of taxation was transformed in the 1640s, when by necessity revenues came under the control of parliament, and this transformation was not undone at the restoration. Thus, the 1640s are a key moment in both processes. Before that date revenues were expanded, but not more quickly than the economy grew, and much of the expansion came through extended exploitation of prerogative powers. The crown raised a number of prerogative or concealed taxes. After the 1640s finances were public, based on taxation and represented an increasing proportion of national wealth.

Taxation as a political issue appears throughout histories of this period. One way of explaining this is by saying that stress within the system of national government finance, which seems mainly attributable to escalating military costs (see chapter 2), led to other political problems. In this sense, the experience of early modern England resembles that described Schumpeter's model. Down to 1640 the ordinary revenues of the monarch were proving less and less sufficient. Parliamentary taxation was resorted to in ways that may have represented a new constitutional principle. In the long run, however, it did not provide an easy way of filling the gap between expenditure and income. This forced Elizabeth and the early Stuarts to test the limits of the prerogative by raising a variety of concealed or prerogative taxes. Unfortunately these strategies had a high political cost. An attempt was made at a systematic solution to this revenue problem in 1610, in the negotiations for a Great Contract between parliament and the crown. The Great Contract was to have replaced many concealed and prerogative taxes with a regular parliamentary supply. In short it would have shifted the basis of finances away from the demesne and towards taxation proper. What parliament was prepared to offer did not hold out the prospect of increasing the scale of public revenue, however, and the negotiations failed. Instead a more decisive moment came in 1641–2, and the changes to public finance made in those years were confirmed in 1660. Between 1558 and 1640, then, we can see particular political problems arising from the failure to resolve the balance between demesne and tax revenues. In 1660 we are in a different financial world, in which demesne revenues are marginal and the customs are unequivocally tax revenues akin to the excises. The financial basis of the monarchy was provided by forms of taxation that survived until the late eighteenth century. This new tax system had its own political problems, however. For example, the capacity to tax predated the creation of secure arrangements for borrowing. As a result individual financiers were able to secure considerable political influence and this was a source of concern to many contemporaries. The increasing incidence of taxation made it a political issue, as did the development of more professional agencies of collection. The final phase of the story begins in the 1690s, when revenue levels again increased dramatically. In this case the most remarkable innovations lay in the way in which the government borrowed rather than in the way that it raised taxation. This transformation of borrowing raised new economic, political and social questions.

This is not, therefore, a book about the timelessness of resistance to taxation. It is quite specific to a period in which the scale of taxation increased markedly after centuries of rough stability, and in which there were significant changes in the nature of taxation and its contribution to revenues as a whole. It saw the emergence of a state funded by taxation which, after 1694, secured a permanent national debt. Within the context of this transformation the political, legal, constitutional, social and economic ramifications of taxation are of central importance. The book seeks to offer a brief introduction to these issues. However, it is more explicitly concerned with a single theme in this complex story – why this outcome? Why was it that by 1714 the taxes on which government depended were the excise, customs and the land tax? What were the political, administrative and economic advantages that they possessed? Although, as we have seen, there were changes in the legal and constitutional issues raised by taxation there was considerable continuity in the reluctance of taxpayers to pay (if there was some prospect of not doing so) and in the administrative repertoire of the government in seeking to overcome this.

It is not possible to give a full account of these issues, not least because our knowledge of many aspects of this history is very partial. This is intended only as an overview, an essay in the old-fashioned sense, seeking to outline the general issues and to suggest the answers that are currently available. Clearly, behind this transformation lay increasing demands for expenditure. Chapter 2 provides further context by sketching out what these demands were and by considering the demands of the government as borrower. Chapters 3, 4 and 5 examine the sources of revenue available to national government to meet the demands for spending and for security for creditors. In each case there are a number of political, legal and economic issues which we need to explore. We will need to outline the authority by which these revenues were raised, how they were administered and who did the assessment and collection. A sense of how much was raised and who was most affected is also, of course, important. Chapters 6, 7 and 8 explore reactions to taxation thematically. This discussion is not intended to be comprehensive. Illustrations of general points are drawn from the experience of a variety of exactions but examples could be multiplied for any of the exactions mentioned in chapters 3–5. It is left to the reader to test the usefulness of the general thematic treatment for any particular tax. Chapter 9 offers a summary of the argument, a chronological review and an attempt to appraise the success of the English state in harnessing economic, administrative and political resources in this period.

Notes

1 P. K. O'Brien and P. A. Hunt, 'The rise of a fiscal state in England, 1485-1815', *Historical Research*, LXVI, 1993, pp. 129–76.

2 *Ibid.*, pp. 148–50.

3 These estimates are very approximate and the term 'publicly controlled' is ambiguous. The figures are based on unpublished and provisional findings of P. K. O'Brien and T. Griffiths. Before 1640 non-parliamentary revenue consisted of crown revenues, sales of assets and mint profits as well as portions of direct and indirect taxation. Direct taxation is here broken down according to the figures in table 1.2: columns (a) and (d) for 1560–1602 and column (a) only for 1626–40 (because the quota taxation of Charles' reign was mainly ship money). Indirect taxation is more approximate. The only indirect taxation controlled by parliament before 1640 was tonnage and poundage. In 1625 this was worth £150,000, that is 44.6 per cent of all indirect taxation (A. Thrush, 'Naval finance and the origins and development of ship money', in M. C. Fissel (ed.), *War and government in Britain, 1598–1650*, Manchester, 1991, pp. 133–62, p. 140; European State Finance Data Base (ESFDB) \Obrien\engg001. The ESFDB is accessible on the world wide web at http://indigo.stile.le.ac.uk/ubon/STILE/esfdb.html). This is assumed to be constant for the two periods covered here. This assumption is doubtless wrong. Under Elizabeth the importance of impositions and monopolies was less marked and tonnage and poundage consequently more important. The inverse is true of the period 1626–40 when the reality of parliamentary control over tonnage and poundage was extremely questionable (see pp. 52–3). Figure 1.3 shows a slight trend towards crown control. In reality this was probably much more marked. I am very grateful for permission to cite this unpublished material.

4 J. A. Schumpeter, 'The crisis of the tax state', *International Economic Papers*, IV, 1954, pp. 5–38.

5 W. R. Scott, *The constitution and finance of English, Scottish and Irish joint-stock companies to 1720*, 3 vols., Cambridge, 1910–12, III, p. 487.

6 A. Thrush, 'Naval finance and the origins and development of ship money', in M. C. Fissel (ed.), *War and government in Britain, 1598–1650*, Manchester, 1991, pp. 133–62; pp. 140–1.

7 J. Hurstfield, 'The profits of fiscal feudalism, 1541–1602', *Economic History Review*, 2nd series, VIII, 1955, pp. 53-61, p. 53.

2

Spending and borrowing, 1558–1714

In seeking to understand what lay behind the transformation described in the previous chapter there are two questions that we need to consider. Firstly, why did governments need more money and, secondly, what were the constraints on their action that forced them to adopt the specific measures that they did? We are primarily concerned here with the second of these questions and will examine the administrative and political pressures which meant that demand for revenue was met through taxation and borrowing. Nonetheless, as a preliminary to this it is important to consider sources of the demand for increased expenditure. We must also consider borrowing, because governments could not survive without spending in advance of their income. The demands of this part of the financial system also had a substantial effect on the development of the revenues.

Expenditure

Expenditure has received much less systematic attention from historians than has revenue, and there is no definitive account which would command the agreement of all historians. For example, many historians would disagree as to whether the principal cause of financial pressure was financial mismanagement, royal extravagance or the pressure of war. The main concern of this section is therefore to appraise the relative importance of civil and military spending in creating financial pressures on government. There is a further question, however, since accounts of increases in the costs of government often give considerable prominence to the supposed extravagance and financial mismanagement of royal courts. In general, inflation in the costs of civil government, which may or may not have reflected 'extravagance', was of relatively limited significance. These costs may have caused short-term problems for the crown but the long-term and sustained increase in the level of revenues is to be explained primarily by the increase in military expenditures.

Measuring the cost of government

There are considerable problems in seeking to recover the costs of government in this period. The cost of some activities is concealed for the simple reason that the money was raised and spent locally. As a result it does not appear in the national accounts. The best example of this is government activity in relation to welfare and social order. There was a rapid expansion of economic and social regulation, the responsibility for which lay with the hierarchy of local officeholders. Much of this activity was 'free' to national government, however, either because it was cost-free (in that officeholders were more or less unpaid) or because the cost was borne by local rates. It might be said that one of the most remarkable extensions of the activities of English government in the sixteenth century was the Elizabethan poor law, which imposed some considerable costs on the localities, but which was no charge at all to the exchequer. Other initiatives, such as the licensing of alehouses, the regulation of pre-marital sexual relations or responses to the plague, likewise very noticeable increases in the level of government activity in some places, were no charge to national government. One implication of this is that what national taxation was spent on does not accurately reveal the full range of government activities.

However, it was not just the case with these measures in relation to social order that local rates are important: the same can be said of some military charges. In particular, the militia forces mustered for defensive purposes twice each year were paid for out of local rates and the cost did not represent a pressure to raise more national taxation. Indeed, a substantial part of the cost even of expeditionary forces fell on the locality directly (in the form of 'coat and conduct money' for the equipment and transport of troops through the locality, the provision of arms and billeting of

22

troops, for example) rather than in the form of national taxation.

The cost of government then, consisted not just of national taxation, but also of a 'dark figure', costs of government passed on in other ways. A second important component of this dark figure was the variety of means by which government servants were rewarded, or government services were procured, without a direct cost to the exchequer. For example, provisions for the royal household before 1640 were procured at below-market prices (see chapter 4 for this right of 'purveyance'). This meant that part of the cost of provision was met from national revenues (the price paid for the goods) but part was not (the costs to local communities of selling goods at below-market values).

Another good example of this kind of hidden cost of government is provided by the remuneration of government servants. The crown could grant commercial privileges at no cost to itself but which offered the possibility of considerable revenue to the recipient (see below, for monopolies, for example). The scale of the difference between the level of expenditure by government and the cost of government could be striking. It has been estimated that in the 1630s the annual cost to the crown of its servants was £340,000–£360,000 per annum. The cost to the subject, in fees and gratuities, amounted to a further £250,000–£400,000 per annum. This added substantially to the cost of government – in the period 1631–5 total revenue averaged £636,000 per annum. If the fees and gratuities are added it is increased to a minimum of £890,000 and perhaps £940,000.[1] In other words, a significant transfer of wealth into the hands of the servants of government was taking place, but only a portion of it derived from taxation.

As a general rule most aspects of early modern English government were poorly bureaucratised and the agents of government were frequently unsalaried or derived much of their income from fees paid by the public rather from moneys paid out by the government. Offices were part of the battery of patronage and reward with which the crown sought to secure support and consent. In this sense their political function was much more diffuse than the simple implementation of government 'policy'.[2] These observations are revealing of the nature of early modern government in general. The government was caught in a kind of poverty trap, lacking the cash to pay sufficient wages to full-time administrators. As a result office had to pay its own way. Here, though, government was powerful because it could put people in positions from which they could derive income from fees and perquisites. This way of using public offices was attractive and can be seen in the reward of political friends, the administration of the crown lands and in the enforcement of criminal statutes, for example. There were, in some cases, further invisible costs to the government when officeholders' profits represented lost potential income for the crown. However, for a cash-poor monarchy this was an attractive solution.

The picture is more complicated because the size of the 'dark figure' of the cost of government was almost certainly changing in this period. The cost of fees and gratuities in relation to total government spending was probably declining down to 1642.[3] The scale of fees and gratuities taken from the subject declined, and there was a notable 'professionalisation' of some branches of administration, particularly the excise. It has been suggested that 'it is hard to believe that anything like as much money changed hands annually in fees, gratuities, presents and bribes [after 1649] as had done before 1640–2'.[4] This might have put more pressure on government budgets: the salary bill for government servants, even excluding the rapidly expanding armed forces, was increasing. Much of this increase is to be explained by an increase in the number of government servants connected with the military.[5] During the seventeenth century the number of offices probably increased and this may have meant that there was a wider redistribution, transferring wealth to a broader range of social groups. In short, more of the cost of government was met directly from the exchequer, and this may have produced a pressure to increase national revenues. On the other hand, much of this expansion would have been self-financing, since in most periods the expansion was most marked in revenue raising departments. Even at the end of our period, however, much of the cost of civilian government would not have been met directly from taxation. For this reason, the costs of bureaucracy are unlikely to have been a direct cause of the increase in national taxation.

There are other ways in which the dark figure was reduced in this period, too. The right to procure goods at cheap rates was abolished in 1640. As a result the exchequer had to bear the full cost of obtaining goods and services and this must have represented a considerable extra charge on national taxation. An increasing proportion of military costs was also met by the exchequer direct as local rates became less important to the financing of military operations. Thus, a contraction in the size of the dark figure may have represented one important pressure on national budgets in this period.

It is difficult to measure the cost of government because there was an important difference between cost to the exchequer and the burden of government on the economy as a whole. One pressure for increased national spending might have been that this gap was closed: a higher proportion of the total cost of government was borne directly by the exchequer at the end of our period. Finally, the difficulties of discerning what the cost of government was should act as a further caution against attributing too much accuracy to the figures quoted in chapter 1. The percentage of national wealth being commanded by national government was greater than the percentage of national wealth being received as government revenue. More importantly, though, the difference was almost certainly not constant. In fact, the figures in chapter 1 probably overstate in the increase in the 'size' of government between 1558 and 1714 because at the beginning of the period the cash cost of government was a lower proportion of total cost than it was at the end.

These are broader questions than the one with which we are primarily concerned, however. What forced governments to increase the scale of revenues so dramatically in this period? The change in the size of the dark figure is one (relatively minor) component of the answer. We now consider the relative importance of military and civil expenditure in driving government to try to increase their spending power.

Civil expenditure

Table 2.1 gives some rough indication of the scale of the increase in civil spending. The figures before 1640 are derived from 'snapshots' of spending under particular heads, and they may be exceptional. For example, some of the expenditures for Elizabeth are from the later, parsimonious years of her reign. They may, therefore, underestimate her expenditures. At the same time that level of expenditure may have been politically unsustainable. Thus, the increased levels of expenditure under James may be exaggerated. Moreover, some of the figures represent spending in the very early years of his reign when pressures for spending of this kind were more acute than for his reign as a whole. Some of the increase in spending before and after 1640 is to be explained by the fact that government had to pay full price for its provisions in the later period. To an extent, then, these figures are probably unrepresentative and may not be comparing like with like, but they do give a rough indication of the scale of the inflation in the civil costs of government.

Table 2.1 *Annual 'court' expenditures, 1558–1688 (£000s)*

	Elizabeth I	James I	Charles I	1660–1688
Household	50–60	70	70+	96.3
Wardrobe	13	26+	26+	20.3
Chamber	12–16	25	28–30	27.0
Sub-total	75–89	121	126	143.6
Privy purse	?1	?5		27.0
Fees	27.6	49.6		83.2
Gifts	9.2	23.4		24.3
Total	111.8–125.8	199		325.4

Source: F. C. Dietz, *English public finance 1485–1641*, London, 1964, II, pp. 81, 107, 111, 112, 401–7, 408, 410, 413–4; C. D. Chandaman, *The English public revenue 1660–1688*, Oxford, 1975, appendix III.

It is well-known that increased spending of this kind caused financial problems for the Stuarts. Their ordinary revenues were insufficient to meet their ordinary expenses with the result that there was an accumulating deficit. This reduced the capacity of the government to meet war-time expenses because there was no accumulated surplus with which to meet the initial costs of war. This contrasts with the Elizabethan situation, where an annual surplus was achieved, which allowed the accumulation of something of a 'war-chest'. In the short term, then, the increase in the levels of expenditure revealed by table 2.1 were of considerable significance. Over the longer term, however, this inflation was of more limited significance: even if the low level of expenditure under Elizabeth had been politically feasible for a sustained period, the additional annual expenditure was only £213,000 while overall budgets expanded by much more than that: from around £450,000 per annum in the 1590s to £4 million per annum a century later.

Over the period as a whole, then, civil expenditure remained a small proportion of total expenditure. The formal provisions of Instrument of Government of 1653 and the civil list act of 1698 give some indication of this because they reveal the proportions of total expenditure devoted to civil expenditure. The Instrument set aside £200,000 per annum 'for defraying the other [ie. non-military] necessary charges of administration of justice, and other expenses of the Government'.[6] By making these things a direct charge on national government, then, the Instrument increased the potential demand for taxation. However, they were a less significant expense than military spending, as we will see. This level of expenditure was roughly the same after the restoration, too. In the period 1660–88 £5,151,163.02 (less than £184,000 per annum) was spent on ambassadors, envoys, the secret service and the fees and gifts already considered under the heading of court expenditures.[7] These were the principal costs of civil 'administration' (although it excludes payments to pensioners and messengers). The civil list act of 1698 granted revenues to the crown for life that were estimated to yield £700,000 per annum, from which the crown was 'to meet the costs of the civil government and the royal establishments', a list much more extensive than is included in table 2.1.[8] We might conclude, then, that there was inflation in the costs of administration and of the court. This was not simply a matter of extravagance and increasing display, however, since in part it may reflect the fact that more of the costs of government were being charged directly to the exchequer. This inflation caused budgetary problems for the early Stuarts in particular. However, taking the period 1558-1714 as a whole, the impact of these costs was relatively minor compared to the expenses of war, as we will see.

Military costs

Military spending was not restricted to periods of active campaigning. Nonetheless, the expansion of war-time expenditure was striking. Wars were extremely expensive, and increasingly so, and a single campaign could cost much more than could be saved by all sorts of stringency in controlling household expenditure. For naval campaigns and war expenditure in Flanders, France and Ireland, Elizabeth's government paid £3,632,226 between 1590 and 1603: £260,000 per annum.[9] This should be placed beside the increase in expenditure in wardrobe, household and chamber under James I of £32,000–£46,000 per annum. Taking the larger figure, had James been able to live at the parsimonious Elizabethan rate, it would have taken seventy-nine years to generate the savings to pay for a similar series of campaigns. The accumulating deficits of the early Stuart period, caused by inflation in civil expenditures, weakened the capacity of government to respond to these military shocks, but even without that inflation the shocks would have been severe. More than this the impact of military expenditures were increasingly shocking.

Table 2.2   *Revenues in peace- and war-time in the reigns of Elizabeth I and Charles II*

	Total (£000s)	Annual (£000s)	(a)	(b)	(c)	(d)	(e)
1558–1585	8,975	320.54	32.33	40.46	23.63	2.91	0.91
1586–1603	9,385	521.39	25.49	44.54	23.61	6.36	0.00
1661–1674	23,558	1,682.71	5.96	41.54	45.59	6.91	0.00
1675–1685	17,508	1,591.64	4.67	22.89	71.54	0.85	0.05

Notes: (a) Percentage of total revenue from crown income
(b) Percentage of total revenue from direct taxes
(c) Percentage of total revenue from indirect taxes
(d) Percentage of total revenue from sales of assets
(e) Percentage of total revenue from mint profits
Source: ESFDB, \obrien\engg001.   The figures for total revenue and annual average revenues, 1558–85 are depressed because data for 1561 and 1574 are incomplete.
Dates: see note to table 1.1, p. 10.

Mobilisation for war created a constant inflationary pressure in this period, and this is reflected in the figures quoted in chapter 1. In the comparatively lightly taxed period 1485–1690, it was during war-time that revenues represent substantial proportions of national wealth – the 1540s, the 1640s, 1650s, 1660s and 1670s. To a lesser extent this is true also of the period 1585–1610 and of the 1620s. Table 2.2 demonstrates this for two long periods. Dividing Elizabeth's reign around 1585 produces a rough sense of the difference between peace-time and war-time budgets. The increase in annual average revenue is striking, representing an increase of more than 60 per cent. The composition of the revenues is also interesting in that the contribution of direct taxation to the total increased. In effect, receipts from direct taxation increased more quickly than revenues generally. This is less true of the period 1660–85, but here the first period is not one of continuous war, and during the years of active campaigning the contrast would undoubtedly be more marked. Thus, if we are interested in why increasingly large amounts of taxation were raised during the period 1558-1714 as a whole, we might look to military rather than civil costs of government.

The costs of active campaigning rose dramatically in the seventeenth century: the 1625 expedition to Cadiz cost four times as much as had Drake's.[10] The military forces assembled during the 1620s were unequal to the task before them, but it seems that they cost more than £1 million per annum.[11] The point hardly needs making in relation to the 1640s and 1650s, but less familiar is the fact that the second Dutch War, again not notable for the military success achieved by the mobilisation, cost £5.25 million and over £5 million was issued to the navy, ordnance and military forces during the third Dutch War.[12] In the two periods 1689–97 and 1702–13 £100,998,000 was spent on war, excluding the costs of servicing the debts incurred in order to sustain the campaigns.[13] If we take any long-term view these figures must persuade us that the primary pressure on the budgets of national government came from warfare and its increasing costs – these figures dwarf those arising from royal extravagance and civilian costs. Their impact was made more noticeable by the suddenness of the peaks as well. An impression of what this meant for governments is given by John Childs:

William's armies in the Low Countries, usually totalling around 100,000 men, needed 150,000lb. of bread, or its equivalent, per day, 300,000 pints of beer, and 120,000 lb. of other consumables such as wood for fuel, wine, meat and cheese. The horses devoured 1,600,000 lb. of green fodder during the summer months on campaign but had to be supplied with 624,000 lb. of straw, hay and oats for each of the hundred days that they spent in winter quarters. To provide flour for this amount of daily bread, 270 windmills were required to grind grain for 120 field ovens which were fired by 2,800 waggon-loads of wood and served by 480 bakers. To maintain William's armies in the Low Countries for each year of the Nine Years' War, 400,000 tons of provisions had to be purchased, stored and distributed.[14]

Military spending was not restricted to periods of war, however. Elizabeth and James had to maintain expensive establishments in Ireland and garrisons (notably Berwick in the sixteenth century and Tangier in the late seventeenth) could also cost fairly significant sums. The most dramatic illustration of the increase in the general cost of military spending is in the case of the navy. In the early years of Elizabeth's reign £12,000 per annum had been assigned to the navy aside from the costs of construction, and this was reduced to £6,000 in the mid-1560s, while construction ceased. This level of expenditure was unsustainable once preparations for war began in the mid-1580s. The peak, in 1588, was £92,222 plus £59,221 for victuals, and in the period 1598–1603 the fleet cost around £90,000 per annum. Peace-time expenditures never declined to the early Elizabethan base, however, and from 1618 to 1623 about £51,000 per annum was spent on ten new ships, victuals and the ordinary expenses. Further expansion in the 1630s was funded by ship money, allowing the construction of new ships, putting a fleet to sea and additional spending of about £55,000 per annum.[15] This spending represented considerable pressure, but this was relatively minor by comparison with the very rapid expansion of the fleet after 1649.

What lay behind the expanding costs of military establishments and of the cost of campaigns was an increasing specialisation and professionalisation of military activity. The Elizabethan naval successes were built on an amalgam of naval and private enterprise and, until 1618, this was institutionalised through the payment of a bounty to merchants who built ships of sufficient size to be serviceable in war-time. The increasing specialisation of navies led to the development of state-owned and state-run navies, which obviously required more direct government spending on construction and maintenance. More than this, larger ships required larger crews – at the height of the first Dutch War the English fleet was manned by nearly 20,000 men, and during the restoration period the peace-time complement was between 3,000 and 4,000. Nearly 31 per cent of total issues recorded by Chandaman was spent on the navy between 1660 and 1688: over £500,000 per annum on average.[16] This is ten times more than the sums spent in the early 1620s and nearly 100 times as great as the spending of the 1560s. The expansion continued as we can see from the table 2.3.

Table 2.3   *English naval strength, 1578–1715*

	Total ships	Ships of the line	Men borne
1578	24		6,290
1603	42		8,346
1633	50		9,470
1660	156		19,551
1676	148	58	30,260
1688	173	100	41,940
1702	224	130	38,874
1710	313		48,072
1715	224	131	13,475

Source: M. Duffy (ed.), *The military revolution and the state 1500–1800,* Exeter Studies in History, I, Exeter, 1980, table N, p. 82.

This expansion in spending was notable in respect of other military establishments, too. The creation of a standing army in the 1640s, and its retention in the 1650s (and, in attenuated form, in the restoration period) represented another long-term charge to the state. The Instrument of Government provided for the maintenance of a permanent force of 10,000 horse and dragoons and 20,000 foot in England, Scotland and Ireland.[17] In the mid-1680s there were about 25,000 troops and numbers increased very rapidly in the later 1680s to reach about 40,000 before the Glorious Revolution.[18] Over the restoration period as a whole £9,474,953.96 was spent on military forces (£338,391 per annum). The ordnance office was responsible for buying and forwarding supplies to military forces. It was allowed £6,000 per annum under Elizabeth although it actually spent £14,000 per annum during the last decade of Elizabeth's reign.[19] The allowance remained £6,000 during the 1620s although this was 'seldom paid'.[20] In the restoration period a total of £2,451,512.68 was issued to it (£87,554 per annum). This increased capacity allowed the subjugation of Ireland, the occupation of Scotland and convoying duties in the Mediterranean, but it was an expensive business operating over this larger territorial base. The garrison at Berwick had cost Elizabeth £15,000 per annum in her later years whereas Tangier cost £506,082.98 in the two periods 1660–73 and 1680–8.[21]

Expenditure under these four headings between 1660 and 1688 – navy, military forces, ordnance office and Tangier – total £27,170,156.60, a fraction under £1 million per annum. To this could be added, stretching a point perhaps, £2,142,938.69 for ambassadors, envoys and secret service. This military cost represents 57 per cent of total expenditure. Moreover, much of the debt incurred, the cost of which is not included here but which would have inflated the expenditure during years of peace, would, in fact, have been related to military spending. This completely overshadows court expenditure (household, wardrobe, chamber, privy purse, fees and annuities, gifts and rewards and payments to individual members of the royal family) totalling £8,039,114.41 (17 per cent).[22] From about 1688 onwards through the eighteenth century the cost of civil expenditure ('the domestic expenses of the monarch and his court') were stable: rising from an average of just under £1 million per annum to about £1.5 million by 1780. The civil list usually accounted for about 15 per cent of government spending, and in the early years after its creation there was, in fact, a small surplus from the £700,000 set aside for civil expenditure, which was appropriated by parliament for other purposes.[23]

The spending of the period 1690-1714 was, of course, dominated by military costs, as the British government undertook campaigns on an unprecedented scale and, in the intervals between active campaigning, struggled to repay debts. These costs were enormous by Elizabethan and Jacobean standards. An impression of this commitment is given by table 2.4. A consequence of the gap between income and expenditure revealed by this table was, of course, escalating debt. In 1689 there was no debt, by the end of the Nine Years War it had reached £16.7 million. At the start of the War of the Spanish Succession this had been reduced to £14.1 million but had risen by 1713 to £36.2 million.[24] In 1710 military spending represented the equivalent of 9 per cent of national income.[25]

Table 2.4   *English military commitment, 1689–1713*

		Men		Annual average	Tax
	Navy	*Army*	*Total*	*expenditure*	*revenue*
1689–97	40,262	76,404	116,666	5,456,555	3,640,000
1702–13	42,938	92,708	135,646	7,063,923	5,355,583

Notes: 1689–97 Nine Years War

1702–13 War of the Spanish Succession

Source: J. Brewer, *The sinews of power. War, money and the English state, 1688–1783,* London, 1989, p. 30.

All this is not to suggest that the financial problems of the crown derived only from military commitments. In particular, the financial problems of the early Stuart period resulted from overspending in a variety of directions. The accumulating deficit that this produced made it more difficult to fight wars, so that we might almost reverse the causal link – peace-time extravagance made it more difficult for the government to support extra-ordinary military expenditure.[26] It is equally true, however, that the revenues available specifically for military purposes were inadequate, the capacity to sustain a military campaign limited. Ship money (chapter 4) was a fairly successful response to the need to develop a new way of financing the navy. However, the greatest advance in this fiscal-military capability came in the 1640s: military engagements forced fiscal reform. Once parliamentary means were found to raise revenues on this scale, however, it is easy to see why the same or similar sources were used for non-military spending. Thus, the pressure to increase taxation was felt most acutely in times of war, but this is not to say that the sole cause of early Stuart fiscal problems was military spending or that the increased capacity was useful only for fighting wars. Nonetheless, the expansion of the revenues in the 1640s, and after, was driven spectacularly by military commitments.

It is also important to emphasise that this does not necessarily mean that the state was a fiscal–military construct. Although there was clearly a fiscal–military state, there was also a state with other purposes whose activities are not revealed by an analysis of exchequer spending. The principal cause of increased national revenue raising then, was military, but also the assumption by parliament of responsibility for expenditure that would previously have lain with the monarch, the cost of which would have been met in non-tax ways. Welfare, social and economic regulation and law were negligible or non-existent costs to national government. This does not mean, however, that 'the state' was exclusively a war-making apparatus. National revenue raising and changes in its means were a product of warfare in the main, but the whole structure of government was more complex and embraced a broader set of goals than this.

Borrowing

Figure 1.1 reveals a narrowing of the gap between peace- and war-time revenues during the eighteenth century. This reflects the role of government borrowing, specifically the creation of a funded national debt which allowed war-time expenditure to be spread over a number of years. Increasingly taxes were granted at least partly with a view to the security that they provided to creditors. There were several stages in the evolution of this system.

Government borrowing before 1640

The development of government borrowing in this period is complicated since it is not only related to the structure of public finance but also to the private money market – the sources of credit. In several important respects the development of public borrowing and of the tax regime were closely related and in order to demonstrate this it is necessary to consider the history of the public debt as a whole. There are two major themes to be considered here: the development of what we might call respectively the machinery and instruments of credit. By *machinery of credit* is meant the ways in which government was brought into contact with potential lenders, the intermediaries and institutions which allowed government access to sources of loanable funds. *Instruments of credit* are the means by which these potential lenders were persuaded to become creditors to the government.

Before considering this in more detail it is worth pausing to consider some further important terms. On the whole creditors are willing to lend money because they expect some return on it. There is though some risk. One consideration affecting the decision of a lender is therefore the *security* of the loan, the certainty of getting the loan repaid. Borrowers, therefore, offer some form of security, usually in the form of assets already owned or of future income. Clearly some lenders offer more security than others and some forms of security breed more confidence than others. In order to make a relatively risky loan more attractive, borrowers might offer higher *returns*, a higher rate of interest. On the other hand, borrowers who are offering good security do not have to pay so much in order to borrow. Other considerations might also affect a lender, particularly the *liquidity* of their loan. By this is meant the ease with which the right to collect the loan can be sold on to someone else should the creditor want his or her money back before the loan is due for repayment. These variations of security, returns and liquidity combine in a wide variety of possible loans, each enticing a different kind of lender. For the government, as we will see, the rules were slightly different, since it was open to governments to coerce lenders or to offer incentives other than interest. In the long run, however, a system of government credit developed offering combinations of security, returns and liquidity that tempted increasingly large numbers of people to lend voluntarily.

In the later sixteenth and early seventeenth centuries the money market was poorly suited to the provision of loans to the government.[27] The instruments of credit (bills, bonds and pledges) were designed primarily to facilitate trade. They allowed short-term credit to merchants between receipt of goods and payment for them, and were usually for relatively small amounts of money. The crown, by contrast, sought loans of large sums for longer periods. Secondly, these forms of credit were essentially *personal*, depending on the word and reputation of individual traders. Whereas the security offered by a merchant, whose livelihood depended on maintaining his credit, was usually sufficient, the word of the king offered less security. This problem of security led the crown to borrow on the security of others – prominent individuals or corporations (notably that of London). Lenders were also coerced to provide forced loans. The crown did not have a very elaborate machinery at its disposal and tended to operate through intermediaries who could tap funds from a wider range of sources. Despite the problem of security, however, the crown had some advantages in these operations. Above all, without necessarily offering direct cash rewards, the crown could offer economic privileges or threaten withdrawal of them: unlike most borrowers the crown wielded both a big stick and could offer very juicy carrots. The shortcomings of the London money market had driven the crown to seek funds abroad in the sixteenth century, notably in Antwerp, but in this market it suffered many of the disadvantages of the London market without being able to bully or bribe lenders so effectively. After 1574 the crown tried to avoid borrowing altogether, but if forced to seek credit it sought it at home where the pressure applied to lenders made borrowing very cheap: only £461,000 was borrowed between 1574 and 1603, and of this only £85,000 bore interest.

Under the early Stuarts demands for credit increased as ordinary expenditures outstripped ordinary supply and a cumulative deficit developed. However, there was little innovation in the ways in which credit was secured. The corporation of London raised considerable sums to lend to the government, either from rich aldermen or by organising subscriptions in the wards. By the late 1620s the city had been treated so badly that it was reluctant to act in this way. As a result the crown fell back increasingly on the offices of customs farmers. These syndicates of great merchants rented the right to collect the customs from the crown. This arrangement guaranteed the crown a certain level of income in the form of rent while the farmers were able to make a profit by collecting more than they paid to the crown. Tax farming had some advantages from a revenue point of view, then, offering a guaranteed return and devolving responsibility for collection onto others. Throughout the century, however, a counter-case was made that it cost the crown potential revenue. The farmers' profits were often an unknown quantity because to publicise them would invite an increase in rent. In general they were suspected to be very large and this was resented because it was, in a sense, profit at the expense of the crown which might have collected these duties itself. In the 1630s this case was made with some force by John Harrison and others who had been involved in customs farming. The crown had other interests apart from maximising revenue, however. The farmers' profits were clearly dependent on the power of the crown, and this gave the opportunity to pressure farmers to provide credit. The crown's preference for continued farming seems to owe much to the advantages of farming as a means of securing credit which obviously outweighed the cost in lost revenue. These credit operations thus provide 'a perfect example of the connexion between loans and economic privileges'.[28] Tax farmers continued to perform this important function as creditors of the crown in the mid and later seventeenth century, too.

Government borrowing, 1640-1688

During the 1640s and 1650s the scale of government borrowing increased dramatically and there were some changes in the mechanisms by which it was done, particularly after 1649.[29] Initially resort was made to the corporation of London, but the city was reluctant to lend after 1647. The gap was filled by tax farmers and prominent merchants such as Sir Martin Noell and Thomas Vyner. Some of these men became tax farmers and commissioners as well as government creditors. This represented a significant alienation of the control of finances by the executive. We will see how the perceived security of lending to government increased as the tax system appeared more reliable, but also as the personal influence of the monarch declined. The fiscal potential of parliamentary taxation was vastly increased in the 1640s and 1650s and this provided the security for important changes in credit techniques during the 1650 and 1660s.

The career of Martin Noell offers an illustration of the opportunities that the developing relationship between public and private finance offered in the later seventeenth century. Noell was an important shipper in the West Indian trade and an influential London alderman. During the 1650s he built up extensive contacts in government circles. He acted as a contractor for the army and navy, securing beds, blankets and saltpetre. In 1655 he was appointed to the Committee of Trade. The same year an expeditionary force captured Jamaica from the Spanish and Noell organised the shipping of royalist prisoners to Jamaica in conditions that caused something of a scandal at the time. He also sold saltpetre to the Spanish when the English government would not buy and there are suspicions that he used his government influence to evade the restrictions imposed on trade by the navigation act. In part his eminence, and his leverage with government, depended on his activities as a government creditor. In 1645 he was acting as a creditor and bought sequestered lands in Lancashire and Yorkshire. The salaries and allowances of all English diplomatic representatives during the 1650s were paid by bills of exchange in Noell's name. In other words, local people were willing to supply money and goods to government officials because they could reclaim the money from Noell. The security was as much his name as the creditworthiness of the regime. In any case it reflects a remarkable degree of influence on his part. He also farmed the revenues of the Post Office and various excises (including that on salt). His interests in the revenue expanded during the 1650s and at the restoration he received further preferment. More revenue farms, a free gift of £8,000 from the king and a knighthood confirmed his usefulness to government. The government continued to be helpful to him. One of his interests was the farm of the customs duty on tobacco and it was he who suggested that the cultivation of tobacco in Gloucestershire should be stamped out. The role of government finance in his rise was significant. 'We may safely claim that no merchant-financier of such towering eminence had emerged in England in the years before the Great Rebellion.' His own account of this rise to wealth and influence commenced with his acquisition of the farm of salt excise revenues in the late 1640s.[30] Other men, such as Sir Thomas Vyner and Sir Edward Backwell, proved equally valuable to successive regimes. Backwell, in fact, received a knighthood from Cromwell and a baronetcy from Charles II.[31]

In a way these men were similar to previous great merchants who had been able to act as intermediaries for government borrowing. Credit continued to be raised through the corporation of London and through the East India Company, and through the farmers of the customs and excise, too. There were some significant developments in the machinery of credit, though. In particular, two new sources of credit were being tapped. Another important group of government creditors were the 'Goldsmith bankers', men who went into banking initially as a side line. Their principal other commercial interests generated cash balances that they were able to lend at a profit, and this came to be an increasingly important part of their business. These men had begun to develop techniques of deposit banking that attracted loans from a large section of society, and these funds could be reinvested with government for good returns. Another important group of intermediaries were people acting as government creditors who were able to attract loans from others by virtue of their position in government. This came to be seen as offering good security. Cashiers of the customs and excise and the paymaster general, Sir Stephen Fox, made short-term loans to the government in anticipation of the moneys that would be paid in to them. Fox, after 1674, controlled both receipt and issue of money, and gave a comprehensive guarantee to raise whatever money was needed to pay the army. This sets him apart from other individuals in the early seventeenth century who had acted as contractors to the government: the security he offered was the control he had over tax revenues. The Goldsmith bankers did not have these institutional links, but they mobilised funds from a very wide public through deposit banking – Edward Backwell, for example, held deposits from 1,372 clients, averaging £520, in 1664-5.[32] Here, the development of government borrowing depended on the development of banking, but equally the attractiveness of investing with men such as Backwell was increased because they had good opportunities to reinvest, at high rates of return, in government.

These changes in the machinery of credit were complemented by changes in the instruments of credit. These are rather technical issues but would bear some explanation here. During the 1650s the navy was financed with the help of borrowing on an unprecedented scale. Lenders were induced to lend by the dependability of the taxes available to the governments of the 1650s and apparently became reluctant to lend only when levels of taxation were reduced for political reasons. At the same time, however, new instruments of credit also offered greater security. Specifically, a system of payment orders was introduced which guaranteed repayment of debts in the order in which they had been contracted. Thus, lenders were freed from the fear of endless procrastination while lenders with more political leverage secured preferential treatment.[33]

In the 1660s there were further developments, particularly the increasing use of two new forms of credit – the repayment order and the fiduciary order (see pp. 41–2). The success of these orders ultimately depended on the security offered by parliamentary control of revenue, in other words on the tax system. Short-term credit had in the past been raised using exchequer tallies, of which there were two kinds. The tally of *pro* had the name of the creditor inscribed on it and guaranteed repayment from a particular part of the revenue. It was thus very secure but offered less liquidity. The tally of *sol* had the advantage to the government of leaving its hands free – it was not limited in the way that it was by the tally of *pro*. For the lender the reduced security that it offered was offset by increased liquidity. After 1665, 'repayment orders' were issued with tallies of *sol*, guaranteeing repayment in strict order from the proceeds of the tax. This made the tally of *sol* as secure as a tally of *pro*, while retaining liquidity. To make this work, however, a strict power of appropriation was necessary. This meant that the tax had to be spent for the purposes for which it had been granted. Put another way, the crown had to be prevented from diverting the funds elsewhere, causing it to default on its debts. In order to achieve this, powers of audit were necessary – the power to check that appropriation was being honoured.

Increased powers of audit and appropriation represented a loss of control by the crown. This is not the only instance of security being improved by reducing the crown's freedom of action. For example, when the city of London made loans to the crown in the 1660s the city took over the tax altogether – the chamberlain received money directly from collectors and made payments from the Guildhall (the treasury of the city).[34] Other intermediaries were also able to raise credit in part at least because they had a significant degree of control over revenues. This was plainly true of the cashiers of the excise and customs and Sir Stephen Fox, as we have seen. In effect their success in raising loans depended, to an extent, on the fact that they secured control over receipts and issues at the expense of the crown.

Taken together these measures of the 1650s and 1660s made

government credit more attractive. They depended on parliamentary powers of appropriation, audit and, above all, the availability to government of predictable and lucrative taxes. After 1649, then, the system of government borrowing had developed considerably. Great merchants like Noell operated on a scale that was unknown before the revolution, and their creditworthiness depended in part on their connections with government. Noell, though, was not completely unlike his predecessors. More innovatory was the way in which cashiers and contractors in the later period were able to use their office to secure credit. The most important change in the machinery of credit in this period, however, was the use the government was able to make of the developing banking system. Goldsmith bankers tapped the wealth of a wide circle of lenders and was able to put this capital at the disposal of government. There were also important developments in the instruments of credit, particularly the order systems of the 1650s and 1660s. These improved the security offered to short-term creditors to the government: those who supplied goods or services in advance of payment to government departments. These instruments of short-term credit were of great importance to government finance and the developments of the mid-century of long-term significance. An important feature of these developments was the loss of the monarch's personal influence over these borrowings.

Government borrowing after 1689

There had been important changes in the nature of short-term borrowing during the 1650s and 1660s, offering increased security to lenders. There was also an important development in long-term borrowing. During the 1660s another kind of short-term credit had developed – the fiduciary order. This was a credit note secured against the credit of the exchequer as a whole, not against a particular source of revenue. It was secure as long as not all were presented at once, and in this respect resembled paper money. It circulated among the commercial population and was respected as a means of settling accounts, so long as the credit of the exchequer remained good. Unfortunately too many fiduciary orders were issued and their holders lost confidence. There was run on them and the exchequer had to stop honouring them. This failed experiment led to another one, this time successful. Those who were owed money were issued with annuities: credit agreements offering an annual payment in return for an initial investment. In this case, the 'investment' was the sum that the government owed. This converted a short-term debt into a long-term one, and the confidence of the investor depended on their confidence that the government would make these payments over a long period. These annuities were a success, and there was a lively market in them. This reflects, again the way in which the security of government borrowing had improved. Again, an important part of this increased confidence derived from the taxing capacity of the government.

The most dramatic changes in long-term borrowing, however, came after 1689 with the creation of a *national* debt, as distinct from a royal one which might depend on 'the Breath in a Man's Nostrils'.[35] Using credit instruments developed for the private market – insurance, mortgages, stocks and shares – a vast debt was accumulated. Much of the capital of this debt was irredeemable, that is it did not have a particular date for repayment or that date may have been many years in the future. Creditors gained their profits from interest or by the selling the title to the sum that they were owed. In order to make their money back lenders would have to receive interest payments for a number of years. The dependability of these returns was also essential if the title to the debt was to have any value on the market – it was this that would attract potential buyers. These forms of long-term debt, more even than the instruments described above, therefore required a very considerable degree of confidence in the durability and fiscal probity of the regime. Indeed many contemporaries observed that it created a vested interest in the constitutional settlement of 1688–9, since it was not at all clear that a future Stuart monarch would honour the debts accumulated during the 1690s and thereafter. There were also developments in the machinery of credit, notably in the creation of the Bank of England in 1694. This was part of an attempt by the government to raise a long-term loan of £1.2 million. Part of the inducement offered to potential creditors was that if a certain proportion of the sum was raised within a particular period of time, the creditors would be incorporated as the Bank. This would allow them to undertake other commercial operations. Increasingly, the government turned to the Bank to raise further loans and to handle their administration.

As in the 1660s, however, innovation was not wholly successful at the first attempt. In order to induce lenders the government offered, among other things, long-term annuities at fixed (high) interest rates. These had proven extremely popular but they had disadvantages for the government. The high interest rates saddled future governments with a heavy burden following the end of the wars, one on which the interest rate could not easily be reduced. Equally, the debt could not be redeemed by paying of the capital sum. The solution was to lure investors to exchange their government debts for stock in the newly created South Sea Company which was granted trading privileges in return for lending money to the government. Many government creditors gave up their government securities hoping for quicker returns on the stock exchange. Many lost out, for reasons we do not need to consider, but the whole exercise illustrates how complex government borrowing had become. The complexities were so great, in fact, that they were handled, increasingly, not by the exchequer but by the Bank of England.

Although the sums raised in the 1690s created new mechanisms of long-term borrowing by comparison with what came later their yield was relatively modest: £6.9 million out of total expenditure of £72 million between 1688 and 1702. This was partly because the cost of the wars was underestimated, the yield of the taxes overestimated and because the government was nervous about borrowing. One result was heavy short-term borrowing: £32 million between 1688 and 1697 for example. This forced down the value of exchequer tallies, which began to look less secure. On two occasions tallies were exchanged for stock in order to forestall credit crises. As in the 1660s the security of short-term borrowing depended on maintaining a safe proportion in relation to tax receipts. The exchequer and other departments began to issue bills akin to fiduciary orders which could be passed on and circulate like money. So long as not all were presented at the exchequer at once, they could be issued to a value beyond the actual cash reserves. Two chartered companies, the East India Company and the South Sea Company, also lent money to the government. This provided the security by which they, too, could borrow, again suggesting considerable confidence in the security of government credit. These companies also began issue bills that circulated like paper money. The connection between the development of public and private credit was clearly intimate.

The 'financial revolution' as defined by Dickson lasted for seventy years after the glorious revolution, and only the opening phase has been covered here. By the end of the period covered by this book, however, many of its central features were established. It has also been suggested that we should give greater prominence to the developments of the 1650s and 1660s in understanding this transformation.[36] Certainly by 1714, or at least by the 1720s, the sheer scale of the debt, the range of government creditors, the means by which they were induced to lend and the administrative measures to control the debt were largely established. Most important for present purposes though, were the implications for taxation. These elaborate credit arrangements depended on making government security attractive. In this the expansion of the tax base of government in the 1640s was crucial and so was the process by which, in stages from the 1660s onwards, control of the flow of these funds was taken out of the hands of the monarch by means of appropriation and audit. In this way the royal debt became a national debt, and 'it is with the national debt that modern finance begins'.[37]

Public borrowing increased the spending power of the British government by nearly 34 per cent in the 1690s and by up to 40 per cent in the eighteenth century. This considerably increased the military capacity of the British state and is an important part of the history of the capture of empire. It is also important to the history of the eighteenth century economy: the financial revolution was important to subsequent industrial growth. The centrality of borrowing on parliament security and against parliamentary taxation to the military effort of the eighteenth century state had obvious political implications – parliament itself became essential. Indeed, many contemporaries thought that the financial measures of the 1690s represented a political plot by the enemies of monarchical power. It has been suggested that the measures of the 1660s, which improved the security offered to lenders by reducing the power of the monarch, provided a foretaste of the financial revolution. Some of the implications for the authority of the monarch were already clear at that point: Clarendon thought that they were 'introductive to a commonwealth'.[38] In the later period there were also accusations that it shifted the balance of power between social classes. Landowners possessed a visible form of easily taxed wealth and bore the burden of taxation while merchants were not only relatively lightly taxed, but profited from the creation of a tax state by lending money. The essential arguments were much elaborated, and we will return to them later, but we should note again the relationship between finance, taxation and political and social history.

In order to understand the development of the tax system we need to know more than just what the money was being spent on. Government credit developed dramatically in this period and the demands of the credit system were an important influence on the revenue system (see document 17, for example). Public borrowing changed radically in the period covered by this book with consequences that were far from narrowly financial. A necessary preliminary to this, and the consequences of profound importance that followed from it, was the existence of a productive and reliable tax system, operating at an acceptable political cost. But the relationship was not just one-way: the demands of borrowing shaped the evolution of the tax system, too, notably in the adoption and long persistence of tax farming. This was feasible only for indirect taxation granted for long periods, and these also became security for long-term borrowing. We have also noted the role of excise cashiers in offering advances to the government as an example of the way that tax administration was affected by the development of borrowing. Another might be the way in which, during the 1660s, government handed over the receipt of extraordinary supply to creditors with the result that the interests of these people began to figure in the collection of taxes, either directly or as a means of pressurising tax collectors. The next three chapters now consider the sources of revenue available to meet these spending requirements and to offer security to potential government creditors.

Notes

1 G. E. Aylmer, *The king's servants. The civil service of Charles I 1625-1642*, London, 1961, p. 248.

2 W. MacCaffrey, 'Patronage and politics under the Tudors' in L. L. Peck (ed.), *The mental world of the Jacobean court*, Cambridge, 1991, pp. 21-35; M. Gray, 'Power, patronage and politics: office-holding and administration on the crown's estates in Wales' in R. W. Hoyle (ed.), *The estates of*

the English crown 1558–1640, Cambridge, 1992, pp. 137–62.

3   Gray, 'Power, Patronage and Politics', p. 252n.

4   G. E. Aylmer, *The state's servants: the civil service of the English republic 1649–1660*, London, 1973, p. 323.

5   *Ibid.*, p. 324.

6   Reprinted in S. R. Gardiner (ed.), *The constitutional documents of the puritan revolution 1625–1660*, 3rd edition, Oxford, 1906, p. 414, article 27.

7   C. D. Chandaman, *The English public revenue 1660–1688*, Oxford, 1975, appendix III.

8   'The civil government expenditures included the fees and salaries of the ministers and many other public officers, the salaries of many of the small fry in various government departments, the salaries and pensions of judges, the salaries and allowances of ambassadors and consuls, and the maintenance of buildings for Parliament and the public offices. The expenditures for the support of the king, royal family, and the dignity of the Crown included the king's privy purse, allowances for the heir and other members of the royal family, the cost of the royal household, and the maintenance of the royal palaces and parks. Pensions and charities came out of the Civil List, as well as the undefined expenditure for secret service and special service.' E. A. Reitan, 'The civil list in eighteenth-century British politics: parliamentary supremacy versus the independence of the crown', *Historical Journal*, IX, 1966, pp. 318–37, p. 319.

9   W. R. Scott, *The constitution and finances of English, Scottish and Irish joint-stock companies to 1720*, 3 vols., Cambridge, 1910–12, III, p. 505.

10   D. Hirst, *Authority and conflict. England 1603–1658*, London, 1986, p. 57.

11   R. Cust, *The forced loan and English politics 1626–8*, Oxford, 1987, pp. 1–2. In 1624/5, £278,494 4s 11d was spent for castles, forts, clothing and supplies alone, with another £68,000 spent by the ordnance office: R. W. Stewart, 'Arms and expeditions: the ordnance office and the assaults on Cadiz (1625) and the Isle of Rhé (1627)', in M. C. Fissel (ed.), *War and government in Britain, 1598–1650*, Manchester, 1991, pp. 112–32, p. 129n.

12   Chandaman, *English public revenue*, p. 211. Over £5 million was granted by parliament to meet this expenditure. *Ibid.*, p. 228. Not all of this was 'war' expenditure – some of it would have been required in peace time, too.

13   J. Brewer, *The sinews of power. War, money and the English state, 1688–1783*, London, 1989, p. 40.

14   J. Childs, *The Nine Years' War and the British army 1688–97. The operations in the low countries*, Manchester, 1991, pp. 47–8.

15   F. C. Dietz, *English public finance 1485–1641*, vol. II, *1558–1641*, London, 1964, pp. 436–48.

16 M. J. Braddick, 'An English military revolution?', *Historical Journal*, XXXVI, 1993, pp. 965–75; Chandaman, *English public revenue*, appendix III. The figures are £14,735,050 out of £47,613,550.

17 Gardiner, *Constitutional documents*, p. 414.

18 G. Holmes, *The making of a great power. Late Stuart and early Georgian Britain, 1660–1722*, Harlow, 1993, pp. 170–1.

19 Chandaman, *English public revenue*, appendix III; Dietz, *English public finance*, pp. 81, 109.

20 Stewart, 'Arms and expeditions', pp. 112–13.

21 Chandaman, *English public revenue*, appendix III; Dietz, *English public finance*, II, p. 109. The costs of Tangier in the period 1673–80 are included in the figures for military expenditure cited above.

22 Chandaman, *English public revenue*, appendix III.

23 Brewer *Sinews*, p. 40; Reitan, 'Civil list in eighteenth century British politics', p. 319.

24 Brewer, *Sinews*, p. 30.

25 *Ibid.*, p. 41.

26 R. Ashton, 'Deficit finance in the reign of James I', *Economic History Review*, 2nd series, X, 1957, pp. 15–29; Scott, *Joint-stock companies*, III, pp. 488–9.

27 The following paragraphs are based primarily upon R. Ashton, *The crown and the money market 1603–1640*, Oxford, 1960; R. B. Outhwaite, 'The trials of foreign borrowing: the English crown and the Antwerp money market in the mid-sixteenth century', *Economic History Review*, 2nd series, XIX, 1966, pp. 289–305; and Outhwaite, 'Royal borrowing in the reign of Elizabeth I: the aftermath of Antwerp', *English Historical Review*, LXXXVI, 1971, pp. 251–263.

28 Ashton, *Crown and money market*, p. 103.

29 The following paragraphs are based primarily upon: M. P. Ashley, *Financial and commercial policy under the Cromwellian protectorate*, London, 1934; W. P. Harper, 'Public borrowing, 1640–60', unpubl. MSc, London, 1927; G. O. Nichols, 'English government borrowing, 1660–1688', *Journal of British Studies*, X, 1971, pp. 83–104; Nichols, 'Intermediaries and the development English government borrowing: the case of Sir John James and Major Robert Huntingdon, 1675–79', *Business History*, XXIX, 1987, pp. 27–46; H. Roseveare, *The financial revolution 1660–1760*, London, 1991; W. A. Shaw, 'The beginnings of the national debt' in T. F. Tout and J. Tait (eds.), *Historical essays by members of the Owens College, Manchester ...*, London, 1902, pp. 391–422; J. S. Wheeler, 'English financial operations during the first Dutch War, 1652–54', *Journal of European Economic History*, XXIII, 1994, pp. 329–43; Wheeler, 'Navy finance, 1649–1660', *Historical Journal* (forthcoming). I am grateful to Professor Wheeler for allowing me to consult this work prior to publication.

30 E. Hughes, *Studies in administration and finance 1558–1825 with special reference to the history of salt taxation in England*, Manchester, 1934, pp. 133–5.

31 Roseveare, *Financial revolution*, p. 12.

32 *Ibid.*, p. 19.

33 Wheeler, 'Navy finance'.

34 Nichols, 'English government borrowing', p. 89.

35 P. G. M. Dickson, *The financial revolution in England. A study in the development of public credit 1688–1756*, London, 1967, p. 16.

36 Roseveare, *Financial revolution*; Wheeler, 'English financial operations' and 'Navy finance'.

37 Ashton, *Crown and the money market*, p. 187.

38 Roseveare, *Financial revolution*, p. 15.

3

The customs

The customs consistently produced 30 or 40 per cent of total revenues in this period. This reflects the fact that their yield, quite exceptionally among the revenues available to the Tudors, expanded very rapidly. The customs were worth £89,000 in 1558/9 rising to £1 million or more per annum in the late 1680s, a level sustained throughout the 1690s.[1] For this reason alone they deserve detailed consideration. But they must also be treated separately from the demesne and parliamentary revenues because they do not fit neatly into either category. Before 1640 their status was ambiguous and contested, but after 1660 they were more firmly under parliamentary control. Before considering the local administration of the customs, and the administrative reforms that allowed their yield to keep pace with the increasing scale of revenues as a whole, we must first examine the origins and constitutional status of the customs.

The evolution and constitutional status of the customs

The history of the customs in the late sixteenth and early seventeenth centuries is marked by serious legal and constitutional dispute. In order to understand the grounds for these arguments it is necessary to understand how the customs had evolved. The customs system was very complex. Successive layers of duties, of different origin and raised by different authorities, overlay one another, with the result that a single item might have owed duty under several different headings. The most lucrative duties were those of tonnage and poundage (see pp. 51–2, below). These were parliamentary taxes to the extent that the right to collect them depended on parliamentary grant. Since the reign of Henry VI this grant had been made at the beginning of each reign. Other, less lucrative duties were the crown's 'own', however, either having prerogative origins or having been granted to the crown in perpetuity. These are usually referred to as the ancient customs. Moreover, the monarch had two further powers that mitigated the extent of parliamentary control. Although parliament granted tonnage and poundage, the rates at which these duties were levied was determined by the book of rates, and the issue of the book of rates was in the power of the crown, not parliament. Secondly, Tudor and early Stuart monarchs successfully imposed new customs duties – the impositions – without parliamentary sanction and with (apparent) legal backing. Thus, although the right to collect a part of this complex system of duties rested on parliamentary grant, the customs before 1641 appear in many ways to have been, effectively, prerogative taxation.

The origins of the practical and constitutional complexity were historical. The origins of the duties are obscure.[2] Some authorities argue that they represent a commutation of seizures of goods into a cash payment, others that they built on local systems of tolls raised by towns or manorial lords. By the thirteenth century, it has been suggested, a semi-national system of rates, collected on the initiative of the monarch and by prerogative right overlay these local tolls. They were only 'semi-national', however, because parts of them (particular tolls or tolls in particular places) were granted away to individuals in a process referred to by Gras as 'subinfeudation' or were subject to exemptions. The 'new aid' of 1266 seems to have been a duty on all imports and exports, possibly of an *ad valorem* kind – that is a percentage of the value of the goods. However, 'it lasted only a few years and met an unknown fate'.[3] Although it was subject to some exemptions it was not prey to subinfeudation, and was therefore a forerunner of the truly national customs system which, all authorities agree, was founded in 1275.

The duties raised in 1275 became known as the ancient (or great) customs. They were granted in a full parliament but at the request of the merchants.[4] The duties admitted no exceptions and fell on three exported commodities – wool, woolfells (the skin with the wool still on it) and hides. A second set of national duties was added in 1303 (the *carta mercatoria* duties), this time not by parliamentary grant but by agreement between king and foreign merchants. These duties (the new or petty customs) were imposed on imports and exports by aliens in return for a charter granting a variety of privileges. The principal commodities affected were wine, wool, woolfells and hides exported, and imported and exported cloth. This grant was, according to Gras, of royal origin, although clearly there is some evidence of a con-tractual arrangement. He suggests, however, that there is no evidence of parliamentary confirmation. A further royal grant was the cloth custom of 1347, later known as pannage, which imposed further rates on the cloth trade, payable by alien merchants.[5]

There were, then, three distinct grants of customs duties, only one of them by parliament. The same commodities though, were named in different grants. This is the first of the complications of the customs duties – that the same commodity could pay duty under different heads. Thus the 1303 duties on wool, woolfells and hides became, in practice, amalgamated with the 1275 duties, while the duties on cloth imposed in 1303 merged with those of 1347: in effect particular commodities paid duties that were an amalgamation of grants of differing origins. What became known as the great custom was the combination of duties on wool, woolfells and hides, the petty custom the combination of duties on cloth. By our period, the petty custom was in fact the more profitable. Of these duties, the 1275 and 1303 rates (all the great customs and part of the petty customs) rates required no renewal.[6]

These customs duties, of diverse origin, became the king's by right. A second general class of duties remained under parliamentary control, the subsidies and tonnage and poundage. In the later medieval period these were the most lucrative duties.[7] They were extensions, for limited periods of time, to the existing duties and were essentially of two kinds: the subsidy of wool, woolfells and hides; and tonnage and poundage. Subsidies augmenting the wool customs were collected continuously from 1336 onwards and in 1362 it was accepted that they required parliamentary grant. In practice, however, they were granted continuously. In 1398, 1415 and 1453 life grants were made to the monarch, autho-rising retrospectively collections since the beginning of the reign.

This, as we will see, is relevant to the history of the duties under Charles I. Tonnage and poundage had its origins in the 1347 grant of a rate on wine and all other commodities. It was made by the council but was subsequently a parliamentary grant, usually tied to the defence of shipping. In 1433 tonnage and poundage raised a little less than the wool custom, but by the sixteenth century had become very valuable. As it developed it became a lifetime grant to the monarch, and from Richard III's reign onwards was made in the first year of a monarch's reign until the failure to secure agreement in 1625. To an extent then, these subsidies and tonnage and poundage were parliamentary taxes, supplementary to the king's right to collect customs on particular commodities in perpetuity, and they were more valuable than the ancient customs duties.

However, the precise nature of the constitutional position of these duties was unclear, the practical realities of parliamentary control still less so. The habit of granting the duties to the monarch at the beginning of the reign was observed from the accession of Henry VI until the accession of Charles I. At that point, however, it was broken, and this used to be interpreted as evidence of an attack on the independent financial powers of the monarchy. Recent work, however, has suggested that, at the very least, parliamentary reluctance to grant tonnage and poundage to Charles I did not amount to a desire to exercise the 'power of the purse'. Instead, it has been suggested, the grant was regarded as belonging to the king by right. In 1625 parliament had wanted to review the customs duties in general. Accordingly the king was offered the duties of tonnage and poundage for twelve months to tide him over while these negotiations went on. The intention was, it seems, to incorporate some impositions into the tonnage and poundage act. Unfortunately parliament was dissolved, for other reasons, before this grant was made and long before the negotiations were complete. Rather than representing an insult to the crown we could regard it as an attempt to a review all indirect taxation and to reduce some of the political frictions arising from its levy (see chapter 7 for the political problems of some of these duties). In the event the discussions never reached fruition and in the meantime Charles continued to collect the money. Parliament declared this illegal in 1626, but prepared a bill to indemnify the king. The privy council certainly interpreted events in this way and the account given in the privy council register clearly does not support the view that parliament withheld the grant deliberately (see document 22). Even in 1628 it was quite willing to reach agreement on the issue until the argument over the petition of right soured the atmosphere.[8] Only during 1640 and 1641 was the grant used deliberately and consciously to force the king's hand in negotiations.[9] It does also suggest, however, that even these parts of the customs duties were far from 'parliamentary' in their nature: they were collected for fifteen years or so without parliamentary authority, but on the authority of the privy council. On the other hand, parliament was clearly eager to extend the range of its sanction and to forestall the use of these events as a precedent.

The third component of the customs, the impositions, was really a Tudor innovation, although there were some medieval precedents. The impositions were of diverse origins, at least in the way that they were justified, but all derived from prerogative rights, and they were of increasing financial significance under James I and Charles I: by 1640, together with the praetermitted customs (see p. 133), they brought in nearly £250,000 per annum.[10] Some were openly imposed, to regulate trade (document 21) or as fines for the evasion of trade regulations, but others were introduced by manipulation of the books of rates. For example, Mary granted Southampton a monopoly on the importation of sweet wines, something that was clearly within her prerogative. In order to enforce this she imposed heavy import duties on wines landed at other places. It was increasingly common to lay such penalties and entirely new duties after 1558.[11]

Some impositions, then, were produced by manipulating the books of rates. These were lists of taxable commodities and the values at which duty was to be levied. Customs duties on the commodities listed were, therefore, paid not at the market rate but at a value set by the government. This simplified the administration, making rates uniform across the country and removed dependence of the administration on the merchant's own declaration of the value of the goods. The earliest book of rates seems to have been issued in 1507 in relation to the port of London, confirmed in 1532 and applied nationally in 1536. It was reissued in 1545 and 1550, but the rates remained the same until 1558.[12] In that year a new book was issued, introducing 300 new rates (mainly on imports) bringing the list of dutiable items to 1,100. Willan was able to compare the rates on 570 of these duties and found that 525 of them increased, some by 12.5 per cent, some by 1,100 per cent, the average of the sample being 119 per cent. There was no further revaluation, despite minor revisions, and sustained interest in the 1590s, until 1604. In this case the rates of 871 items can be compared. This reveals that 216 increased (by an average of 64 per cent), 590 remained the same and 65 decreased (by an average of 35 per cent). As a result the overall increase in the sample was 13 per cent, clearly a less significant response to inflation than the Marian revaluation.[13] Further revisions followed in 1613, 1615, 1622 and 1635.[14] There are some important points to note here. Clearly the levels of receipt from customs were largely dependent on the rates set down in the book of rates, and the issue of the books was not under parliamentary control before 1641. Instead it was done by cooperation between the crown and assemblies of merchants. Secondly, the issue of a new book of rates offered the government a means by which new impositions could be laid without parliamentary consent.

There were three elements in 'the customs' in the early seventeenth century then: the customs proper; the subsidy of wool etc. and tonnage and poundage; and the impositions. The grant of the second of these sets of duties lay in the power of parliament, although the practical reality of the power that parliament exercised over that revenue was clearly questionable. Moreover, the receipts from the customs were heavily influenced by the rates set out in the book of rates, and the issue of such books was not in the hands of parliament. Impositions, of course, lay entirely within the prerogative, if they were legal at all. In these ways, then, before 1641, the customs resemble prerogative income rather more than they resemble taxes. The book of rates was negotiated with merchants rather than with the representatives of taxpayers. This places these duties, politically and legally, in a different category from other potential indirect taxes on consumption, such as excises, which were regarded with horror in the 1620s. Simonds D'Ewes, not obviously eager to pay duties, was clearly aware of the distinction between these forms of customs duty in 1641:

> and now when his majestie hath not onlie received this subsidie of
> Tonnage and Poundage without law, but hath alsoe received vast

sums in another illegall way (I meant shipp-monie) and hath advanced his customes to an higher rate than ever anie of his roial progenitors enjoied, wee may well wonder that the Fleete should be now unprovided for.[15]

Parliament acknowledged certain duties to be the king's in 1642 – such as the ancient custom on wool, prisage and butlerage (see below) and the *carta mercatoria* duties of 1303.[16] The tonnage and poundage acts also tacitly acknowledged the king's independent rights to some duties. The acts granted tonnage and poundage and subsidies, noting that 'that the sums of money hereby granted upon merchandize are not the rates intended to be continued but the same to be hereafter in this present parliament altered in such manner as shall be thought fit'. They reduced the duties on tobacco and explicitly discounted the praetermitted customs and subsidies raised by letters patent. More generally the acts threatened a charge of *praemunire* against officials collecting any duty not granted by parliament or, alternatively, collected continuously from the end of the reign of Edward III to the beginning of the reign of Mary I. This last clause therefore included all the duties that were the king's own, but excluded all the impositions.[17] This clause was highly dubious, one would think, given the legal judgements in favour of a number of impositions (see below, chapter 7).

Important changes overtook the customs in 1641, and were confirmed in 1660. Firstly, Charles I lost control of tonnage and poundage, having conceded that collection depended on parliamentary grant, and was forced to negotiate on other issues in order to secure successive grants. Secondly, the impositions had been made illegal and this had a third consequence. Since the books of rates stated the values for impositions separately a new book of rates was necessary, adjusted to compensate for the loss of revenue from impositions. This book of rates was issued by parliament, not by the king and council. Hereafter, customs were collected by parliamentary authority according to rates set by parliament. They were clearly tax income after 1640, before that date their status had been more ambiguous.[18]

The administration of the customs

There are a number of complications in studying the 'customs' before 1640 then, arising from the variety of duties and the authority by which they were levied. This could result in one commodity paying several different duties on import or export. This complexity was exacerbated by the way in which the duties were collected. The right to collect particular duties was sometimes granted to different people, with the result, potentially, that the same commodity paid not just different duties but made the payments to different people. This complicated system evolved from what was, in origin, a very simple system of local administration.

We lack a detailed study of the local administration of the customs in our period before 1696, but it appears that it had changed very little in principle since 1275. The administration was shaped by the bureaucratic weakness of national government in the face of potential corruption or negligence in the ports. From 1275 onwards there is strong evidence of concern at collusion between customs officials and merchants in order to evade the duties (see chapter 8 for a discussion of evasion). To overcome this the crown established a fourfold division of responsibility. Each port had a collector who received the money, paying it to the exchequer or to an assignee. They also issued 'cockets' to merchants importing or exporting goods. Cockets were documents that certified the nature and quantity of the cargo being carried. A comptroller (or controller) in each port kept a counter-register against which the records of the collector could be checked. Usually the king appointed controllers to check his own collectors, but the thoroughness of the check could be increased by making the two officers responsible to different interests. In the medieval period, for example, the customs were sometimes collected by appointees of the king, but the money was due to assignees, not to the exchequer. In these circumstances the controller was appointed by the assignees, not the king. Alternatively, if the customs were being collected by assignees, the king appointed the controller to check the collector.

The third major officer in the port was the searcher. He was responsible for checking the cockets issued and the receipts for moneys paid against the cargoes being carried. He also checked, for example, that the victuals being carried duty free did not exceed the allowances or that passengers were not carrying gold or silver. The fourth official was the surveyor, who had oversight of the records of the other three, over all the traffic in the port and over all cockets, receipts and certificates, which were to be signed by him. It has been noted rather gloomily, that '[t]he necessity of such an officer is commentary enough upon the morality of the customs branch of the early English civil service'.[19]

As the medieval system developed there were normally three sets of collectors and controllers in each port: one for the old and new customs; one for cloth custom; and one for the subsidies and tonnage and poundage. In 1568 London had collectors for the petty custom on imports, the petty custom on exports, the tonnage and poundage on imports, the tonnage and poundage and imposts on exports, the great custom (or custom and subsidy on wool) and the impost on wines.[20] Collectors were usually substantial local merchants, sometimes locally chosen but more often appointed by the king. The controller was a salaried post, from the mid fourteenth century onwards usually filled by a royal appointee, sometimes local men of lesser substance, sometimes a royal clerk whose duties were performed by deputies. Searchers were salaried royal appointments. In all cases fee income was more significant than the salary, and there were ample opportunities for corruption (document 20). We know very little about this level of administration in our period before the later seventeenth century, by which time there was a multiplicity of offices, many of them useless, as we will see in a moment.

Initially, such officials were appointed to London and the 13 outports. The coast either side of each port was the responsibility of these officers. Thus, London's 'port' extended to Gravesend, that of Great Yarmouth from Blakeney to Woodbridge.[21] Gradually the numbers of ports increased (by 1671 there were 20 ports in addition to London). Each headport, as they were now termed, had member ports (51 in 1671) and creeks (113 in 1671) over which the officers also had jurisdiction. For example, Poole had the member ports of Weymouth and Lyme Regis attached, had two creeks of its own (Wareham and Swanage) and two attached to each member port (Lulworth and Portland to Weymouth, Charmouth and Bridport to Lyme Regis).[22] This required the appointment of subordinate officers, and in the head ports themselves a range of further offices were created – watchers, waiters, wharfingers and so forth – to keep a closer watch on the traffic in the port.

Two other factors served to confuse the administration of the duties in the ports. One was the multiplication of duties after 1660, and particularly after 1690, and the other was the use of the customs administration to enforce trade regulations of a more general kind. The 1660 tonnage and poundage act listed only three kinds of duties – tonnage on wine imports, poundage (a rate of one shilling in the pound of the value of imports according to a new book of rates) and the ancient duty on wool. Subsequent additions had made the system difficult to understand by the 1680s, and the reign of Queen Anne saw more additions than the previous three reigns put together. Some were new duties on commodities already taxed, others were duties on new commodities. Under this system a merchant importing 20 reams of French paper (10 Atlas fine, 10 super royal) paid revenue under thirteen different headings. By 1784 100 separate accounts were being kept in the customs houses.[23] The complexity of these duties was a problem by 1713:

> The great difficulty that attends the knowledge of the Customs, especially the computation of the several Duties payable upon Importation or Exportation, arises chiefly from the many Branches of that Revenue, which are all to be kept separate & distinct, for the uses & purposes to which they are respectively applicable; from the multiplicity of Statutes relative to the same;-and from the frequent alterations by subsequent, additional or explanatory Acts; or by repealing & sometimes again reviving Clauses in several of them, according to the exigencies & emergencies of the Nation, or as they were found to be good or bad in their consequences.[24]

These complexities were increased by the various embargoes, quarantines and prohibitions the customs men were asked to enforce.[25]

In order to understand the structure of the local administration in detail in the late seventeenth century it is again necessary to narrate something of the history of the customs. As we have seen, in the medieval period there were three officers and a surveyor. For much of the Tudor and early Stuart period the customs collection was farmed. In those periods the three officers were still appointed by the monarch, and they became known as patentees. At the same time it became usual, it seems, for the farmers to appoint a collector. The officer previously known as the 'collector' was now known as the 'customer'. Increasingly the customer's role became less demanding, as collectors representing the farmers undertook most of the work previously undertaken by him. In 1671, when farming was ended, the two offices survived, that of the customer largely a sinecure, that of the collector functional. A similar division occurred in other offices.[26] In the fourteenth century, Chaucer had appointed deputies to conduct some of his business for him and by the late seventeenth century it was standard practice for the royal appointees to claim their fees, leaving the actual discharge of their duties to deputies. The number of such offices multiplied as the number of ports and creeks increased, all requiring oversight.

The end result was a customs service filled with useless offices held by sinecurists. This was a considerable expense – perhaps one-sixth of the costs of the outports is accounted for by spending on these offices.[27] It also meant that the patentees, not the treasury, controlled appointment to many local offices. Moreover, the patentees claimed large fees and allowances, often leaving insufficient remuneration for the active officers. This must have increased the temptations for officers to collude in evasions or fraud, accepting bribes to do so.

There was, then, an elaboration of local administration, and a separation between patentee officers and the active deputies. Larger numbers of officers were needed to patrol the expanding range of ports and creeks and to oversee the traffic of the ports. However, in general the principles of the administration were unchanged. They rested on a division of responsibility between the customer (collector), searcher and controller, with a degree of oversight from a surveyor, or equivalent. What Hoon says of the eighteenth century seems equally true of the earlier period: 'There was little systematic change.'[28]

Administrative reform in the customs

The national scheme of collection of these duties was very complex, with particular people licensed to collect particular duties in particular places. Under this system it was possible that a single commodity could pay its several duties each to a different person. This was one of the administrative problems that was progressively tackled in this period. Administrative reforms aiming to improve the customs revenue were usually made at this level, and were aimed at increasing the rigour of local administration. This was done in two ways – the issue of books of orders or administrative instructions; and closer supervision of the work of local officials.

The essential problem was to ensure a degree of accuracy in the work of local officials for whom the temptations to laziness or corruption were considerable (documents 19–20). Throughout the period, from 1573 onwards, instructions and orders were sent out with this intent and many historians interpret this as indirect evidence of the prevalence of such practices. For example, the 1573 book suggested that officers in London were attending for two and a half hours each day and that officers in the outports bought their positions at such high prices that they were forced to cheat the Queen in order to make their money back.[29] Various procedural changes, such as enlarging the wharf next to the customs house to increase the traffic there, and the recommendation that the book of rates be open in the house, suggest a similar concern to regulate administration. When the crown took over direct collection of the revenues in 1671 it took over also an elaborate manual of administration, the *index vectigalium*.[30]

Making these measures stick was another matter, and one that clearly tested the administrative capacity of the early modern state. One solution, adopted for much of our period, was farming.[31] Men with experience of the customs administration, such as Sir Thomas Smyth in the 1570s and 1580s, or great merchants in the period 1603–71, bought from the crown the right to collect the duties. The attraction of this scheme to the crown was partly the promise of credit and an advance on the revenue. However, the appeal of farming in the sixteenth century was certainly the promise of tighter local administration, although at other points (the 1560s, 1590s, 1642–62 and after 1671) closer administration was sought by other means. One of the initial obstacles to centralisation, however, was the interest of the exchequer where each royal official accounted separately and paid a fee for doing so. Any threat to this system therefore threatened the income of the exchequer officials.

In 1552 a commission was appointed to consider the royal revenues and recommended, among other things, farming the customs for two to three years at a time in order to check frauds and abuses, ensure enforcement of trade embargoes and to save on fees (presumably exchequer accounts were to be necessary only for the rental payments, not for all the separate payments made in the port). Municipalities and ports were envisaged as potential farmers. The scheme was not implemented, and neither was the obvious alternative of more widespread use of informers: both seem to have suffered from potential hostility. Instead, in the 1560s, two general-surveyors were employed to oversee the activities in all the custom houses in the country. They were given a share of any improvements in the revenue that they secured. In this sense their office was analogous to that of the hunters after concealed lands who also tried to locate and exploit fully crown resources that had been lost or neglected.

The surveyors lost office in 1568, possibly due to the unpopularity of their activities. Instead reliance was placed on searchers with extensive powers, on common informers and on detailed instructions to local offices. At the same time an alternative strategy was developing – farming. Since the 1560s duties on particular commodities had been farmed – notably the wine duties – and this resulted in less hostility. Farming particular commodities apparently upset fewer vested interests. However, farming did affect the interests of Sir Thomas Smyth and in the late 1560s he petitioned for a customs farm to compensate his loss. He was granted farms involving various combinations of duties and ports between 1570 and 1588, as was Francis Walsingham. Some goods and duties were not farmed, and the customs officers continued to account for them separately, but for much of this period the farms secured efficiencies. For example ports were grouped together under sub-farmers and deputies, and accounting was simplified. Rather than recording all payments the farmers only had to record their rental payments at the exchequer. Exchequer officials were given compensation and annuities to make up for the loss of income. This simplification of accounts also had a disadvantage, however, in that the government never knew how much the farmers were collecting. From 1585 onwards the farmers' own books had to be deposited at the exchequer in order to provide the basis for negotiation of new leases.

During the 1590s there was a return to direct collection for most duties, while retaining the improvements secured by the farmers, under the oversight of general-surveyors. Eventually these officials had jurisdiction over all the duties except wine and over all the ports except London. They retained the local administration established by the farmers, including the increased number of local officers. The central office was in London, but the officers travelled. Money was handled on their behalf by receivers, not by the customers, and was paid to the exchequer via the general-surveyors. This system was unpopular, not least with the exchequer, and customers were allowed to resume separate accounting at the exchequer. In the early seventeenth century there was a piecemeal return to farming, this time, it seems, driven by shorter-term financial considerations rather than a desire for administrative reform. During the 1590s the government was put under financial pressure by the costs of war. Hoping for better returns a series of leases were granted. This proved to be a prelude to farming on a national scale in 1604.[32] It was probably motivated partly by a desire for certainty in the revenue since there had been considerable fluctuations in receipts in the later 1590s. Farming also offered the promise of harnessing the anticipated improvement in trade following the war by handing administrative control to men with a financial interest in maximising receipts.

In this sense farming taxes was like farming land. A lease was negotiated which took account of the current value and the possible future value of the revenue. The crown received a regular rent, which may not, by the end of the lease, have reflected the full, improved value of the customs. This shortfall was made up at the renewal of the lease by enhancing the rent. Both landlord and tenant were able to profit from improvement. This was the system of administration that dominated from 1603 to 1671, with an intermission from 1642 to 1662.[33] The Great Farm of the customs, in 1604, covered most commodities (except tonnage on wine, prisage and the impositions). The initial rent was £112,400 per annum, rising with each lease to reach £172,500 in 1638. There were further increases after 1660, too: the farm was leased for £390,000 in 1662 and for £400,000 in 1667. The crown officers remained in place under the farm, and continued to keep accounts, but they deposited their books with two newly appointed general-surveyors. These books were to help with future negotiations for the leases. Although the impositions were not farmed they tended to be collected by the same financiers who leased the farms.

As with any landlord–tenant relationship there were disagreements about responsibility for various payments. If the king placed embargoes on trade with particular countries, or went to war, this obviously affected the value of the customs and could make the lease unfair. Similarly, new impositions could affect the volume of trade and hence of receipts. In the 1660s in particular, plague and (uniquely) the great fire posed serious threats to the income of the farmers. This was a disadvantage of all tax farming, and there were similar pleas from the excise farmers in the 1660s.[34]

Farming, then, offered a certain revenue and increasing rental value because the farmer had an incentive to make improvements. Moreover, farmers were, by offering advances, anticipating the revenue and frequently acted as willing creditors to the monarchy because they were anxious to secure renewals of their leases. These features explain the dominance of farming for much of the seventeenth century. However, there was always a suspicion that farmers were making unjustifiable profits from their leases and that the government could get more by cutting them out and resorting to direct collection. This, and the difficulties of negotiating leases, might explain the abandonment of farming.

During the 1640s and 1650s, for reasons that are not clear, the customs were administered by commissioners, initially taking their own accounts. Enforcement rested on the justices of the peace, before whom recalcitrants could be summoned, but this responsibility was later taken over by the commission. In 1649 exchequer accounting was restored and in 1654 the exchequer discipline was also restored. Commissioners were paid a percentage of receipts, and so had the same vested interest in efficiency that farmers had, and there were frequent changes of personnel to encourage competition. In 1657, however, apparently as a result of disappointment at the levels of receipt, an attempt was made to return to farming. It failed when Martin Noell, heavily committed already as a creditor of the regime, pulled out of the lease.[35]

The restoration government resorted to farming again in 1662 in an attempt to improve receipts. The 1660 tonnage and poundage act had introduced new rates but the yield of the customs proved to be 25 per cent lower than expected. This first farm

(1662–7) though, was disrupted by war, fire and plague and although the initial rent had been £390,000 per annum, in the event, in the final two years, receipts were only £210,000 after allowances to the farmers. A second, more successful farm (1667–71) with an annual rental of £400,000 improved receipts and a third lease was negotiated in 1671, setting the rent at £480,000 for five years. At the last minute, however, negotiations broke down. There were fears that the successful bidder, William Bucknall, had secured control over too large a share of national revenues. More importantly, it seems that the farmers over-played their hand in negotiations. They had previously advanced £200,000, much of which was already spent. With the end of the previous lease imminent they seem to have believed that they had the government over a barrel and tried to add new conditions. These probably related to conditions for future loans and guarantees of defalcations in the event of war. As a result of these demands, however, the government pulled out and the administration of the customs reverted to commission. This proved a great success, building on the improved administration of the farmers and benefiting from expanding trade. The commissioners saw steadily increasing yields until, in the 1690s, the customs were worth about £1 million per annum.[36] In these circumstances the leases and rent payments now appeared to have been not means by which to enhance or guarantee revenues, but to have acted as artificial restrictions on government receipts from a naturally expanding source.

We can briefly summarise this discussion of the customs. In the early seventeenth century there were three kinds of duty: the customs which were the king's own; tonnage and poundage and subsidies over which parliament had a degree of control; and the impositions raised by prerogative. The rates at which the customs duties were collected were based mainly on notional values, set down in the book of rates, rather than by market rates, although a number of duties were taxed *ad valorem* on the oath of the merchant. After 1640 the customs duties were securely under parliamentary control. In order to collect these duties collectors, controllers and searchers (and increasing numbers of auxiliary and deputy officers) were appointed by the crown to customs houses in London and the outports (of which there were about twenty by the late seventeenth century). Each customs house had jurisdiction over a number of member ports, and 'creeks'. In terms of receipts London dominated, probably yielding between two-thirds and three-quarters of total customs revenue for most of our period.[37] It had the most elaborate administration, and frequently separate provision was made for it in the organisation of the customs. The chief administrative problem, besides keeping rates up to date, was to ensure accuracy in registering the values of imports and exports. This problem was addressed by creating a division of interest in the ports, between collectors and controllers and searchers, and by increasing the level of oversight. This was done at a national level by the leasing of the right to collect the customs to farmers, or by employing crown officials in the collection – the general-surveyors. In general, farming was favoured until 1671 when, for short-term reasons, collection was placed in the hands of crown officials. This proved a great success. Direct collection witnessed constantly increasing revenues as trade increased and removed the potential tensions between farmers and government arising from the effects of changes in trade or foreign policy. Despite the problems of sinecurists in the port offices, underpay and the temptations to collude in evasion or smuggling, this administrative structure was largely unchanged between the late seventeenth and the late eighteenth centuries.

Notes

1 P. Williams, *The Tudor regime*, Oxford, 1979, p. 72; C. D. Chandaman, *The English public revenue 1660–1688*, Oxford, 1975, p. 35; C. G. A. Clay, *Economic expansion and social change. England 1500–1700*, 2 vols., Cambridge, 1984, II, p. 268.

2 On the early history of the customs see N. S. B. Gras, *The early English customs system. A documentary study of the institutional and economic history of the customs from the thirteenth to the sixteenth century*, Cambridge, Mass., 1918.

3 *Ibid.*, p. 57.

4 Brown suggests that behind it was an agreement with the merchants to pay duties in return for the re-opening of the Flanders trade: A. L. Brown, *The governance of late medieval England 1272–1461*, London, 1989, p. 66.

5 These grants are described in Gras, *Early English customs*, pp. 59–77.

6 Brown, *Governance*, p. 66

7 See *ibid.*, pp. 67–9 for the following.

8 C. Russell, *Parliaments and English politics 1621–1629*, Oxford, 1979. See also W. J. Jones, *Politics and the bench. The judges and the origins of the English civil war*, London, 1971, pp. 74–7.

9 C. Russell, *The fall of the British monarchies 1637–42*, Oxford, 1991, esp. pp. 256–8, 346–50, 357–64, 436–7.

10 R. Lockyer, *The early Stuarts. A political history of England 1603–1642*, London, 1989, p. 249.

11 For the early history of impositions see F. C. Dietz, *English public finance 1495–1641*, London, 1964, I, pp. 206–8, II, chapter 16; Gras, *Early English customs*, pp. 89–94; G. D. G. Hall, 'Impositions and the courts 1554–1606', *Law Quarterly Review*, LXIX, 1953, pp. 200–18.

12 N. S. B. Gras, 'Tudor "books of rates": a chapter in the history of the English customs', *Quarterly Journal of Economics*, XXVI, 1912, pp. 766–75. See also Dietz, *English public finance*, I, pp. 25, 207–8.

13 T. S. Willan (ed.), *A Tudor book of rates*, Manchester, 1962.

14 Dietz, *English public finance*, II, pp. 372–6.

15 Quoted in C. Russell, *The causes of the English civil war*, Oxford, 1990, p. 179.

16 H. Atton and H. H. Holland, *The king's customs*, 2 vols., London, 1908–10, I, p. 87.

17 *Statutes of the realm*, London, 1963, V, pp. 132–3. Repeated pp. 135–7, 139–41, 143–4, 174–6 (the latter differs in some details).

18 Jarvis notes the significance of the change, emphasising the confirmation of the change by the issue of the rates in 1660: R. C. Jarvis, 'Books of rates', *Journal of the Society of Archivists*, V, 1974–7, pp. 515–26, pp. 518–19. For books of rates see also the debate in *Journal of the Society of Archivists*, VI, 1978–81, pp. 227–9, 365.

19 Gras, *Early English customs*, p. 99. See *ibid.*, pp. 94–100 for an account of the early customs administration.

20 Dietz, *English public finance*, II, p. 310. For the administration of the late medieval customs see Brown, *Governance*, p. 70.

21 N. Williams, *Contraband cargoes. Seven centuries of smuggling*, London, 1959, pp. 3–4.

22 Atton and Holland, *The king's customs*, pp. 106–8.

23 E. E. Hoon, *The organization of the English customs system 1696–1786*, New York, 1938, pp. 26–7.

24 Quoted by *ibid.*, p. 32.

25 *Ibid.*, pp. 37–44.

25 *Ibid.*, pp. 5–25.

27 *Ibid.*, p. 14.

28 *Ibid.*, p. 4.

29 Dietz, *English public finance*, p. 313.

30 Chandaman, *English public revenue*, p. 29.

31 For the history of the Tudor and Stuart customs farms in general see Dietz, *English public finance*, II, chapters 14–15.

32 For this farm see, in particular, A. P. Newton, 'The establishment of the great farm of the English customs', *Transactions of the Royal Historical Society*, 4th series, I, 1918, pp. 129–55.

33 For customs farming under the Stuarts see Dietz, *English public finance*, II, chapter 15; R. Ashton, *The crown and the money market 1603–1640*, Oxford, 1960, chapter 4; and Chandaman, *English public revenue*, pp. 22–8.

34 For more routine disputes of this kind involving the excise farmers, see M. J. Braddick, *Parliamentary taxation in seventeenth-century England. Local administration and response*, Royal Historical Society Studies in History, 70, Woodbridge, 1994, pp. 204–7.

35 M. P. Ashley, *Financial and commercial policy under the Cromwellian protectorate*, London, 1934, chapter 6.

36 Chandaman, *English public revenue*, pp. 21–36.

37 Dietz, *English public finance*, p. 312; Ashley, *Financial and commercial policy*, p. 51–2; Chandaman, *English public revenue*, pp. 30, 89n.

4

Demesne revenues, prerogative income and concealed taxes

In the first chapter we saw how the balance of revenue shifted away from the demesne in our period. This chapter briefly describes the various revenues that derived from the demesne or from the king's personal rights in his realm. Many of them were taxes in most respects but, crucially, they were not necessarily so in the political sense implied by Schumpeter. In this chapter we need to consider the demesne income properly understood (that is, revenue from the crown lands), its extension to the king's vestigial feudal rights, and also a third category of 'prerogative taxes'.

The crown lands and forest fines

The crown lands did not yield a good revenue in our period. In part this was due to the unique nature of the crown estates.

> As a landowner, the Crown possessed every sort and type of landed property known to sixteenth- and seventeenth-century society. Much of its estates consisted of unexceptional leaseholds and copyholds of rural and urban tenements. ... Like most other landlords of status, it devoted a proportion of its land to unproductive ends for recreation, maintaining parks and forests.

Unlike many other landlords, however, the crown had estates so large that it was difficult to keep track of them and it was forced to delegate management on a scale that other landlords could avoid. It was also unusual among landlords in that its estate revenues were a small proportion of its total income. These differences help to explain the poor performance of the crown estates as sources of revenue in our period.[1]

The failure was also, partly, a managerial one. Under Elizabeth the emphasis of the management of the lands seems to have been to reduce the costs of administration and to stabilise income. This meant that even though the crown sold land the annual revenue to the crown was not reduced: savings in costs compensated for the loss of income from the alienated lands. The hands of the crown were, to an extent, tied by a traditional paternalism which sought to avoid over-burdening the tenantry. Limited administrative resources made it difficult even to keep track of landholdings, let alone ensure that they yielded the best possible income and tenurial arrangements were often formidably complex. One way of increasing revenue was to tempt improvers to take over the lands by offering long leases or reversions (a reversion means here the right to take up a tenancy on the expiration of the existing lease). This gave potential tenants the prospect of a long period in which to make a profit and so they might be willing to take on lands that were unimproved. In the long term it meant that an asset of the crown would be of increasing value and to this extent the arrangement might be mutually beneficial. However, there was a problem with both reversions and long leases in that they tied the hands of government for the future, too. In effect it lost control of its assets for long periods.

There were other reasons why the lands did not yield as much as they might have done. Perhaps most importantly, the lands were not simply a financial resource, and their use for other purposes reduced their financial value to the crown. For example, granting leases at low rents was a low-cost means of reward which had consequences for the income of the crown. The lands were used, therefore, as a means of patronage and reward as well as a source of regular income. They had two further important functions as well: they were used for recreation and, periodically, they could be sold to realise large sums of cash in an emergency – particularly war. There were, for example, heavy sales in the fifteen years after 1598.

In the seventeenth century improvements of marginal lands were made by speculators who sometimes made good profits. To an extent, these profits came at the expense of the crown. In this sense, the improvements harmed the revenue of the crown. On the other hand, the crown did benefit in the long term from the improvement of its assets, that could be leased for more money in the future. Also, in the short term the crown was able to get some money for an asset of little immediate value. On the whole, however, more aggressive management in the Jacobean period ran up against problems familiar from Elizabeth's reign. In particular careful management of the lands was hampered by the temptation to sell lands in moments of financial stress. By 1640, when the temptation was acute, there was little left to sell, and this strengthened the position of parliament.

Thus, the royal lands offered little prospect of self-sufficiency. In 1560 gross yield was about £115,000; in the last five years of Elizabeth's reign the average was around £142,066; in 1605 £145,000; 1621 £115,362; 1630-5 £127,960 and in 1641 £123,914.[2] Over the eighty years as a whole, then, the income had not increased by much. In the same period the average price of agricultural products had increased by 124 per cent, that of industrial products by 29 per cent.[3] Heavy sales during the 1650s reduced still further the stock of lands and the prospects of the restored monarchs deriving a substantial proportion of their income from them had disappeared. Although much of this land was recovered at the restoration the king received little because much of it was assigned to provide jointures for the Queen Mother and Queen Consort. They were further reduced by the sale in the early 1670s of the crown's right to various fees from the lands. This was done to relieve a debt crisis arising from the first Dutch War and to secure further funds. This latter expedient is familiar from the earlier period, but it left a negligible annual revenue produced by the crown lands: the king received just over £3,000 per annum in the 1670s and £10,000 in the 1680s.[4] These figures obscure the other purposes of the crown lands, however, and it is anachronistic to consider them only a potential source of revenue.

Another way in which the demesne was directly exploited for revenue under Charles I was through the revival of the forest laws.

A forest was neither more nor less than a piece of land precisely limited by a perambulation and designated as forest by the crown ... It was neither necessary for the crown to own any land in a forest, nor did it have to contain a single tree. Apart from a monopoly in the hunt, the forest law created the equivalent of a nature reserve, in which the use of land must not be changed without permission, so as to offer free movement, shelter and food for game and hawks.[5]

This overrode common law to some extent, and arable within the limits of the forest was not protected from the marauding game. However, the compensation was generous common rights to timber for building and fuel, and grazing where this did not threaten the interests of the game. Like other landlords the crown made concerted attempts to make use of its resources in the sixteenth and seventeenth centuries, and this extended to attempts to exploit the forests more fully. This was done through the resurrection of the traditional instrument of enforcement in the forests – the forest eyre. Under Henry, earl of Holland, this became very active in the 1630s. Two aspects of its activities yielded direct profits, but at the cost of considerable resentment.

The two parts of the policy that aimed to yield a revenue were the imposition of fines on those who had offended against the forest law and attempts were made to restore the ancient bounds of the forests. This latter scheme aimed at penalising encroachments on these ancient bounds, through compositions with the offenders. Anzolo Correr argued, in 1637, that this procedure seemed 'to be a question of depriving men of their property which they have held for many centuries without the Crown raising any claim'.[6] The fines for infringement were clearly legal, depending on long precedent for the holding of justice seats. It has been suggested, however, that by comparison with the previous operation of the laws the level of fines was unjustifiably high.[7] The perambulation of the ancient forest bounds was more contentious. In Northamptonshire it was undertaken from 1637 onwards, and caused considerable indignation. Those found to have encroached on the ancient liberties were liable to a variety of obligations associated with the forest, and many chose to compound for their offence. In five years after 1635 £38,667 was raised from the forests of Dean, of Essex and three forests in Northamptonshire.[8] It was, apparently, this latter aspect of the process that rankled most: 'The validity of titles to land – a most sensitive point – was questioned in pursuit of moderate gain.' Overall, 'The crown had … abused its dignity for a mess of pottage.'[9] The lands

71

and forests, the demesne in the strictest sense, were unlikely to generate the revenue necessary to meet the commitments outlined in chapter 2, any more than it had been able to in the medieval period.

Fiscal feudalism

It has been argued that in the period 1215-1540 English feudalism was 'to all intents and purposes, a fiscal system'.[10] It has been suggested that:

> Latter-day feudalism ... had nothing to do with the feudal relations upon which medieval society had been originally constructed. What was left may be described as fiscal feudalism, feudalism kept alive for no other reason than to bring in revenue to the government.[11]

Tenants owed obligations to their lord, the original justification having been that their lands had been carved out of his demesne.[12] Long before our period these obligations had become encumbrances on the land and sources of revenue to the lord. There were numerous such feudal incidents all of which could be made to realise some kind of profit. *Escheat* was the reversion of the land to the lord on the death of a tenant without heir, or on forfeiture for felony or treason. *Aids* were cash payments to the lord in financial difficulties such as for ransom, to knight his son or marry off his daughter. *Wardship* gave custody of the body and inheritance of an under-age (under twenty-one for males, under sixteen for females) heir to the lord and marriage gave the lord the right to chose a partner for heirs who inherited under-age. *Reliefs* represented a charge paid on inheritance by an heir of age before the lord would receive his homage and allow entry into the tenure.

For many people these obligations were owed to lords but were also due from tenants: only the crown was always a recipient.[13] The crown's position was distinct in further ways. Firstly, it had a special right, of 'prerogative wardship'. If a tenant-in-chief died leaving an heir who was under-age, wardship was exercised not simply on the lands held in chief, but from all lands held by the heir. This had been a grievance in magna carta, but by the mid fifteenth century was established as a lawful right. A second

feudal 'incident' peculiar to the crown was *primer seisin*. On inheritance there was an interval between the death of the old tenant
and the homage of the new tenant. Normally the heir inherited
immediately and could hold the land before paying homage.
When the lord was the crown, however, there was an interval
during which the crown took possession. This interval could last
until homage was paid, or for a full year, depending on the
tenure. In the meantime, of course, the crown could enjoy the revenues from the estate. Additionally, an heir to lands held of the
crown had to 'sue for livery', that is, the right to enter the inheritance. This involved the payment of one half-year's profit.[14]

This collection of rights consisted of the power to administer
lands and dispose of heirs by marriage (wardship) and a series of
cash payments (aids, fines, reliefs etc.). Many of these incidents
were subject to strict regulation from 1215 onwards – sums due
for reliefs were of fixed value, and the value of aids likewise
(except in the case of ransom). The rights of wardship and marriage were not regulated in this way, and although magna carta
prohibited lords from commiting 'waste', this was a rather vague
limitation. This lack of regulation enabled lords, and the crown in
particular, to tap the wealth of the estate more effectively. As a
result, royal administration concentrated on making the most of
these rights in particular. In the thirteenth and fourteenth centuries the office of escheator evolved, a local official in each shire
whose purpose was to enable 'a more intensive and efficient
exploitation of wardship and marriage and primer seisin'. By the
fourteenth century 'each shire ... contained an official whose sole
duty it was to safeguard the royal rights to feudal incidents'.[15]
This ensured closer observation of crown rights, but also allowed
business to be expedited with a degree of local contact.

The period covered here is associated with the final phase of the
administration of wardship and related incidents. The Tudors created a court responsible for enforcing these rights, and it enjoyed
considerable financial success until its abolition in 1646
(confirmed in 1660), but as with the crown lands its usefulness as
a source of revenue was in some tension with other functions.
Over the period 1558-1597 the court of wards produced about
£650,000 for the crown, an annual average of £14,700 (table 4.1).
These figures conceal some important changes, however. The
highest profits were made in the decade prior to 1561, and in the

1560s the yield was only about 80 per cent of this, falling further
to about 68 per cent in the 1570s. There was slight recovery in the
1590s, but the decline in revenues was marked when the figures
are adjusted for inflation.[16] During the Elizabethan period, then,
the profits of wardship, like those from the crown lands were
declining. This decline was probably quite severe when adjusted
for inflation in the costs of government, for which the indices
used here are only a rough guide.

Table 4.1 *Revenues from wardship, 1558–1597*

	(a)	(b)	(c)
1541–51	9,004	9,004	9,004
1551–61	18,026	12,263	14,898
1561–71	14,403	11,903	7,581
1571–81	12,300	7,785	9,840
1581–91	12,963	5,866	9,002
1591–97	14,575	5,319	11,568

Notes: (a) Annual average net profit
  (b) Profit adjusted to take account of the Knoop/Jones index of
    wheat prices
  (c) Profit adjusted to take account of the Kerridge index of rents
Source: J. Hurstfield, 'The Profits of fiscal feudalism, 1541–1602', *Economic
History Review*, 2nd series, VIII, 1955, pp. 53–61; p. 56. The corrections
according to the two price series in the above notes are quoted from
Hurstfield.

The decline of the net profit to the crown was the result of
increasing profits for middlemen. Wardships continued to yield a
near-market value and the difference between this and the
receipts at the court of wards were kept by private individuals.
Taking into account estimates for the size of this intermediary
profit, 'the overall net profits from fiscal feudalism throughout
the reign rise from £650,000 to £2,600,000'. In other words, about
£2 million went to her subjects, not to Elizabeth. The explanation
for this difference lies in the importance of such things as wardships as a means of reward which was low cost to government but
high yield to the recipient. 'The significance of the feudal rev-

enues in the Tudor period lies not in their direct yield to the state but as a method of payment, albeit indirectly and capriciously, to ministers and civil servants.' Lord Cecil tried to secure a greater share of this money for the crown and, in the Great Contract, to replace it with a more systematic arrangement. Under the early Stuarts this programme of increasing the revenue function of the wardships continued: by the end of James' reign they yielded £40,000 per annum, in 1635 £54,000 and 1641 £75,000.[17] These were significant increases, but if Hurstfield's estimate for the profit to intermediaries was correct for the Elizabethan period, it suggests that these other functions of wardships, as with the crown lands, continued to be of great significance. The loss of some of these means of reward may have exacerbated the inflation of the direct cost of civil administration and the court noted in chapter 2.

These feudal incidents were not taxes in the full sense in that they derived, however remotely, from a personal and tenurial relationship, not from a public relationship. They were financial obligations of an intermittent kind, more akin to rent than to taxation. 'The incidents of feudal tenure formed a body of legal rights enjoyed by the lord over the lands held of him, giving him on a number of occasions a share of the revenues of the lands of his tenant.'[18] Royal exactions were an extension of this relationship. Their incidence was to a degree capricious and inequitable:

> Wardship and Livery in effect provided a small irregular tax on *all* estates any parts of which were held in chief of the Crown, and a much heavier tax (which can be thought of as a primitive capital levy or death duty) on *some* of them, this being almost entirely dependent on the accidents of mortality.[19]

To this extent they were like purveyance before the introduction of composition agreements (see below pp. 79–83). These agreements, as we will see, helped to spread a burden which had previously fallen erratically and unpredictably. The desire to even out, over time and between people and places, the burden of financial obligations seems to have been an influence on the evolution of the fiscal system over the whole period. A minor but significant indication of this, perhaps, is the way in which the rate produced in Cumberland to pay purveyance (the purvey) became the basis on which direct taxes were collected in the 1690s.[20] These rates were not necessarily fair, but they were more predictable than the patchwork of feudal incidents and prerogative exactions of the late medieval system.

The forest fines exacted by Charles I were distinct from these tenurial obligations, involving fines for infringement of the king's rights: they were not a recurring tenurial obligation akin to rent, but a 'fine' in our sense of a punishment for an infringement. A similar revenue was derived from distraint of knighthood. In 1227 men were summoned by Henry III to assume the responsibilities of knighthood. The intent had been to meet a military challenge and it was hoped that large numbers would attend. In the sixteenth century the intention was to raise money by imposing fines on non-attenders, and the summons was issued at a coronation rather than in moments of military emergency. This had been done in 1558, but in 1603 the effort was fairly desultory and no fines were collected. What distinguished Charles I's exercise was not novelty or legality, but vigour. Sir Julius Caesar, the oddly-named master of the rolls and renowned antiquary, put together various records of previous exercises. He recognised their financial potential but Charles appears to have been reluctant to exploit it. He initially refused to sign the necessary proclamation and the machinery of enforcement was set in motion only hesitantly. There were innovations, however. The obligation for compiling the lists passed from the sheriffs to county commissions. These commissions were given broad powers to use local officials and documents in order to summon people and compound according to their wealth. This systemisation and the procedure for relating the level of fine to an assessment of wealth made this procedure appear rather like non-parliamentary taxation. In fact, the level of the fine was even related to subsidy ratings.[21] Not all these commissions were compliant, of course. That in Northamptonshire, headed by Lord Montagu, seems to have been dogged by doubts. Montagu himself made a kind of connection with non-parliamentary taxes, arguing that the imposition of fines should be limited to those who had refused other non-parliamentary taxes.[22] Other commissions appear to have resisted and individual taxpayers mounted legal challenges. Nonetheless, it was a financial success. The sum of £173,537 was raised by Easter 1635 (£747 subsequently). It took longer to collect and involved more work than parliamentary taxes, but on the whole the effect must have seemed worth it. It has been suggested that the success probably encouraged Charles I's government to pursue ship money, on the evidence that grumbling could be overridden with administrative commitment and legal backing. In this sense, it was a dangerous precedent, 'a staging post on the road to collapse'. Because it generated 'false optimism, it delayed a more fundamental approach to the problem of royal finance, [and] sent the council in a dangerous direction in search of a solution'.[23]

In chapter 2 we saw how the power of government to grant commercial privileges could be harnessed to induce potential lenders to extend credit to the crown. In particular, the creation of chartered companies and/or the granting of leases to farm taxes could be a prelude to securing substantial loans. This principle was also manifest in the patents of monopoly. The crown was the source of authority for the regulation of economic activity, and monopolies granted by the crown could be made to encourage innovation or to protect domestic industry. In these respects the policy was not always successful. It was also an activity that could be turned to financial advantage and this was a further source of opposition. The rate at which patents were granted accelerated in the early seventeenth century, motivated to a significant extent by the profit that could be turned by the crown. More grants were made in the period 1603–24 than in the previous half century.[24] The profit to the crown could be made in a variety of ways. Some patents were a means of writing off old debts, such as the monopoly of playing cards granted to Sir Richard Coningsby by James I, who owed him £1,800.[25] One of the most notorious Jacobean monopolies granted to alderman Cockayne. Until the grant of the monopoly the Merchant Adventurers had enjoyed a monopoly over the export of cloths, which were shipped unfinished to producers in the low countries and Germany. Cockayne proposed that English cloth should be finished at home in order to maximise domestic profits and was granted a monopoly to this end. It was a commercial disaster, however, as foreign countries banned the import of finished cloth and this led to serious problems in the cloth trade. The original monopoly, although justified on commercial grounds, probably owed much to the fact that Cockayne had wanted to attack the privileges of the Merchant Adventurers. It might have been significant to his prospects of success in seeking this monopoly that he was a creditor to the crown.[26] Other recipients of patents were required to make payments to the crown, justified as compensation for lost customs duties in some cases, or as a simple royalty or rent. The soap makers paid a royalty to the crown of £8 per ton during the 1630s, for example, the Newcastle host-men, the chartered company of coal-shippers in the city, 2s. per chaldron. In this form the grant of a monopoly was very like indirect taxation, since the cost of the royalty or rent was presumably passed on to the consumer. In this sense it may be regarded as a kind of excise taxation (for which see pp. 90–101). Patents could also be granted for the enforcement of economic regulations. Sir Walter Raleigh was given a patent to issue licences for taverns, William Carr to license brewers of beer for export, for example. Robert Kirke and William Cater obtained a patent to enforce in East Anglia a law ordering an acre of hemp to be sown for every 60 acres of arable. Their profit came from the collection of fines for non-compliance.[27]

The profits of the monopolists derived from the enhancement of prices and from the prosecution of those who infringed the patents, and these profits were often much larger than the sums received by the crown. In effect, then, monopoly patents could be regarded as indirect taxes on the subject: those of the 1630s have been described as the 'delegation of indirect taxation ... to monopolistic companies'. However, the cost of collection (the profit to the patentees) was enormous by comparison with other taxes. The customs probably produced £350,000 at a cost to the consumer of £420,000; monopolies produced £100,000 at a cost of £750,000. This latter figure was 'about the same sum as all the receipts of the Exchequer from all other sources'.[28]

Whilst not all patents of monopoly were revenue devices then, an increasing number were, and these attracted considerable hostility (documents 7–8). Elizabeth headed off an attempt to make them illegal in the 1590s and James suspended many on his accession, pending consideration by the king and council. But his subsequent use of the device for revenue purposes resulted in renewed hostility. There were attacks on monopolies in 1621 (see frontispiece) and in 1624 the grant of monopolies to individuals was made illegal by statute. Subsequently patents to corporations were granted, and in the 1630s this became fairly lucrative: in 1640 they produced about £100,000 per annum.[29] The most notorious monopolies were those on salt, soap, starch and coal, and excises on salt, soap and coal all attracted criticism subsequently.

In the 1630s some monopolies were particularly egregious. Overall the revenue was significant, therefore, but in many cases individual monopolies were unpopular out of all proportion to their yield. This unpopularity should not persuade us that the purpose of the grants was solely financial, however.[30]

The royal power to regulate the economy could be turned to profit, and in some cases this came to resemble indirect taxation, but it was inefficient. It was, in fact, a good example of the inefficiencies of a cash-poor government, making a profit through the offices of private interests. Monopolies imposed a high cost on the consumer and yielded a relatively small profit to the government. Those patents which resemble forerunners of excise taxation were, then, particularly expensive prototypes to run. They also involved a high political cost, resulting from suspicion of the patentees who were thought to be (and sometimes were) making large private fortunes at the expense of the public.

Prerogative taxation

These forms of cash exaction were unpopular and not, as we have seen, particularly fruitful or suited to long term exploitation. More promising in these respects were forms of 'prerogative taxation'. Many of these taxes, particularly the impositions and ship money, were effectively national taxes but they were raised as a personal right of the monarch. Purveyance, impositions and ship money all provoked serious political and legal disputes, some of which seemed to raise fundamental questions about the power of the monarch. It is worth considering their organisation in some detail therefore.

Purveyance was a right of very ancient origin, to commandeer provision for the royal household, or to purchase goods at the 'king's price' rather than at the full market price. It was organised through the Board of the Greencloth, the spending and purchasing agency of the royal court. There were two kinds of purveyance. Firstly, there was that taken from particular merchants for specific commodities. For example prisage was originally the king's right to seize wine directly from merchants for his own use. In time, however, this had been transformed into a cash payment. This cash payment became one of the 'customs' although it was of quite different origin to some duties. Little is known about this kind of purveyance, although it appears that in the late sixteenth century, in response to price inflation and consequent pressure on the household budget, composition agreements were entered into with merchants for supply to particular departments of the household.

The second type of purveyance, and the one on which we concentrate here, involved purveyance from the counties rather than from individual merchants – the purchase of provisions at a price determined by the king. Obviously, such a right was potentially arbitrary and tyrannical and the practice of purveyance had been subject to regulation for centuries. There were provisions in magna carta limiting its administration and forty statutes regulating the activities of the purveyors were passed between the thirteenth and the sixteenth centuries. These culminated in a statute of 1555 which confirmed all previous legislation and set new regulations. This statute provides a useful point at which to describe the administration of purveyance in the sixteenth century.

Purveyors were sent to the counties under commissions issued by the clerks of the crown. By the provision of the 1555 act the commission had to name both the specific counties in which the purveyor had powers and the amounts of commodities he was to raise. The commissions were to be English, so as to be easily understood locally, and attached to parchment blanks on which the purveyor was to enter records of his transactions. These records were to be countersigned by high or petty constables, or headboroughs. These blanks could then be passed to the Board of the Greencloth via justices, so that the purveyor's accounts could be verified. All these measures were clearly designed to prevent fraud, or over-burdening of the localities. The commissions were also issued for limited periods only, again a significant restriction.

The purveyors themselves were men of moderate status – often from the London business community, but not merchant princes. It seems that they were outsiders to the localities they visited, and perhaps this probably contributed to the oft-expressed suspicion of sharp practice. Their fees and allowances were small, and the principal source of income a percentage of the purchases that they made. These purchases were made, generally, in three ways. Firstly, the purveyor could visit a village, summon the constable and negotiate with him. Alternatively, the purveyor could attend market and purchase supplies there, or from farmers on their way to the market. The taking of purveyance on the highway was regarded with particular suspicion because the farmer had no protection from the constable and was unlikely to know the law of purveyance. Finally, the purveyor could go to large estates and take supplies from there. It is easy to see why this could be unpopular. Even with a scrupulously honest and fair-minded purveyor the burden could fall very unevenly, on particular places or individuals (document 1). There were, in fact, attempts to force purveyors to avoid repeated visits to the same place.

In the course of the period covered here, there were important changes in the nature of purveyance which effectively trans-formed it into a tax. Firstly, counties were encouraged to enter into composition agreements. Justices entered a contract to supply commodities of an agreed quality at the king's price. They purchased the goods at market price and sent them to court, where they were paid the lower, agreed, 'king's price' for them. In order to reimburse themselves, they levied a rate on the whole county to cover the difference. These agreements had several advantages. For the crown they guaranteed a supply of goods at below market price and household expenditure was thus pro-tected from inflation. The counties, on the other hand, avoided the intrusion of rapacious and shady purveyors, and could spread the cost of purveyance more widely. These composition agreements were successfully sold to the counties on this basis, and by the end of Elizabeth's reign most had compounded. This was a second advantage to the crown – it had secured these arrangements while also avoiding further parliamentary regula-tion, despite complaint about purveyance in the early parlia-ments of Elizabeth and those of 1571, 1581, 1587 and (most seriously) 1589. Instead, eventually, privy councillors had formed the lords commissioners for household causes in 1591, and had recommended to the counties that they report on the abuses of purveyors. Having heard the complaints the commissioners were able to commend this composition scheme by way of remedy.[31]

One further development, apparently a feature of the seven-teenth century, was for counties to raise a rate to cover the differ-ence between the agreed price and the king's price, and to pay this direct to the household. The household then used this to sub-sidise purchases made in the market. In this form, clearly, pur-

veyance had become a tax raised to subsidise household consumption, by authority of the royal prerogative. Few counties
compounded for all the goods they supplied, and so purveyors
continued to operate in most counties. For the goods for which
there was an agreement the justices of the peace were supposed
to raise a rate and purchase the goods. In many cases, however,
they accepted the suggestion of the Board of the Greencloth, that
they secure the goods through the offices of an 'undertaker', frequently someone who had previously been a purveyor. One other
officer, finally, was important in this system, the clerk of the
market. It was his job to ensure the use of uniform and honest
weights and measures and that fair prices were charged, mainly
(but not only) where the king's officers were buying. In general,
he would incline to keeping prices down, obviously.[32]

The cash receipts of purveyance were not equivalent to its
value to the crown. Sometimes purveyance produced surplus
goods that could be resold at a profit, such as unconsumed wheat.
One particular example might illustrate the complexities of
putting a value on purveyance. During the 1620s the king
acquired 7,000 mutton carcases at below market price and a further 498 at the market rate. This cost £2,397 per annum. One cost
to the country at large was the difference between this sum and
the price the mutton would have commanded on the open
market, which amounts to £4,352 per annum. There was a further
cost however, in that the king made £1,874 by selling hides and
tallow from the carcases and wool from the living animals kept
for 'store' on royal pasture. The king's gain then was £6,226 in all.
What at first looks like a purchase at £2,397 in fact amounts to a
£6,226 charge to the country.[33] Overall, purveyance was probably
worth £40,000 to £50,000 per annum 'although its operation had
also provided for the comfortable lining of not a few private pock-
ets'.[34] Perhaps this gap between the cost to the country and the
worth to the crown contributed to the hostility to purveyance,
and its agents. As we will see below, it was not without its problems, and it came close to abolition in 1641, before its ultimate
demise in 1660. It was bracketed together with wardship, ultimately, in the revenues to be surrendered by the monarchy in
return for half the receipts of the excise.

We have seen how pressures arising from household costs led
to the transformation of a prerogative right of purveyance into

what was, in economic terms, a tax. Certain prerogative dues, attached to particular purposes, could be pressed in order to meet part of the escalating military cost incurred by early modern governments. Some of the impositions were like this. For example, in 1591 a new impost on French wine and other goods was successfully raised, without challenge. It was effectively a 'convoy duty', the proceeds of which were to go to 'waftage', 'the maintenance of war vessels to defend the merchant fleets that periodically visited Bordeaux'.[35] We consider other examples below, in our account of Bate's case. In this respect ship money was similar – it could be claimed that it was not a tax for a general purpose, but an extension of a previously acknowledged and much more restricted service to the crown. In these ways the crown could meet 'non-war' military costs by these 'marginal taxes'. That is, not all military costs were associated with active campaigning, and these were marginal in the sense that they were marginal extensions of prerogative rights. It is significant, though, that they were taxes in our, economic, sense but not in contemporary political and legal terms.

The most notorious of these 'prerogative taxes' was ship money. This arose from an ancient prerogative of the crown to commandeer ships from coastal towns to provide for their defence in time of danger. In two stages this right was transformed into, effectively, a form of national direct taxation. Firstly, towns commuted the supply of a ship into a money payment. Secondly, and this is associated with what has been called a 'revolution in naval finances', such payments were raised from the whole country and deployed directly for the support of a national navy.[36] In this sense, then, ship money was the most direct attempt to push prerogative rights to meet the inflated costs of military activity in the seventeenth century.

During the 1630s a number of writs were issued demanding the payment of the ship money. It was the second of these, in 1635, that transformed the levy into a national direct tax. However, historians are not agreed that it was intended as a permanent addition to the revenues: neither could it be, since it was raised for a specific expenditure not as a substitute for parliamentary subsidies. As was the case with other prerogative taxes, then, there was an ambiguity attendant upon the raising of ship money. From this ambiguity arose, as we will see, a significant political cost. In other respects, however, the ship money levies faced difficulties of administration common to direct taxation throughout the period. The administration of the tax was simple in essence. The privy council issued writs each year from 1635 to 1640 to sheriffs instructing them to supply a certain number of ships and men. The sheriff was responsible for rating the county, and organising collection through the high and petty constables. In a sense this gave the administration great strength. Collection could be expedited by leaning on a particular man and the application of a quota was, therefore, virtually a guarantee of success. As a result, yields of the tax were impressive until 1639. There were disadvantages, however. Some sheriff's ratings were controversial. Moreover, men held the shrievalty for one year only and successive sheriffs frequently changed the basis of the tax. The turnover of sheriffs also posed problems for collection – in Somerset in the late 1630s the privy council was chasing four different men for arrears.[37] By the late 1630s in many parts of the country the offices of sheriff and of constable had become much less attractive as a result of the consequent headaches.[38] Beside these administrative difficulties the tax did push a legal right to a new limit, and although there is no agreement on how seriously to take legal objections, no historian seems to have suggested that there was no opposition on legal grounds.

There was then, a repertoire of prerogative taxes that could produce an annual revenue. Finally, there were forms of prerogative exaction, amounting in effect to taxes, which would yield large sums for intermittent, or 'extra-ordinary' purposes: the various forms of loan and benevolence to which resort was made. Both were required by the monarch, authorised under the privy seal, and collected through the lieutenants and justices. A forced loan, in theory, was repayable (although most writers treat this claim with considerable scepticism) whereas a benevolence was a 'free gift' to the monarch. Apart from this distinction the two forms of exaction were similar.

There were long medieval precedents for soliciting loans from the general public, approached either through letters of the privy seal or itinerant commissioners. The commissioners were armed with explanations of the occasion of the loans, urging the necessity of the loan either arising from 'a threat to the safety of the realm, or an opportunity for removing such a threat'.[39] Feudal law insisted that such aids were of 'grace', but they were not free of force. 'The aid could not merely be taken, it had to be asked, and the subject was assured a clear right of consent; but having been asked – under appropriate safeguards – it could not be refused.'[40] The instructions for these loans did not contemplate refusal, only resistance. In the fifteenth century similar loans became known as 'benevolences', and operated on similar principles. To some extent it was a money payment in lieu of war-time service due from certain of the king's tenants, but these benevolences clearly cast a wider net. In all 'the Middle Ages furnished not only a statutory general obligation to unpaid service in defence of the realm, but some precedents for developing this as a tax upon the wealthy, non-noble subject'.[41] Benevolences were a free gift limited by subjects' generosity in lieu of active service. Loans were a general obligation to aid the king in time of need. They rested, formally, on consent and the sum was granted on promise of repayment.

The medieval precedent was for the commissioners for the loan or benevolence to summon the men of a locality or town to hear the justification for the levy. They sent letters under the authority of the privy seal to individuals of known wealth. Individuals were pressed to agree on a sum to be loaned, sometimes with considerable force. Having agreed a sum the money was paid either to the commissioner or to the exchequer. Commissioners issued bills, the exchequer tallies, which promised repayment from the exchequer. The commissioners were local gentlemen, the men who formed other crown commissions. All this was done 'within the terms of [a] notion of obligation'.[42] Outright refusal was impossible without denying the necessity claimed by the crown. Instead there was negotiation and formal excuse, but in essence the aids, loans and benevolences successfully employed the idea of a subject's obligation to aid the crown in time of necessity.

Such levies were made at various times in the sixteenth century and early seventeenth century.[43] Forced loans were raised in 1557, 1563, 1570, 1588–91, 1597, 1600 (from aliens), 1604–5, 1611, 1617, 1621–2, 1625, and 1626. Another had been suggested in 1568. Benevolences were raised in 1599, 1614, 1621–2, 1625, 1626 and 1639, and another had been planned in 1594. The clergy were asked for benevolences in 1577 (to contribute to the cost of repairing Dover harbour), 1596 and 1628. This form of exaction then, was a feature particularly of the war decades of the 1590s and

1620s. The record of repayment was not good: between the accession of Charles I in 1625 and April 1635 £290,365 was raised in loans on the privy seal and by other means, £25,069 by gifts for the defence of the palatinate. In July 1635 £177,192 was still owed on privy seal loans, including £17,192 to the earl of Holland.[44]

We know surprisingly little about these loans but the instructions to a Norfolk collector in the period 1589-91 are in print and there is an excellent case study of the (rather exceptional) loan of 1626. In February 1589 the privy council sent to the lord lieutenant of Norfolk and Suffolk, Lord Hunsdon, a batch of letters under the privy seal to individuals specifying sums that they should lend. These letters were to be distributed via the deputy lieutenants to justices of the peace. The justices were to summon the potential lenders to 'encourage them to yealde both willingly & speedily to the soomes conteyned in the ... privie seales'. Those who proved reluctant were to be brought before the deputy lieutenants. If further persuasion failed they could be threatened with accurate valuation of their wealth. The threat was not simply immediate, either: the assessment would be kept on record at the privy council as the basis for future payments of all kinds (document 10). In August, dissatisfied with the progress of the loan, the council wrote again, threatening to summon slackers before them. The letter acknowledged the possibility that the loan was causing hardship, however. It empowered the deputy lieutenants to arrange for the burden of an individual to be spread among a number of contributors and appropriate provision made for the repayment. In February 1590 repayment was promised within a year to those attending personally with the letter under the privy seal. Although this was a clumsy procedure, and one likely to raise many hackles, it was apparently regarded as a credit arrangement, not a revenue measure, and in January 1591 further letters were sent suggesting that the Queen intended this to be an annual procedure. As a credit measure, offering no choice and no interest, it was a less attractive means of raising money than those hit upon a century later. It is not clear that this scheme made much headway, although in Norfolk a thirty-eight page memorandum book listed the lenders and those given temporary respite.[45] The loans seem to have continued to produce cash at the centre into 1592.[46]

The political implications of such proceedings might be

considerable, as the detailed study of the forced loan of 1626–7 has shown. Legal objections to the loan are considered below, but it is useful here to offer a brief outline of the levy and the reasons for its grant. In 1627 England was at war with the two major European powers, Spain and France. The cost of the war was reaching £1 million per annum, money which was not provided by parliament. Parliament had voted in principle to provide four subsidies to the king, but had proceeded to attack the duke of Buckingham, leading to a dissolution. The crown appealed for a benevolence, in the form of letters under the privy seal. This was a failure, largely because the counties were reluctant to pay a non-parliamentary grant. In response to this objection an alternative plan was conceived to proceed by loan. This would be raised via letters under the privy seal addressed to justices of the peace through the lieutenancy. There are several ways in which the loan seems to have differed from earlier grants. One is that the circumstances, the manner of its implementation and the fact that promises of repayment were very vague, encouraged the view that it was not a loan, but a prerogative tax. Secondly, the measures taken to enforce it were very heavy-handed. Finally, the money was demanded from men of comparatively modest means. The result was a fiscal success, with £243,776 being accounted for (£161,532 actually collected) by November 1627. This compared favourably with the £275,000 raised by the five subsidies of 1628.[47] This money, however, like many forms of prerogative taxation came at high political cost in the localities and in the fora of national political debate. It is significant that in the early stages of the loan the king had been moved to give assurances that it would not be repeated and that it was not a threat to the usual sources of supply. Such devices were not regarded as infinitely renewable resources, clearly.

The prerogative could be pushed, then – impositions, wardship, purveyance, monopolies, forest fines, distraint of knighthood, ship money and forced loans all produced significant sums of money with the cooperation of local officeholders. Increasingly, these sources appeared more lucrative than the parliamentary alternative. As we will see in the next chapter, the administrative means by which they were collected was similar to the means employed by parliamentary taxes, and some of the problems were much the same. Generally, however, the political difficulties of parliamentary taxation rested in securing grants. Once granted, questions of legality and legitimacy did not arise. For the prerogative taxes this was not the case: nearly all of the revenues discussed in this chapter were subject to serious legal challenge and/or political objection. This did not, as we have seen, rule out the possibility of high levels of receipt, but it was a cost that had to be considered. By the late 1620s, it has been argued, this balance could plausibly have been thought to have favoured prerogative revenues against the kinds of taxes to be considered in the next chapter.[48]

Notes

1 R. W. Hoyle (ed.), *The estates of the English crown 1558–1640*, Cambridge, 1992, pp. 5–6. The following account of the lands is drawn from this work.

2 *Ibid.*, pp. 10–11.

3 Comparing average prices in the 1560s with those in the 1630s: C. G. A. Clay, *Economic expansion and social change. England 1500–1700*, 2 vols., Cambridge, 1984, I, p. 50.

4 C. D. Chandaman, *The English public revenue 1660–1688*, Oxford, 1975, pp. 110–15.

5 G. Hammersley, 'The revival of the forest laws under Charles I', *History*, XLV, 1960, pp. 85–102; pp. 85–6.

6 Quoted in P. A. J. Pettit, *The royal forests of Northamptonshire. A study in their economy 1558–1714*, Northamptonshire Record Society, 23, for two years ending 1963, Gateshead, 1968, p. 83.

7 *Ibid.*

8 *Ibid.*, p. 89.

9 Hammersley, 'Revival of forest laws', p. 102.

10 J. M. W. Bean, *The decline of English feudalism 1215–1540*, Manchester, 1968, p. 6.

11 J. Hurstfield, 'The Profits of fiscal feudalism, 1541–1602', *Economic History Review*, 2nd series, VIII, 1955, pp. 53–61, p. 53.

12 For the following see Bean, *English feudalism*, pp. 7–20.

13 H. E. Bell, *An introduction to the history and records of the court of wards and liveries*, Cambridge, 1953, p. 1.

14 In the case of some tenancies this was known as 'ouster le main': Bean, *English feudalism*, p. 11.

15 *Ibid.*, pp. 16, 19.

16 Hurstfield, 'Profits of fiscal feudalism', pp. 55–7.

17 *Ibid.*, pp. 57–61. Receipts under James I and Charles I from R. Lockyer, *The early Stuarts. A political history of England 1603–1642*, London, 1984, p. 249 and K. Sharpe, *The personal rule of Charles I*, New Haven and London, 1992, p. 129.

18 Bean, *English feudalism*, p. 7.

19 G. E. Aylmer, 'The last years of purveyance 1610–1660', *Economic History Review*, 2nd series, X, 1957–8, pp. 81–93; p. 81.

20 W. R. Ward, 'The administration of the window and assessed taxes, 1696–1798', *English Historical Review*, LXVII, 1952, pp. 522–42; p. 526. See also J. V. Beckett, 'Local custom and the "new taxation" in the seventeenth and eighteenth centuries: the example of Cumberland', *Northern History*, XII, 1976, pp. 105–26.

21 H. H. Leonard, 'Distraint of knighthood: the last phase, 1625–41', *History*, 1978, pp. 23–37, LXIII; p. 27.

22 *Ibid.*, p. 27.

23 *Ibid.*, p. 36.

24 C. Wilson, *England's apprenticeship 1603–1763*, London, 1965, pp. 101–2.

25 J. Thirsk, *Economic policy and projects. The development of a consumer society in early modern England*, Oxford, 1978, p. 59.

26 Lockyer, *The early Stuarts*, p. 5.

27 P. Williams, *The Tudor regime* Oxford, 1979, p. 162.

28 W. R. Scott, *The constitution and finance of English, Scottish and Irish joint-stock companies to 1790*, 3 vols., Cambridge, 1910–12, I, pp. 199, 222–3.

29 *Ibid.*, p. 223. The yield would have been higher during much of the 1630s when the lucrative salt monopoly was in force.

30 Sharpe, *Personal rule*, pp. 121–3, 257–62.

31 A. Woodworth, *Purveyance for the royal household in the reign of Queen Elizabeth*, Transactions of the American Philosophical Society, 35, Philadelphia, 1945.

32 Aylmer, 'Last years of purveyance'.

33 *Ibid.*, pp. 83n., 85.

34 *Ibid.*, p. 92.

35 H. Atton and H. H. Holland, *The king's customs*, 2 vols., London, 1908–10, I, p. 65.

36 A. Thrush, 'Naval finance and the origins of ship money', in M. C. Fissel (ed.), *War and government in Britain, 1598–1650*, Manchester, 1991, p. 156.

37 L. M. Hill, 'County government in Caroline England', in C. Russell (ed.), *The origins of the English civil war*, London, 1973, pp. 66–90; p. 85.

38 For a general account of ship money see Sharpe, *Personal rule*, pp. 545–95. Some of the arguments made there are controversial. For the reluctance of constables to serve see J. Kent, *The English village constable 1580–1642: a social and administrative study*, Oxford, 1986, esp. pp. 240–52, 298–306. The best account is A. A. M. Gill's unpublished PhD thesis, 'Ship money during the personal rule of Charles I: politics, ideology and the law 1634 to 1640', Sheffield, 1990.

39 G. L. Harriss, 'Aids, loans and benevolences', *Cambridge Historical Journal*, VI, 1963, pp. 1–19; p. 4.

40 *Ibid.*, p. 6.

41 *Ibid.*, p. 10.

42 *Ibid.*, p. 17.

43 G. R. Elton, *The Tudor constitution*, Cambridge, 1960, 43–4; R. Ashton, *The crown and money market 1603–1643*, Cambridge, 1979, pp. 35–6; Williams, *Tudor regime*, chapter 2 *passim*.

44 F. C. Dietz, *English public finance 1485–1641*, London, 1964, II, *passim*, pp. 270–1; L. L. Peck, *Court, patronage and corruption in early Stuart England*, London, 1990, p. 213.

45 A. H. Smith and G. M. Baker (eds.), *The papers of Nathaniel Bacon of Stiffkey, III, 1586–1595*, Norfolk Record Society, LIII, 1987 and 1988; *passim*, p. 114.

46 Dietz, *English public finance*, p. 64n.

47 R. Cust, *The forced loan and English politics 1626–8*, Oxford, 1987, pp. 1–4.

48 C. Russell, 'Parliament and the king's finances', in C. Russell (ed.), *Origins of the English civil war* London, 1973, pp. 91–116.

5

Parliamentary taxes

In the first part of our period parliamentary taxes were a relatively minor part of national finances and were of diminishing importance. Even that part of the customs duties that was nominally under parliamentary control (tonnage and poundage) was in decline relative to the expanding receipts from non-parliamentary impositions. Parliamentary grants of taxation were occasional and supplementary to the ordinary revenue. By their nature therefore, they were subordinate in terms of aggregate value. The forms of direct taxation available before 1640 were also fatally flawed, with the result that their yield was increasingly disappointing. These flaws are considered in more detail in chapter 8, but the chief problem with these taxes was administrative, and in this brief account of their administration we need to draw attention to these potential difficulties. We then consider direct taxation after 1640, which was far more effective, and parliamentary indirect taxation, an innovation of the 1640s.

Direct taxation before 1640

There were two direct taxes prior to 1640, the fifteenth and tenth, and the subsidy. The fifteenth and tenth had originally been an assessed tax, but in the fourteenth century this had been commuted into a quota tax. The total amount to be raised from the whole country was fixed, and particular portions of this total were assigned to particular counties or boroughs. These apportionments were revised in the fifteenth century, and from then on various exceptions were made in response to pleading from particular places. From the point of view of national revenue raising, this was a fatal weakness of the tax. The yield was fixed in the fifteenth century and later revisions resulted in reductions, rather than increases in the burden. In a period of inflation, which was particularly severe in military spending, this was a very serious problem. This method of raising taxes was not without its advantages, however. The yield was known in advance and the machinery of collection was very efficient. As with the later levy, ship money, the apportionment of the burden was a matter of local discretion. Unlike the ship money payments the responsibility for assessing the tax did not rest with a single man. In this case it was achieved by meetings of substantial local inhabitants, as in Hereford, where it was done by 'every of the citizens and inhabitants of the said city which have been thought able and sufficient to pay any part of the said fifteenths and tenth'. It was not always this encompassing, however. For example, in Southwell, Nottinghamshire, it was done by 'divers of the chief inhabitants' and in other places the tax was allocated according to customary arrangements which might be very complex. In Moulton, Lincolnshire, the lands of foreigners were rated first, then pasture and arable lands of inhabitants were taxed in order to make up the total sum due.[1]

The enforcement of collection was achieved through the exchequer. Those responsible for the collection entered a personal bond for payment of the sum due from their jurisdiction. In effect they gave a personal guarantee to the exchequer that they would pay. If they failed to satisfy the exchequer then the exchequer would issue a writ to the sheriff giving power to seize the goods of the defaulting collector. The exchequer thus had a legal guarantee that it would receive the money due. There was obvious potential injustice in holding the collector responsible if the default in payment was not due to him but to the refusal of others. This, it would seem, would make the office of collector an unattractive one. However, collectors could shift the blame for default by declaring that they could not pay by reason of debts owed to them: they declared that they could not satisfy the debt they owed to the king because they themselves were owed money. In these circumstances the exchequer would help the collector to recover the debts in order to be able to claim the money owing to the crown. Thus, the debt could be collected not from the goods of the debtor himself, but from those who owed him money. In the case of tax collection this would include those who had not paid the taxes assessed on them. Thus, in a rather roundabout way the exchequer could force taxpayers to meet the sum due from them. This was an effective system – the quota set by the fifteenth and tenth was usually paid nearly in full. For example, in the period from 1590 until the tax was abandoned in the 1620s, the yield of the tax in Norfolk hardly varied. The result was that, as the yield of the subsidy in the county declined, the relative significance of the fifteenth and tenth increased considerably. The principal problem with the tax was that the quota was insufficient, and increasingly so. But there were also problems arising from the local allocation of the burden, which in many places was determined by an outmoded and often unjust custom (See below, pp. 111–12).[2]

The subsidy, by contrast, was not a quota tax, but an assessed tax. As such, as we will see, it stands out as one of the most ambitious taxes of the period from the fifteenth to the late eighteenth century, during which taxation was usually of the quota kind. It was a Tudor innovation which had initially been quite successful, remarkably so given the ambitious administrative task which was set – the assessment of national wealth for each grant. So significant was this administrative task, and the participation required to perform it, that the tax has been regarded as a test of the political limits of the Tudor state.[3] Following a parliamentary grant, commissions were appointed by the crown to oversee the assessment and the collection of the tax in the localities. In the later sixteenth century these commissions were drawn from the same group of county gentry that provided the magistracy and the militia commissioners. In the towns, the commissioners came from the same group of prominent inhabitants who provided the town government. These commissions activated collection by appointing assessors for each parish or ward in their jurisdiction. These assessors were, characteristically, drawn from the groups who acted as constables, churchwardens and overseers. They produced a valuation of the wealth of the inhabitants of their jurisdiction which was returned to the commissioners for scrutiny. The commissioners heard any appeals and could excuse people from payment if, for example, they held land in other places and wished to pay tax elsewhere. Having reviewed the valuations the commissioners sent copies to London and to local collectors. Collection was enforced in the same way as for the fifteenth and tenth – collectors became personally liable to the exchequer for collection of the tax. The tax due was a per centage of the valuation made by the assessors.

Subsidies were granted with increasing frequency in our period, and collection worked well. The crucial weakness lay in the assessment of the wealth on which the tax was rated. Valuations became increasingly unrealistic as assessors protected the wealth of their neighbours, particularly after 1566 when assessment on oath was discontinued (documents 9, 12). In London the yield of a subsidy fell by about 50 per cent between 1558 and 1590. This was partly because, after a change in the legislation in 1559, many payers were able to pay tax on lower assessments outside London. In Norfolk the effect of this was less marked and in this period the total yield only fell by about 16 per cent. The principal cause of the decline of the subsidy was the increasing inaccuracy of assessments. If this repeated voluntary evaluation of the wealth of the nation is seen as a political test of commitment, we can fairly say that the late Tudor and Stuart state failed. The result was a dramatic fall in the yield of the tax. Between 1590 and 1630 it fell by a further 70 per cent in Norfolk and London, for example. As assessments declined, many taxpayers appear to have fallen off the bottom of the scale – in 1566 there were 6,700 subsidy payers in Essex, by 1628 there were only 3,700. At the same time, assessments became concentrated at the lower levels. This probably made the tax more regressive because the gap between the assessments of the richer and poorer taxpayers became narrower. Overall, the tax was granted and collected on a constantly contracting tax base. Obviously this was a very serious weakness in a period of inflation. The picture was not as gloomy everywhere: in Cheshire, the yield of an individual subsidy fell by only 17 per cent between 1590 and 1630, perhaps because the county was not paying fifteenth and tenths at the same time. The result was that the total yield of the subsidy actually increased in the county during the 1620s when grants were made more frequently. This experience, however, was almost certainly exceptional and perhaps unique.

The great advantage of the subsidy was its flexibility, however.

Analysis of the assessments for the tax at a very local level confirms that the assessment of wealth was related to perceived ability to pay rather than to actual wealth. Although this weakened the tax considerably as a means of raising money, it did reduce the possibilities for serious dispute. This was particularly the case since any taxpayer who complained about his rating was likely to prove to be under-assessed by a considerable amount. This flexibility, and the fairly easy tax regime that it produced, made the subsidy a much less contentious levy in the localities than the fifteenth and tenth.[4]

Direct taxation after 1640

The most successful direct taxes of the seventeenth and eighteenth centuries were quota taxes rather than assessed taxes. The subsidy was used in 1640 and 1663 but in Norfolk and Cheshire (and probably nationally) the valuations on these occasions were no more realistic than they had been by the end of the 1620s. The fifteenth and tenth was abandoned in the 1620s, probably because it had become so inequitable. The principle of the quota persisted, however. It made ship money effective and productive, as we have seen, until the political problems of that tax overwhelmed it. In 1640, in addition to subsidies, parliament granted a tax of £400,000 to be raised according to stated quotas. The effectiveness of this tax is difficult to gauge because collection was overtaken by civil war. Many collectors were excusing their liability years later, explaining that the money had been taken by one side or another. There is evidence to suggest, however, that it was a productive levy. It was administered, like the subsidy (and unlike the ship money writs), through a local commission. Like the fifteenth and tenth it imposed a quota, enforced by the machinery of bonds in the exchequer. In two respects, however, it overcame the weaknesses of the fifteenth and tenth. Firstly, the quota that it set was a more realistic response to the revenue demands faced by the national government. Secondly, the quotas within localities were set at the discretion of local commissions, so they were more likely to be regarded as fair.

This tax, then, combining the advantages of the fifteenth and tenth (the quota) with those of the subsidy (the role of local commissions in resolving disputes over rating), seems to have offered a recipe for administrative and fiscal success. Its enforcement was unproblematic. It, in turn (and more than the ship money levies), provided a model for the assessments of the 1640s.[5] These taxes imposed monthly quotas on localities which were vastly more onerous than any previous form of direct taxation. In Warwickshire, the burden of the assessment in the 1640s was ten times greater than that of the ship money levies. In Cheshire collection was relatively difficult during the war because parliament did not fully control the county, but soon after collection improved to at least 75 per cent of the quota. For a total of thirty-nine months during the 1650s the collector for the county collected nearly £16,000 with an arrear of only 5 per cent. This compares very favourably with the roughly £10,000 paid in total in subsidies during the twenty-five year period 1590-1614. Most of the sums which were not paid into the exchequer, furthermore, had been collected but disbursed locally. In the counties of the Eastern Association, Kent and Sussex the tax was very heavy and collection even more effective, achieving high yields very rapidly. The same was true during the 1650s and in the mid-1660s when the assessment (under a different name) was equally onerous and equally effectively collected. In Norfolk in the war years of the mid-1660s the burden of parliamentary taxation (excluding the hearth tax) was about thirteen times as great as it had been in the years 1590-1614 and 1621-9. Over 80 per cent of this burden was produced by taxation in the form of assessments. In Cheshire the burden of taxation in the 1660s (this time including the hearth tax) was nineteen times as great as it had been in the 1620s, and the difference between the 1660s and 1590s was even greater. Again the lion's share (about two-thirds) came from assessments. Clearly, it is this direct taxation that accounts for the bulk of the increase in total revenues noted in chapter 1. This must have raised the profile of parliamentary taxation in the localities. The increase in the burden of direct taxation rose much more quickly than the total burden of government.[6]

These taxes were assessed by local people under the direction of commissions composed of substantial local men (even in the 1640s and 1650s). Collection was made through the constables. It was enforced by the county committees in the 1640s and 1650s, and by receivers-general answerable to the exchequer in the 1660s and beyond. This seems to explain its success both in terms of yield and in the lack of sustained resistance. In most counties that have been studied the assessment was considerably more onerous than the excise, but it was the excise that attracted most hostility. The reasons for this are examined in more detail below, but it does perhaps illustrate the advantages of administration by local officeholders. They were better placed to negotiate and mediate the burden of the tax, while the quota imposed a limit on this discretion.

After 1660 the assessment was regarded with some embarrassment by the restored monarchy, but was used frequently nonetheless. The large revenues received in the 1660s owed much to this form of direct taxation, although attempts were made to use alternative forms. The assessments were little changed from the commonwealth period, even using the same quotas until 1664. There were refinements of the basic recipe. For example, a new layer of administration was added in the office of receiver-general, a man who was responsible for chivvying the commission and collectors. More flexibility was added to the implementation of exchequer process by the expanding administrative role of the treasury. The treasury increasingly intervened in areas where there were problems relating to tax collection to negotiate or cajole, often through the office of the receiver-general. As with all the direct taxes granted by parliament though, in the localities these assessments remained the responsibility of existing officeholders. Gentry and burgess magistrates formed the commissions and seem to have provided the receivers-general, their immediate subordinates in local society providing the high collectors and sub-collectors.[7]

The 'administrative repertoire' changed very little with regard to direct taxation. Local commissions oversaw valuation, local officeholders assessed and collected the taxes and collection was enforced by a system of bonds. There was no innovation that enabled national government to value the wealth of its subjects more accurately, but the tax-take was greatly increased by an administrative device of ancient origin – the quota. Although parliament frequently granted these quotas reluctantly, the key to the success of this form of taxation lay, nonetheless, in parliament's willingness, however grudging, to grant large quotas.

In 1688, in response to demands for urgent supply, parliament again resorted to quota taxation in the form of the assessment.

This was succeeded though, in 1689, by an assessed tax. It has been suggested, however, that it was raised with reference to the previous year's assessment, rather than to a genuine valuation, reflecting the fact that the administration was in the same hands.[8] In 1690 and 1691 quota taxes were again used, each twelve month assessments raising just under £1,614,000. Hostility to the distribution, however, led to the adoption of a new tax in 1692. Like the subsidy this required the valuation of the wealth of all individuals in the country. A rate of four shillings in the pound was to be paid on this valuation. This was the foundation of the land tax. Assessors were not on oath (as in the subsidy) and the tax produced £1,922,000. In the following year, with the assessors on oath, it produced £10,000 less. Further declines in the total yield led to the abandonment of the attempt at valuation. Instead, in 1697, quotas were adopted, albeit in a slightly different form from that with which we are familiar. Parliament decided what one shilling in the pound would produce from each commission and thereafter granted the land tax as a number of shillings in the pound. In effect this was, of course, a quota tax. Three shillings in the pound was deemed to be worth £1,484,015, and in 1698 this was apportioned according to the proportions raised in each locality towards the total amount raised in 1692. Again, then, the difficulty of controlling assessment led to the imposition of quotas in order to safeguard yield.[9]

The land tax was very similar to earlier direct taxes and this is reflected in the experience of the administration. The problem with these taxes had never been collection. Exchequer process ensured this, and the elaborations of the restoration period – the receiver-general, the tax office, treasury oversight – were carried over into the administration of the land tax. Ultimately it depended on local men, drawn from substantial local inhabitants. The early Stuart taxes had depended on constables and, although the land tax did not, it was administered at the lowest levels by men from the same social rank as constables. Similarly, assessment was in their hands. Local administration was in the hands of gentry and burgess commissions at county and borough level and, below them, it was in the hands of parish elites.[10] Moulded by the need to control under-assessment and the advantages of harnessing existing elites, direct taxation reached a consistent point of evolution. It was a successful recipe – of the total revenue of £122 million raised between 1688 and 1714 £46 million came from the land tax.[11]

Indirect taxation

Before 1640 there was no indirect taxation in England granted by parliament, with the notable exception of tonnage and poundage. One of the most remarkable innovations in this period, then, was the establishment of an effective and (eventually) professional excise administration. Excises had been suggested as a possible solution to revenue problems in the 1620s but the reaction of most within the House of Commons was extremely hostile. Excises were introduced by both parliament and the royalists in 1643 and figure in the histories of the interregnum as the cause of great hostility (see documents 23, 25–6). By 1660, however, the administration had evolved to the point that the advantages of the excises were such that they were adopted in favour of direct taxation. In fact they had come to be regarded by some as the 'easiest' and 'equallest' form of taxation.[12]

Excises are a consumption tax, paid at the point of retail of particular commodities. In this sense they are distinguished from import and export duties, although in practice in our period excises on imported goods were closely related to customs payments. In the 1640s a broad range of commodities of domestic manufacture and import were subject to the excise, but the range of the duties was reduced. In 1647 excises on domestic salt and meat were dropped and in 1660 the excises on imports were abandoned. The excises were restricted to beer and liquors. Half the receipts were granted to the king in perpetuity in compensation for the loss of various prerogative revenues. Thereafter governments were tempted to impose new duties but such plans were met with hostility. This hostility grew out of a fear of a 'general excise', something associated with the arbitary governments of the 1640s. The comprehensiveness of the range of goods taxed in the early 1640s may have led to an association between excise, tyranny and standing armies (documents 23-4, 37).[13]

The tax was distinctive in its administration in that it was organised from a central office with local agents of collection, either commissioners or farmers. During the 1640s administration of the excise alternated between commission and farming, with parts of the collection being under each at any given time. Farming the excise had the same advantages and disadvantages as it had for the customs. It offered an assured rent and a source of credit but aroused suspicions of profiteering and tended to increase the hostility of taxpayers. The practical difference may have been limited since, in the period 1643–60, farmers and sub-commissioners were often the same men. Moreover, there is some indication that they all depended on a semi-permanent group of subordinate officers who developed an expertise in the administration. These were the sub-collectors and gaugers, frequently known indiscriminately as 'excisemen'. Although many officers – sub-commissioners, farmers and their officials – appear to have been local men, they were less likely to have been drawn from the ranks of the county and borough officeholders. It was partly for this reason that they were often regarded with a mixture of suspicion and contempt. This continued to be the case after the restoration (documents 27–8). In 1660 the farms of the 1650s were ended and direct collection resumed, but in 1662 a new set of leases were granted for the whole collection, dividing the country into groups of counties. In some areas local gentry bid successfully for the leases, and the crown did not always take the highest bid, preferring instead to leave the tax in the hands of men who had the support of the local magistracy. Subsequent leases went for successively higher sums, and consortia of local gentry gradually lost out. By 1677 financiers held the leases[14] although, again, the little work that has been done on the very local level suggests that these changes in management might have taken place over a continuity amongst subordinate officials. In other words, whoever held these higher offices depended on a degree of local knowledge and experience, and often took over minor officials from previous administrations.[15]

Farming was abandoned in 1683 in favour of direct collection and a professional administration developed rapidly thereafter. In 1690 there were 1,211 full-time excise officers, nearly as many as the 1,313 employed in the customs. By 1716 there were 2,778 excise officers, compared to 1,750 in the customs. By 1726 the excise was considerably larger, with 3,466 employees to the 1,911 officers in the customs administration.[16] During the eighteenth century the excise was the most bureaucratised arm of government. This professionalisation of the excise administration has received considerable attention. 'In the late seventeenth century, most of the state revenue was collected by a motley body of private subjects, part-time and amateur officials and employees of the tax-farmers. But after 1713 most of the revenue was collected by employees of the central government.'[17] By 1770 the provinces were divided into 53 collections, each with a clerk, collector and a supernumerary (a kind of trainee). There were about 253 supervisors below them, and at the lowest level 2,704 peripatetic officers, either footwalkers or outriders. Officers were frequently moved from place to place in order to prevent close acquaintanceship with the producers. These local officers worked extremely hard – footwalks were 12-16 miles, rides much further. Many worked very long hours and the work was arduous and demanding. The rewards were certain, however – promotion, salaries and superannuation were clearly defined to reduce the temptations of corruption. It was a bureaucratic achievement beyond the capacity of most European states.[18]

In the light of this long-term success, the notorious problems of the early excises seem puzzling. In fact, argument centred on the range of goods to be subject to duty, on the issue of who was to do the collecting and who was to arbitrate disputes. The basic principle seems to have won a degree of acceptance, but the specific administrative provisions were the subject of dispute. In particular, the employment of salaried revenue agents, collecting taxes as a means of earning or supplementing a living, caused considerable suspicion. It provided a sharp contrast with the administration of the direct taxes which were assessed and collected as part of more general duties by established officers of local government. Although these issues, of what to tax and who should be employed in the service, caused considerable friction we should not overstate its seriousness, given the long-term success of the levy.[19]

The household and poll taxes

Some taxes in this period do not fit neatly into the categories of direct or indirect taxation, notably the 'household taxes': that is the hearth tax and the window tax, and the poll taxes. Additionally, the 1690s saw an interesting variation on the poll tax, a tax on births, marriages and burials.

The hearth tax, sometimes called the chimney tax, was raised between 1662 and 1689, when it was abolished. It placed a tax of one shilling on each hearth in a house, with various exemptions for poverty, or for chimneys used in industrial production. It was a progressive tax in that it assumed a correlation between numbers of liable hearths and wealth. Wealthier taxpayers would, it was assumed, pay more because their houses would have more hearths. The records generated by the administration have been extensively used by social historians who have cast doubt on this assumption. Detailed local studies reveal that while there is a broad correlation, numbers of hearths are by no means a certain guide to wealth. A further problem was under-recording (these problems are considered in more detail below, chapter 8).[20] In principle the advantage of the tax was that it counted very visible indicators of wealth, but in fact it appears that the tax was evaded. This explains, again, variations in the pattern of administration. Initially constables were responsible for recording the numbers of hearths and collecting the money, returning it via sheriffs to the exchequer. This sheriff's administration lasted from 1662 until 1664. Disappointment at the yield led to the appointment of royal officials, the receivers, who assessed and collected the tax until 1666. Further disappointment led to the adoption of farming. In the event it took some time for the total revenue to regain the levels achieved under the sheriff's administration when it had been valued at £170,000 per annum and yielded £115,000 net at the exchequer. This was a significant sum, of course, but does not compare with the revenue potential of assessment taxation, which in the mid 1660s was reliably producing £120,000 each month. Between 1668 and 1671 the excise produced an average annual net yield of nearly £323,000, and this rose throughout the restoration period.[21] The problem of evasion continued to drive administrative reform. The first farm was not a great success, for reasons that are considered later, and direct collection was resumed in 1669. Farming was resorted to again between 1674 and 1679, and there then followed five years of 'management'. Finally, between 1684 and 1688 the tax was again collected directly. The hearth tax was marked by considerable hostility, not just evasion, and it was abandoned in 1689 as a 'badge of slavery upon the people'. These then, were the two chief drawbacks of the tax – evasion and hostility, and we consider both below. We can note here, though, that much of the overt hostility to the tax (and the excise in the 1640s and 1650s) derived from its administration by entrepreneurs (document 29) and not simply from its burden: it was definitely the junior partner among the three principal inland taxes raised during the restoration period.

A successor to the hearth tax as a means of taxing households was the duty introduced in 1696. Each house was to pay a basic rate of 2s, with a higher rate for houses with 10–20 windows (4s) and for houses with more than 20 (8s). In 1709 it was extended, extra duties being placed on houses with 20-30 windows and those with more than 30, and in 1747 it was revised again, imposing a flat rate per house with an extra charge per window. Thus the house tax had become a window tax. The land tax commissioners rated it during its first year before justices of the peace took over. Payments were made via the land tax administration, through the receiver-general, and receipts were audited with those of the land tax. The window tax had several advantages. Like the hearth tax it was raised as a specific sum due from a number of easily visible features which broadly reflected wealth. Unlike the hearth tax it could be assessed without entering the house. These advantages seem to have secured it the much longer life-span that it enjoyed by comparison with the hearth tax. However, the yield was consistently disappointing to the treasury and there were constant expressions of concern about partiality, evasions and misrepresentations. These problems of evasion and under-reporting, again like those experienced in the collection of the hearth tax, drove some administrative changes. For example, professional surveyors were appointed to make valuations of their own. They also represented the interests of national government when taxpayers appealed against valuations to the justices of the peace.[22]

Poll taxes were another way in which wealth was tapped without resort to quota taxation. They were raised in 1641, 1660, 1667, 1678, 1689–90 and on a quarterly basis from 1692 to 1693, 1694 to 1695 and 1698 to 1699. Furthermore, the land tax had additional elements of taxation by poll in 1697 and 1702. It is tempting to see these grants as a series, but 'at the time they were levied they were regarded as specific and almost one-off measures for raising desperately needed revenue for military purposes'.[23] Such taxes were usually granted for a specific purpose therefore. For example, that in 1641 was raised to pay off the Scots army and excused the inhabitants of the counties of Northumberland and Durham where the Scots already posed a considerable burden. The 1660 tax was granted to pay off the commonwealth armies and that of 1667 to support the Dutch War. The tax in 1678 had been raised in preparation for a military campaign against the French and those of the 1690s the campaigns of King William.[24]

The principle of all these taxes was simple, but in practice their provisions varied widely. In general direct taxation was intended for extra-ordinary purposes and the poll taxes were an attempt at direct taxation which would fall less heavily on land.[25] They comprised, generally, a flat rate for payment per head. However, above this minimum payment there were complex gradations according to wealth and status, specific rates being placed, for example, on kinds of income from office, or trade. These variations were new each time, and could be of bewildering complexity.[26] The timing of the grants, and their provisions, bear testimony to the desire to find an alternative to assessment taxation: generally these taxes were raised to meet military expenditure and sought to tax non-landed wealth. Their assessment and collection were usually the responsibility of local officeholders, and their yield was almost always disappointing. This seems to have been the result either of evasion or of over-optimism on the part of the framers of the taxes. Ward was quite clear on this point: 'the treasury was confronted by persistent and contumacious resistance from the commissioners'.[27] The 1641 levy raised £400,000, that of 1660 about £227,000, that of 1667 £246,000 and that of 1678 £261,000. This is more than the annual yield of the hearth tax, but is in all four cases less than had been hoped for. Worse still, this disappointment was compounded by the slow rate of payment.[28] Poll taxes were, generally, regressive, the lowest rate applying to a very broad section of the population. On the whole, it seems, the effort that went into their administration was rarely rewarded by very full receipts.

Related to these taxes was the tax on the registration of births, deaths, marriages and the associated poll tax on bachelors over twenty-five and widowers, raised in the 1690s. This is usually referred to as the marriage duty act.[29] The tax had a short life, only eleven years, but its records have provided an important source for social historians. The tax was closely related to the poll taxes, not just in its general principles, but in its detail. The scale of charges on the registrations was graduated for those of the status of gentleman and above following the gradations of earlier poll taxes. Similarly the poll charges on bachelors and widowers were one-quarter of those imposed by poll taxes in 1678 and 1689.

The tax was the responsibility of a local commission, initially the land tax commissioners. However, the land tax commissions were only appointed for one year at a time since the land tax itself was only granted for one year at a time. As a result, after 1696, the commissioners were the justices of the peace for the relevant area. The commissioners appointed assessors who produced lists of estates, degrees, titles and qualifications under four headings: born, died, married and unmarried. This was obviously a major undertaking, and commissioners had the power to review the results if they suspected under- or misregistration. The collection was complicated by the fact that the events on which the tax fell were unpredictable. Money was returned to a receiver-general who was to check the receipt against a duplicate assessment furnished by the commission. The operation required efficient registration, and in this lies its attraction for social historians. Anglican clergy were required to extend their registers to include not just christenings, but also births. Likewise burials outside the church and non-Anglican marriages were to be recorded too, and there was some confusion over the division of labour between collectors and clergy. This was, then, an onerous administrative task. It fell on substantial inhabitants, some of whom received fees for their work. The return on all this labour was unimpressive: in the first five years the average yield was only just over £50,000 per annum. By the time of its abandonment this had fallen to less than £30,000. The abandonment of the tax was due in part to its complexities and unpopularity. At its peak, therefore, it was worth only about one-fifth of a poll tax each year. 'When one considers the large number of people who were engaged in the raising of such relatively paltry sums, it seems surprising that the experiment was not abandoned earlier.'[30]

Many of these problems with poll taxes were recognised by Sir William Petty, a leading seventeenth century writer on economic matters. 'The Poll-moneys which have been leavied of late' he wrote in 1662, 'have been wonderfully confused; as taxing some rich single persons at the lowest rate; some Knights, though wanting necessaries, at twenty pounds.' Moreover, because they taxed status, they encouraged 'some vain fellows to pay as Esquires, on purpose to have themselves written Esquires in the Receipts'. This made the yield of the tax difficult to predict and difficult to audit: 'by this Confusion, Arbitraries, Irregularities, and hotch-potch of Qualifications, no estimate could be made of the fitness of this Plaister to the Sore, nor no Checque or way to examine whether the respective Receipts were duly accompted for, &c.'[31] The frequent resort to this form of taxation probably reflects the unpopularity of other forms rather more than it does the advantages of poll taxes.

Tax farming and borrowing

All these taxes attempted to widen the tax base, to increase the success of national government in tapping sources of wealth. In the long run, one of the greatest successes of government in this respect was borrowing, which mobilised vast resources from a variety of sources in the eighteenth century. Another way in which this was done was through tax farming, an administrative device that we have encountered in our brief descriptions of the customs, the hearth tax and the excise. In one sense tax farming is of a piece with the use of informers or discoverers of crown lands. It was an attempt by the government to harness private initiative and the profit motive to maximise the exploitation of crown rights, be they prerogative rights or rights granted by parliament. In this sense the use of farmers demonstrated bureaucratic weakness. There was a hidden benefit to tax farming, though, in that it mobilised significant wealth on behalf of the national government, in advances for the leases or in securing loans from the farmers. The customs farmers, as we saw in chapter 2, were important government creditors, advancing lump sums and affording overdrafts on the money due from them. The ability of the syndicates of farmers to mobilise this capital was an important reason for the perseverance of the government with customs farming, as we have seen. In the 1660s this dependence on tax farmers was particularly striking when the three main branches of the ordinary revenue were all in farm – the customs, the excise and the hearth tax. In this period, before the gradual abandonment of farming, a small group of financiers secured a substantial hold over government revenue. Edward Backwell, Sir Thomas and Robert (later Sir Robert) Vyner, Francis Meynell and John Colvill together formed 'The little coterie of bankers, in whose hands the government henceforth placed itself almost without reserve'.[32] However, it was the influence of a group of financiers headed by William Bucknall which threatened to take control of two-thirds of the revenue in 1671 by taking over the customs farm (they already controlled much of the excise). Fears about the consequences of such dominance may have helped to persuade the government to return to direct collection of the customs.[33]

The administrative repertoire of government was limited and improvements in the receipts of indirect taxation came from a mixture of farming and direct collection. The potential of direct taxation was severely limited by a lack of information and a practical dependence on local self-assessment. These administrative constraints limited the capacity of government to tap some kinds of wealth. The most visible and easily taxed form of wealth was land, and the most productive forms of direct taxation fell on land. In trying to tap other resources other taxes were laid, notably on hearths and windows, but also poll taxes on status. In 1671 a reformed version of the subsidy also tried to tax commercial wealth.[34] Administrative reform before 1670 centred on three strategies: seeking to harness private interest to public service, particularly through tax farming; trying to tax easily visible forms of wealth; and applying quotas to grants of direct taxation. From 1670 onwards farming was gradually abandoned in the indirect taxes and the notable professionalisation of the revenue establishment began.

Notes

1 M. J. Braddick, *Parliamentary taxation in seventeenth-century England. Local administration and response*, Royal Historical Society Studies in History, 70, Woodbridge, 1994, pp. 24–5.

2 *Ibid.*, chapter 1.

3 R. S. Schofield, 'Taxation and the political limits of the Tudor state', in C. Cross, D. Loades and J. J. Scarisbrick (eds.), *Law and government under the Tudors. Essays presented to Sir Geoffrey Elton* ..., Cambridge, 1988, pp. 227–55.

4 Braddick, *Parliamentary taxation*, chapter 2.

5 *Ibid.*, pp. 127–30.

6 *Ibid.*, chapters 3, 6.

7 *Ibid.*, chapter 3.

8 S. Dowell, *A history of taxation and taxes in England*, 2nd edition, 4 vols., London, 1888; II, p. 47.

9 *Ibid.*, pp. 47–9.

10 C. Brooks, 'Public finance and political stability: the administration of the land tax, 1688–1720', *Historical Journal*, XVII, 1974, pp. 281–300; W. R. Ward, *The English land tax in the eighteenth century*, Oxford, 1953; Ward, 'The administration of the window and assessed taxes, 1696–1798', *English Historical Review*, LXVII, 1952, pp. 522–42.

11 Brooks, 'Public finance and political stability', p. 283.

12 Braddick, *Parliamentary taxation*, chapter 4; M. J. Braddick, 'Popular politics and public policy: the excise riot at Smithfield in February 1647 and its aftermath', *Historical Journal*, XXXIV, 1991, pp. 597–626; E. Hughes, *Studies in administration and finance 1558–1829 with special reference to the history of Salt taxation in England*, Manchester, 1934, chapter 4.

13 Hughes, *Studies in administration and finance*, p. 122.

14 *Ibid.*, p. 152.

15 Braddick, *Parliamentary taxation*, chapter 4; C. D. Chandaman, *The English public revenue 1660–1688*, Oxford, 1975, chapter 2.

16 J. Brewer, 'The English state and fiscal appropriation, 1688–1789', *Politics and Society*, XVI, 1988, pp. 335–85; p. 353.

17 *Ibid.*, p. 352.

18 See also J. Brewer, *The sinews of power. War, money and the English state, 1688–1783*, London, 1989, pp. 101–14.

19 Braddick, *Parliamentary taxation*, chapter 4; Braddick, 'Popular politics and public policy'; Hughes, *Studies in administration and finance*, chapter 4.

20 N. Alldridge (ed.), *The hearth tax. Problems and possibilities*, Conference of teachers in regional and local history in tertiary education, London, 1983; T. Arkell, 'The incidence of poverty in England in the later seventeenth century', *Social History*, XII, 1987, pp. 23–47; K. Schurer and T. Arkell (eds.), *Surveying the people. The interpretation and use of document sources for the study of population in the later seventeenth century*, Local Population Studies supplement, Oxford, 1992, chapters 3, 4. The material relating to the 1660s is discussed in Braddick, *Parliamentary taxation*, chapter 5.

21 Braddick, *Parliamentary taxation*, pp. 249–50; Chandaman, *English public revenue*, pp. 312, 314–15.

22 Ward, 'Administration of window and assessed taxes'.

23 T. Arkell, 'An examination of the poll taxes of the later seventeenth century, the marriage duty act and Gregory King' in Schurer and Arkell (eds.), *Surveying the people*, pp. 142–80; p. 142.

24   *Ibid.*

25   Chandaman, *English public revenue*, p. 143.

26   For a convenient summary of these provisions, see Arkell, 'Examination of the poll taxes' pp. 144–51.

27   'Administration of window and assessed taxes', p. 523.

28   Braddick, *Parliamentary taxation*, pp. 233–41; Chandaman, *English public revenue*, pp. 176, 181, 188.

29   For the following, see Arkell, 'Examination of the poll taxes', pp. 167–71.

30   *Ibid.*, pp. 170–1.

31   *A treatise of taxes and contributions* (1662), reprinted in Charles Henry Hull (ed.), *The economic writings of Sir William Petty*, New Jersey, 1986 edition, p. 62.

32   W. A. Shaw, 'The beginnings of the national debt', in T. F. Tout and J. Tait (eds.), *Historical essays by members of the Owens College, Manchester ...*, London, 1902, p. 407.

33   Chandaman, *English public revenue*, p. 27.

34   *Ibid.*, esp. p. 149.

6

The politics of taxation: the economic effects of taxation

The next two chapters consider early modern debates about the principles of taxation (in the general, economic sense). All the revenues described in chapters 3–5 are considered, except for the crown lands and forests. The chapters follow the distinction made in chapter 1 between the economic and political implications of taxation. It was suggested that economic historians were frequently concerned with the non-revenue consequences of taxation, with the implications for the distribution of wealth and the structure of demand. Political historians, by contrast, are often more concerned with the authority by which taxation is raised. It is possible to make a similar distinction in discussing early modern debate about taxation. Thus, although in practice both issues are usually present in debate about taxation, in the next two chapters we try to consider them separately. This chapter considers arguments about the burden and political economy of taxation, things we might broadly assume to be related to the 'economic' effects of taxation.

Complaints arising from these issues are frequently assumed to be a cloak for straightforward reluctance to pay. In other words, a claim that a particular tax unfairly burdened the poor or discouraged domestic industry was an argument of convenience. 'For the majority of Englishmen down the centuries the desire to avoid taxation has been permanent. Cheating the crown of its revenues has been almost a national pastime, largely because high rates of taxation have persisted.'[1] The same is true, of course, of arguments defending the property rights of the individual against the power of the state. Questioning the legality of a particular tax might just have been a ruse for avoiding payment. In the next two chapters then, we need to be sensitive to the possibility that arguments put forward in public debate were not sincerely intended. But this cuts the other way, too. These arguments may indeed have been a cover for tightfistednesss. But, on the other hand, arguments about the unfairness of the tax burden might have been a safer way of expressing more deep-seated reservations about the legal and constitutional propriety of an exaction. Moreover, suggestions that a particular tax was illegal might be a spectacular way of acting on a view that their economic impact was unfair. For analytic purposes, then, we divide economic from legal and constitutional arguments. In reality, however, they were closely related and both might simply be rationalisations of reluctance to pay tax at all.

The burden of taxation

By contemporary European standards England in the late sixteenth century was lightly taxed, and yet national governments faced frequent complaints about the burden of taxation, particularly as it affected 'the poor'. In a sense late sixteenth and early seventeenth century taxpayers did not know how lucky they were, how little taxed they were by comparison with what was to come in the 1640s and (still more) in the 1690s. Their pleas about the burden of direct taxation were not groundless, however, given the way that the burden fell: complaint was usually about the relative burden of taxation, not the absolute burden. The fifteenth and tenth, by the time of its abandonment, was very onerous in some places, and what made this unfair was the undervaluation of many more places. The subsidy too, by the early seventeenth century, was becoming increasingly regressive.

The allocation of the burden of the fifteenth and tenth was determined by custom, as we have seen, and this could become a source of conflict. As a general rule it seems that the apportionment of the tax became more inequitable. It was very difficult to shift the burden, and as areas suffered relative economic decline so their share of the fifteenth and tenth became relatively more difficult to shoulder. This could be the case within particular settlements. For example, in some parts of Lincolnshire enclosers were among the richest inhabitants but were exempt from the tax. Similarly the distribution across whole counties could be unfair, too. In Norfolk, for example, Thetford paid the fifteenth and tenth but Great Yarmouth, a much richer place, had a complete exemption. Moreover, Norfolk as a whole was almost certainly overtaxed: only Middlesex paid more. Its share of the total probably reflected the distribution of taxable wealth in the fifteenth century, when the quotas had become fixed, rather more than it did the position in the late sixteenth and early seventeenth centuries. Cheshire, on the other hand, did not pay at all. It also appears that, by comparison with the subsidy, the fifteenth and tenth fell on poorer taxpayers. In some places particular tenements or kinds of tenancy may have been exempt, and as the tax became relatively more heavy and frequent such inequities became more irritating. As some of the inhabitants of Mayden Bradley, Wiltshire, complained in 1602, there were many who were exempt from the tax. They noted that 'in elder times when these payments came very seldom the matter was not much stood on or regarded especially'. With the increasing frequency of grants to pay for the wars of the 1590s, however, many local disputes were occasioned by the distribution of the burden. This increased pressure must have heightened perceptions of the unfairness of the way the burden was distributed in many places. It may have lain behind moves to replace the customary allocation of the burden in Leicester, for example.[2] It was for this reason, apparently, that the fifteenth and tenth was abandoned: not because of its absolute burden on the poor but because of relative inequities. As Robert Doughty put it in the 1660s, the tax 'did at last lie upon so few and that so unevenly, that it made men (if not unable) at least unwilling longer to continue the same'.[3] Those debating supply in parliament in the 1620s were certainly conscious that the fifteenth and tenth might unfairly burden the poor, towns and ancient boroughs.[4]

Similarly, the mechanics of the decline of subsidy valuations seems to have produced inequities in its distribution. The very rich were the most dramatically under-assessed and, as the general level of assessments fell, poorer taxpayers fell off the bottom of the scale altogether. As a result the burden fell increasingly on the middling sort. This was noted by one contemporary in 1641: 'The poorer sort cannot pay the King, the greater sort as having the law in their own hand will pay but what they please, but the middle sort they must and shall pay, and in such disproportion as is insufferable.'[5] This judgement is borne out by analysis of subsidy assessment in London, Norfolk and Cheshire (see below, chapter 8, for further discussion of this). The burden of the tax was not felt as an absolute one, so much as an inequitable one.[6]

These complaints about the burden of direct taxation were not solved by the quota taxes of the mid and later seventeenth century. Given the greater weight of taxation and the lack of precision in its allocation, this is hardly surprising. It is important to note that, despite the great increases in the *total* burden of taxation, complaint continued to focus primarily on the *relative* burden of taxation. What was at stake was usually fairness, not subsistence (documents 13–14, 17). In Chester in the 1660s there was a protracted (and well-documented) wrangle which illustrates this point. Chester had claimed for a number of years that it was unfairly burdened in national quota taxation and, as we will see below, had made a number of attempts to limit its liability. According to the quotas as they had been settled in 1649, the burden placed on the city was equivalent to one-tenth of that on the county of Cheshire. However, in the 1665 quota for the royal aid a single quota was applied, to be met jointly by the city and the county together. This, the city claimed, was to enable the relief of the city. In the event, however, the joint commission, dominated by representatives of the county interest held the city to the same proportion. The city had apparently offered to pay a quota which would have resulted in a pound rate in the city twice as heavy as that paid in the county. This suggests that the quota was unfair, that in order to meet the obligation being imposed a much heavier tax was being raised in the city. The county refused the offer. When another tax, the further supply, was added the city tried to negotiate once more but failed to secure a concession. After that the city refused to pay the sum set on it by the commission as a whole. As a result there was an accumulating arrear. This was exacerbated when, in December 1666, parliament set quotas for another tax, in which the city and the county were to have separate commissions. For this tax the city was expected to produce a sum equivalent only to one-twentieth of the sum due from the county. This provided a parliamentary 'precedent' for the city in trying to reduce its contribution to the earlier taxes.

From that point on the city paid only one-twentieth towards the royal aid and further supply with the result that an arrear of £1,180 developed. The city claimed that it was due from the county but had not been assessed by county commissioners. The county, by contrast, claimed that it had been assessed on the city and was due from taxpayers there.[7]

The dispute demonstrates a problem inherent in quota taxation. It was adopted in place of accurate valuation which had proved administratively and politically impossible. Because of this, however, there was no way of gauging how accurately quotas reflected the actual distribution of wealth: there was no accurate valuation against which to compare them. In these circumstances to follow precedent was the strategy favoured by the government, leaving the fine detail of allocations to be decided according to local discretion. On the other hand, in this case (and one may presume in others too) there seems to have been some justification for the claim that the city was over-burdened: the county does not appear to have challenged an assertion that the pound rate raised in the city in order to meet the quota was much higher than that in the county. Complaints of this kind, about the distribution of quota taxation, were endemic.

Sir William Petty suspected that this reduced the taxing capacity of the government. In 1665 he wrote that

> Whereas many are forced to pay 1/10 of their whole Estates towards the raising of but 70000 l. per mensem, besides what they pay more insensibly and directly, as Customs, Excise, Chimny-Money, &c. ... It must come to pass, that the same Persons must from *Christmas*, 1665. pay 1/3 of their whole Estates, if the war with Holland continue two years longer.

However, 'if the Publick Charge were laid proportionably, no Man need pay above 1/10 of his whole Effects, even in the case the Tax should rise to 250000 l. per *mensem*, which God forbid'. The solution, though, rested on something that was politically contentious, if not unacceptable. The only way of achieving an equal distribution was by accurate assessment: 'Assessments upon personal Estates (if given in as elsewhere upon Oath) would bring that Branch which of itself is most dark, to a sufficient clearness.'[8] The use of oaths in the valuation of direct taxation was consistently eschewed, however.

The burden of taxation on the poor affected the range of commodities on which indirect taxation fell. In general, this became a
matter of political economy – the manipulation of duties to
encourage or discourage particular trades, industries or forms of
consumption. James I, it is widely believed, was responsible for
very heavy duties on tobacco in the early seventeenth century, a
vice he regarded with particular hostility. Yet it was a duty that
produced vast revenues over the seventeenth and eighteenth centuries, too – there were sound fiscal reasons for taxing these lucrative and rapidly growing trades. We consider these questions of
tariff policy below, and concentrate here on the excises – indirect
taxation on consumption rather than import.

For much of our period the excise was a dirty word, but this
was not necessarily because some of the duties were regressive or
because the overall burden was particularly heavy. During the
1620s it was equated with oppression and regarded as a foreign
devil, while the 1640s and 1650s saw an outpouring of hostile
pamphlets attacking both the tax and its agents. Excise taxation is
potentially regressive since taxpayers are charged at the same rate
regardless of their wealth. This is particularly true if the tax falls
on staple commodities, which everyone has to buy in more or less
equal quantities. If the charge falls on luxury goods, this regressiveness is reduced because consumption of those goods is
related to wealth and, hence, to ability to pay. In pamphlet debate
it was assumed that taxing 'necessaries', goods that people had to
buy regardless of their income, was unacceptable (document 37).
However, some of these duties came close to this. Bread was
never taxed (see document 7 for similar comment on the burden
of monopolies) but meat and salt were and there were constant
grumbles about particular excises. Once established, the excise
became extremely attractive to governments, in that it was a
means by which to avoid taxing land, its incidence was not so
noticeable and, increasingly, because parliament would grant it
for longer periods than it would direct taxation. Thus, it offered a
better security for long-term borrowing. There was, therefore, a
tension between executive eagerness to impose excises and political opposition, frequently referred to as opposition to a 'general
excise'.[9]

There were arguments in favour of the excise on distributive
grounds, based on the principle 'that a man's total expenditure is

a good test of his ability; taxation distributed on this basis would make him share equitably in national charges according to his proportion'.[10] Since government could not effectively assess ability, many found this a persuasive argument. Once again Petty is very quotable on the issue. 'It is generally allowed by all,' he wrote in 1662, 'that men should contribute to the Publick Charge but according to the share and interest they have in the Publick Peace; that is, according to their Estates or Riches.' The justification for taxing consumption was that

> there are two sorts of Riches, one actual, and the other potential. A man is actually and truly rich according to what he … actually enjoyeth; others are but potentially or imaginatively rich, who though they have power overmuch, make little use of it; these being rather Stewards and Exchangers for the other sort, then owners for themselves.

Wealth was to be measured by the extent to which it was enjoyed, that is, in consumption. Thus,

> [c]oncluding … that every man ought to contribute according to what he taketh to himself, and actually enjoyeth … [W]e must conceive, that the very perfect Idea of making a Leavy upon Consumptions, is to rate every particular Necessary, just when it is ripe for Consumption; that is to say, not to rate Corn until it be Bread.

Since the practical difficulties of doing this were formidable, however, 'we ought to enumerate a Catalogue of Commodities both native and artificial, such whereof accompts may be most easily taken, and can bear the Office marks either on themselves or on what contains them'. In all, this would harmonise natural justice with administrative ease.[11] Whether many contemporaries ever believed that the excise had achieved this is another question. We consider some of these arguments later, but we can note that if the burden of the excise duties *was* felt to fall unfairly on the poor this acted as a restraint on tax policy. However, this issue was embedded in a more complex set of considerations in the case of the excise, and there was a degree of consensus that the poor should help to support the government.

As a result of the complexity of these issues, and even though many of these principles apparently commanded general agreement,[12] the distribution of the duties between commodities was

still contentious. It was asserted that the tax did not fall on everyone equally because rich householders consumed more, but this
was not automatically accepted. As a result, Petty was keen to
find 'accumulative excises', where this relationship did hold true.
These accumulative excises were to fall on commodities which
were consumed in greater quantities according to wealth. If these
things were taxed then the amount of tax being paid would bear
some relation to ability to pay. Clearly beer, bread and salt did not
fit (although he thought that chimneys did). Petty was also
unusual in arguing that debate should look at the tax system as a
whole (but see document 35). Since the excises were heavier on
the poor, he suggested, so direct taxes should aim at the rich.
More generally, it was accepted that the excises were equitable if
they were optional, that is, if they did not fall on the necessaries
of life. One writer proposed in 1647 that

> a tender care be had of the fundamentals ... of man's life, namely,
> bread, flesh, salt, small beer, etc. – that in all matters of taxes the
> state lay her finger on things necessary for men's sustenance and
> her loins on such things as are merely superfluous. Otherwise it
> would be lamentable that the poor labourer who hath threshed all
> day for a livelihood should himself be threshed at night with uncon-
> scionable payment for things tending to the bare support of nature.

Another asked in 1653 'If excise may not be removed, can it not be
reduced and principally lean upon the richest and most superflu-
ous commodities[?]'[13]

This very general distributive plea on behalf of the poor ran up
against the distributive principles already discussed, however.

> [excise duties] were approved as being paid gradually, insensibly
> and surely, as making the poor man contributary to the cost of a
> benefit which he shared, as distributing the burden of taxation equi-
> tably between rich and poor on the basis of a rough test of ability
> approaching that of expenditure or income, and as in a measure
> making the individual his own assessor. They were looked upon as
> equitable in themselves, and not as part of a compensatory system
> of taxation. They were opposed with great persistence on the
> grounds that it was grievous to tax the necessaries of the poor, and
> that Excises were destructive of personal or constitutional liberty
> and injurious to industry.[14]

Seeking to adjust the relative burden of taxation, with the aim, of course, of making it 'fairer', drove much of the debate about taxation in our period. For example, one of the motivating factors behind the adoption of composition agreements for purveyance was the desire to equalise the burden of the exaction (documents 1–2). A letter from Lord Burghley and other privy councillors to officeholders in Essex in 1592 makes this clear. Its concern was that 'an indifferent and equal charge may be laid generally upon her said subjects in all such cases where purveyors have authority to deal'. Moreover, the Queen herself was 'desirous to have all provisions of her household and stable to be served with the good liking of her loving subjects'. As a result she had instructed

> us to signify her Highness's will and pleasure to you that presently all the justices of the peace in the shire [assemble and select four, three, and two to have authority] to agree upon such order and composition to be taken for that shire … as hath heretofore been taken by commission yearly within your shire for her Majesty's household and stable.[15]

In other words, that the justices should find a locally acceptable means of distributing the burden (document 3).

Once again complaints about the burden of taxation may have been as much about equitability as about the total weight of taxation. As we saw above, the purveyors in the counties were constrained in various ways in order to ensure that they took only the quality of goods authorised by the Board of the Greencloth. Nonetheless, the impact of purveyance could be extremely unequal, falling on places visited by the purveyor only. It was a common complaint that purveyors visited particular places repeatedly or that their exactions unnecessarily burdened the poor.[16] Purveyors were frequently accused of being arbitary in their activities, obviously a related complaint. Another reason for the adoption of composition agreements was to restrain their authority and to bring the whole process under close supervision by the magistracy (documents 2–3). It was these issues that fired a dispute between Sir Arthur Heveningham and Sir Nathaniel Bacon in Norfolk, Bacon fighting a rearguard action against the authority of the Board of the Greencloth, and securing a significant degree of local support in the process.[17] This sense, that the magistracy was a more legitimate authority than outside agencies for overseeing the exaction of local resources, is a theme common to reactions to many of the revenue devices examined here. As we have seen, many counties sent a cash subsidy to the household rather than supply goods. This subsidy covered the difference between the market price of particular commodities and the 'King's price'. In effect purveyance became a tax, and where this arrangement was adopted it was rated and collected under the direction of the magistracy. In Cumberland this was so successful that the rate, known as the purvey, became the unofficial basis for many later national taxes, which were raised as multiples of the 'purvey'.[18] Clearly, magisterial cooperation, if it could be secured, promised success in the raising of taxes.

It seems then, that not all complaints about the burden of taxation can be dismissed as mere reluctance to pay. They frequently related to a sense of unfairness in the distribution of taxation, and this was, of course, a serious matter. No doubt they were attractive arguments to those who did, simply, wish to keep hold of their money, but they cannot be reduced simply to this. To the issue of fairness must be added local disputes and local honour or resentments. The north of England was notoriously under-assessed for the land tax, for example.[19] Equally, legal objections to taxation may have been a device for expressing this more mundane desire to be treated equally with a neighbour or rival. However, it is not always clear that this was the case and the distinction is to a degree an artificial one. The protracted disputes over the apportionment of ship money in Cheshire and Chester illustrate this. Because the tax penetrated well down the social scale, and also because

> the royal authority was so centrally involved in the tax and so often invoked by those trying to collect it, it was not possible to react against ship money without also raising a whole series of questions about the nature and limits of the King's authority. Hence the result of this situation was to give quite humble members of society a direct personal and financial stake in a national political issue of the first importance – the question of the legality or otherwise of ship money.[20]

The political economy and non-revenue effects of taxation

So far we have been concerned with arguments about the burden of taxation. In particular, this has centred on the relative rather than the total burden of taxation, on the fairness of the distribution of its weight. As that burden increased arguments became more elaborate and were wedded to a more 'mercantilist' view of the economy. Taxation was no longer simply portrayed as an unfair burden on the poor or on a particularly over-taxed group. Instead it was deemed to be a potential drag on the wealth of the nation as a whole. In short, there was debate in the mid and late seventeenth century about the political economy of taxation. This was the case both with the direct taxes and in connection with tariff policy. Moreover, taxation strategies were increasingly assessed in relation to the security that they offered for borrowing. Finally, other non-fiscal effects of taxation became more obvious and more consciously manipulated. These new issues were a product of the changing role of taxation in public life.

There is little doubt that the manipulation of customs rates in the interests of trade became more sophisticated in this period. Some historians refer to this as the rise of a 'mercantilist' tariff policy. A mercantilist tariff policy is one aimed at promoting domestic manufactures. In order to do this the government would put high tariffs on foreign imports in order to discourage competition and protect home industries. At the same time domestic manufacture might be helped by lowering duties on imported raw materials and by reducing duties paid by manufactures sent abroad. This pattern of priorities is not reflected in the Elizabethan duties but can be discerned in the tariffs in place after the restoration. At the beginning of our period, it seems clear, customs duties were used simply to raise money. After 1660 this revenue raising purpose was often in tension with other, non-fiscal uses of tariffs.

In order to analyse the economic effects of the Elizabethan customs it is necessary first to describe how they were rated. Elizabethan duties were either specific (a particular sum due from a particular quantity of a number of commodities) or *ad valorem* (a proportion of the value of a particular commodity). The small number of specific duties were generally becoming lighter. This was because inflation eroded the value of the sum payable in relation to the rising value of the commodity. This was particularly true of the duties on cloth. Wine and wool duties, on the other hand, were high enough to be an encouragement to smuggling.

The *ad valorem* duties were nominally 5 per cent, but the value on which the duty was paid was often less than the true value of the goods. This was because duties were raised according to the fixed values in the books of rates, which were probably significantly under-valued. The result was that, despite increases in 1558 and 1604, duties were very low, for many commodities perhaps between 1.5 per cent and 3.5 per cent. Although this reduced the temptation to smuggle, it also made most duties ineffective as instruments of protection.

Equally, those commodities on which high rates were imposed do not fit easily with mercantilist presumptions. Wine imports, for example, on which the specific duties might have amounted to an *ad valorem* rate of 80 per cent, were not in competition with domestic production. Moreover, the chief domestic industry, cloth production, was only protected indirectly. Duties were imposed on exports of its raw material, wool (up to 37 per cent *ad valorem* equivalent), but export prohibitions were frequently suspended for individuals in return for a fee. This too, suggests that policy was driven more by a concern for revenue than by a broader 'economic policy'. Concern was frequently expressed in this period about the balance of trade, and a consistent desire was expressed to secure an inflow of bullion. There is little sign, however, that tariffs were manipulated with this in mind, although the exclusion of wine imports helped to some extent. In short, the generally low level of duties and the pattern of their incidence argues against the existence of any protectionist or bullionist blueprint. Instead their purpose was to raise revenue.[21]

This had changed by the end of our period. Crucial to this transformation was the experience of the period 1640–1660. In the early Stuart period, most writers assume, the impetus to expand the range of duties was financial (with the frequently noted exception of the duties of tobacco, later to be an extremely valuable rate). The pattern of duties adopted in the period 1640–60 suggests that the added weight of customs duties was adjusted with trade in mind. It has been estimated that import duties were four times greater than export duties, for example, and there were other 'non-fiscal' aspects of tariff policy. French wines paid high duties in the late 1640s, probably as a response to the French attitude during the second civil war, and during the 1650s anti-Spanish duties were introduced and preferential tariffs were used, too.

For example, duties on ginger and sugar imported from the West Indies were lowered in compensation for the effects of the navigation acts.[22] The increasing burden of the customs, and the establishment of parliamentary control over the book of rates, seems also to have been associated with the more self-conscious manipulation of the tariffs for mercantilist or trading purposes.

These non-fiscal purposes are present after 1660, too. In the 1660 book of rates one-sixth of the main import headings and one-third of the export headings were modified. In this general revision a pattern is discernible. Over fifty rate changes on imports involved either increases in the duties on manufactures or decreases of the duties on raw materials. An equal number reduced the duties on exports. As a whole this amounts to a 'mercantilist' revision, favouring domestic manufacture and exports at the expense of imports of manufactures and luxuries. Added to this, some duties were clearly aimed against the French, and there is the first sign of a corn law. Rates on imported corn varied according to the domestic price in order to protect domestic farming interests. Coupled with the navigation acts, these changes amounted to an 'impressive reorientation of commercial and colonial policy, [in which] fiscal considerations appear to have played little direct part'.[23]

The trend continued throughout the period 1660–88. In fact, it has been suggested that the Commons tended to regard the customs as a tool of foreign or trade policy, a tendency that was in tension with the revenue concerns of the crown. Sometimes the two interests were congruent, but only in the 1680s can it be said that the revenue interests were dominant.[24] The victory may have been short-lived: one authority recommended a review of the book of rates 'respect being had not so much what commodities will raise the greatest revenue to the Crown, as what is the true interest of the nation'.[25] We need more work here, but the general case seems defensible that after 1640 customs revenues expanded very rapidly (in line with other forms of taxation) and this produced more elaborate debate about their political economy. At points, in the 1660s and 1690s for example, the political and trading purposes of rate changes seem to have been so prominent as to adversely affect revenue. This was not a complete contrast with the earlier period – some duties had always had a non-revenue purpose – but the importance of trade policy seems to have increased in importance alongside the dramatic increase in the burden of customs taxation.

Receipts from the customs, as we noted in chapter 3, grew at the same rate as tax revenues as a whole. Much attention has rightly been paid to innovations such as the excise and land tax; this has been to some extent at the expense of ignoring of the customs. There were, evidently, considerable advantages to this form of revenue. The chief of these was, no doubt, that it was an indirect tax on consumption rather than a direct tax. The expansion of the customs was dramatic, and debate surrounding the purposes and implications of the duties became increasingly complex. In the early part of the period tonnage and poundage had, at least in theory, been applied to a particular item of expenditure – the navy. This continued to be the case, in the sense that particular duties were used to secure particular loans. They were, in effect, mortgaged. This was because long-term loans needed long-term security, and there was considerable resistance to perpetual direct taxation. There was, then, pressure to use indirect rather than direct taxation to secure loans. In periods of war the government undertook emergency borrowing and this was usually secured against new customs duties. During the eighteenth century this pattern became clearer. Warfare usually led to an immediate increase in the rate of land tax because this was easy to change. As a result the share of total income borne by the land tax was highest during periods of war. This money went to pay for immediate expenditure and short-term debt, but this increased revenue could not cover the cost of protracted warfare. The mobilisation of supplies was often undertaken on credit and this formed a short-term debt owed to suppliers which was not secured against a particular source of revenue. In order to prevent the growth of unfunded debt, short-term debt was converted into long-term debt. The security for this was provided by indirect taxation: the customs and excise. 'It is for this reason that increases in existing customs and excise duties or levying of new imposts occurred most frequently toward the end of long wars.'[26]

Overall the structure of finances at the end of our period is probably less bewildering than the confusing network of particular rights and revenues of the period 1558–1640. However, particular parts of the system became extremely intricate and sophisticated. A case in point is the plethora of customs duties and the complicated credit arrangements with which they were associated. In 1660 there were three kinds of rates – tonnage (rates per tun on imports); poundage (rates of one shilling in the pound on imports according to the values set down in the book of rates); and the ancient duty on wool. Rapidly, however, restrictions on trade and additional rates were added for particular periods and the system became considerably more complex. By 1670 the *index vectigalium*, a sort of customs handbook, could note that the various regulations and duties were 'both difficult in the discovery and doubtful in the interpretation'.[27] Under William III there were great increases in the variety and burden of the duties and there were further rapid additions between 1702 and 1714 (more duties were added in this period than in the previous three reigns put together). Because each additional or temporary duty was assigned to secure a particular fund they were all accounted separately. By 1784, as we have seen, there were one hundred separate accounts being kept in the customs houses.[28] This expansion of revenue and the proliferation of duties reflects the political advantages of the customs which were ultimately regarded as the 'ideal form of taxation'.[29] Significantly, it was only the customs that were mentioned in the Instrument of Government as the source from which the permanent military establishment was to be funded. The political frictions caused by the excises and assessment may have discouraged governments from undertaking to collect them indefinitely.

The debate about the broader purposes of taxation was not restricted to the customs of course. One advantage of the customs, as we have seen, was that it was not direct taxation on landowners, and we noted in chapter 5 the variety of taxes employed in order to avoid burdening the land. Indeed, some landowners came to benefit positively from tariff policy in relation to corn imports and exports. We have already noted the use of tariffs to protect producers from competition. After 1674 they could benefit from the payment of bounties from the customs revenue to producers who managed to export corn. Another clear advantage of the customs duties was that they were not a general excise.

There were, then, important non-fiscal effects of taxation and there is some evidence that these effects were being more consciously manipulated (documents 13, 34–5, 38). Some of these consequences begin to touch upon the issues discussed in the next chapter. For example, recent work on the origins and purpose of the marriage duty act demonstrates one of the ways in which attitudes towards taxation were becoming more sophisticated. The tax produced only about one-fifth of the revenue received from a single poll tax, and the administrative effort that went into the exercise was considerable. This could 'provide confirmation ... that the government's prime interest in this tax was not fiscal but social control, which it planned to achieve through annual updated censuses of all its inhabitants, including those who had recently moved house, and the recording of all their births, marriages and burials'.[30] It has been suggested that the elaborate demographic statistics that resulted were the main purpose, not a by-product, of the exercise.[31] Certainly, together with the poll taxes, they provided the basis for Gregory King's much quoted political arithmetic. The connection between taxation and 'numbering the people' seems to have been close. Indeed, Glass seems to hint that objections to and obstructions of the tax derived from hostility to this information gathering as much as to the burden of the tax.[32] There is also a suggestion of social engineering in the imposition of a double poll on bachelors in the poll taxes, giving a positive incentive to marry, and one of the criticisms made of the marriage duty act was that it was a tax on the marital bed.[33]

The quest for information was not in itself new, of course. The military surveys of 1522 sought to collect a range of materials that was 'unprecedented', and has been referred to by one recent commentator as 'the first instance of [a] new appetite for detailed information'.[34] The survey clearly called for more than military information, and was an attempt to gauge the wealth of the nation, information which was 'ruthlessly ... exploited to place financial burdens on the people'. This, it has been suggested, explains the subsequent 'reluctance to give government the means to make further impositions'.[35] Between these two dates the best guide to the wealth of the country was contained in the subsidy returns. This fact goes some way to explain the reluctance of contemporaries to be 'raised in the subsidy book', a misfortune which might entail a number of other financial consequences. This reluctance to supply information exacerbated the chronic shortage of information available to early modern governments. This fact of life is reflected in the use of hunters after concealed lands or the use of common informers to enforce penal statutes.

[The use of hunters] might be compared to the use of paid informers in a society without a professional police force. One can see why
the idea appealed to the Crown and its ministers; public revenue
would be increased without public expenditure; the 'hunter' would
be spurred on by private greed to secure a public good.[36]

Here, then, is a familiar tension between using private interest to
persuade individuals to bypass the magistracy and the political
costs that were entailed (see chapters 7 and 8). The same fears of
a well-informed executive fired opposition to direct valuation
and fears of a general excise, as we will see in the next chapter.
The preferred solution was to secure information or resources
through the magistracy, but this was not easy (documents 9–11,
30).

It was partly for these reasons that in general, in the period
1660–1714, fears raised by the excise outweighed its attractions as
an alternative to direct taxation of landed incomes. The advantage of the latter was that they were the most visible forms of
wealth. Indeed, there was even a preference in the restoration
period for land based taxes over excises on malt liquors on the
grounds that, although the latter clearly fell on land and affected
the price of barley, the impact of the former was at least clear and
predictable.[37] It has been suggested that fear of executive power
led to proposals for other forms of taxation such as polls and the
marriage duty act. These fears of executive power persisted in the
eighteenth century and surfaced, apparently quite unreasonably,
in the excise crisis of 1733 (documents 23–5).

However, in the course of the eighteenth century the arguments
in favour of excises began to win out. The appeal of easy and professional administration contributed to this, but so did arguments
related to the economy. By the end of the War of the Spanish Succession income from excises was greater than that from land tax.
With the breaking out of peace the land tax was banked down
while the excise continued to rise. Thereafter it was the most
lucrative source of revenue throughout the eighteenth century.[38]

In this perspective, and treated as serious debates about taxation
policy, the famous parliamentary and extra-parliamentary battles
about excises begin to emerge as mere 'shadow boxing'. From 1688
down to the introduction of the first income tax in 1799 excises
became more widespread, onerous and effectively collected

because excise duties alone proved capable of paying for imperial
expansion and funding Britain's 'blue water' defence strategy.[39]

Excises fell, by a process of trial and error, on decencies. These are
commodities which are not essential to subsistence but which are
not luxuries either. One concern was that the commodities taxed
should be such that demand would not be depressed by indirect
taxation to the point where revenue was lost. It was also an
advantage if demand for the commodities taxed rose among pros-
pering groups. Thus, excise would not fall disproportionately on
the poor. Similarly, as the public debt burgeoned and parliaments
continued to be reluctant to grant direct taxation in perpetuity, it
was excises that offered the best security. Although opposition to
the expanding power of the crown continued to be directed
against the excise its advantages overbore this kind of argument.
The complexity of the issues, however, provides something of a
contrast with debate in the later sixteenth century.

Taxation has a variety of non-fiscal economic effects. These
include, for example, the redistribution of wealth by taxing particular groups more heavily than others or changing patterns of
demand by affecting prices. In many cases, these effects may be
'unfair' and the cause of dispute. Many taxpayers were concerned with these issues, with the relative rather than the absolute
burden of taxation. This kind of complaint was common to all the
taxes and exactions studied here, and continued throughout the
period. It is sometimes assumed, in fact, that this lies at the root of
all objections to taxation: disgruntled taxpayers were really trying
not to pay or at least not to pay as much. These non-fiscal effects
of taxation may be intended or unintended. In other words, governments may consciously manipulate the tax regime in order to
redistribute wealth or to affect patterns of demand. In the period
covered by this book the visibility of taxation, among all the other
sources of revenue, increased dramatically. The increased revenues of the period 1640–1714 came from a smaller number of
sources that were clearly taxes. As the scale of revenues increased
the proportion derived from taxation jumped dramatically. All
over the country, then, levels of taxation rose much more quickly
than levels of revenue in general. After 1640 the non-fiscal effects
of taxation seem to have been discussed with more sophistication
too, and governments appear to have manipulated them more

self-consciously. This was almost certainly linked to the greater visibility of taxation. Finally, the manipulation of the tax regime was increasingly done in the light of the elaborate credit arrangements of government, and the demands of borrowing affected the range of taxes to which resort was made.

As we have seen, these non-fiscal aspects of taxation also led debate to the issue of individual liberty and its relationship to the power of the executive. We might expect such concerns to have increased in proportion to the amount of taxation being collected. The increasing visibility of the tax regime might have led to more elaborate discussion of the relationship between individual property rights and the political obligation to pay taxes. In fact, however, the history of these more 'political' arguments was less straightforward than this suggests. It forms the subject of the next chapter.

Notes

1 N. Williams, *Contraband cargoes. Seven centuries of smuggling*, London, 1959, p. xi.

2 M. Bateson (ed.), *Records of the Borough of Leicester*, Cambridge, 1905, pp. 413, 445, 446.

3 Quoted in M. J. Braddick, *Parliamentary taxation in seventeenth-century England. Local administration and response*, Royal Historical Society Studies in History, 70, Woodbridge, 1994, p. 23. For the decline of the fifteenth and tenth see *ibid.*, chapter 1.

4 C. Russell, *Parliaments and English politics 1621–1629*, Oxford, 1979, pp. 188, 226.

5 Quoted in Braddick, *Parliamentary taxation*, p. 64.

6 *Ibid.*, chapter 2.

7 M. J. Braddick, 'The centre and the localities in seventeenth-century England: resistance to the royal aid and further supply in Chester, 1664–1672', unpublished paper.

8 *Verbum Sapienti* (1665) reprinted in Charles Henry Hull (ed.), *The economic writings of Sir William Petty*, New Jersey, 1986 edition, pp. 103, 115.

9 W. Kennedy, *English taxation 1640–1799. An essay on policy and opinion*, London, 1913, chapter 4; J. Brewer, *The sinews of power. War, money and the English state, 1688–1793*, pp. 145–9; Braddick, *Parliamentary taxation*, chapter 4.

10 Kennedy, *English taxation*, p. 63.

11 *A treatise of taxes and contributions* (1662), reprinted in Hull, *The economic writings of Sir William Petty*, pp. 91–2.

12 Kennedy, *English taxation*, chapter 4.

13 Quoted in *ibid.*, pp. 76–7, 77n.

14 *Ibid.*, pp. 79–80.

15 Quoted in A. Woodworth, *Purveyance for the royal household in the reign of Queen Elizabeth*, Transactions of the American Philosophical Society, 35, Philadelphia, 1945, p. 15.

16 *Ibid.*, pp. 37–8.

17 A. H. Smith, *County and court. Government and politics in Norfolk, 1558–1603*, Oxford, 1974, pp. 293–302.

18 See above p. 75.

19 Brewer, *Sinews*, p. 201.

20 P. Lake, 'The collection of ship money in Cheshire during the sixteen-thirties: a case study of relations between central and local government', *Northern History*, XVII, 1981, pp. 44–71; p. 61.

21 T. S. Willan (ed.), *A Tudor book of rates*, Manchester, 1962. By bullionist is meant a concern to produce a favourable balance of trade in order to secure an inflow of bullion.

22 M. P. Ashley, *Financial and commercial policy under the Cromwellian protectorate*, London, 1934, pp. 60–1.

23 C. D. Chandaman, *The English public revenue 1660–1688*, Oxford, 1975, p. 13.

24 *Ibid.*, pp. 11–21.

25 Quoted in Kennedy, *English taxation*, p. 35.

26 J. Brewer, 'The English state and fiscal appropriation, 1688–1789', *Politics and Society*, XVI, 1988 pp. 344–6, 346.

27 Quoted in E. E. Hoon, *The organization of the English customs system 1696–1786*, New York, 1938, p. 26.

28 Above p. 58.

29 Kennedy, *English taxation*, p. 28.

30 T. Arkell, 'An examination of the poll taxes of the later seventeenth century, the marriage duty act and Gregory King' in K. Schurer and T. Arkell (eds.) *Surveying the people. The interpretation and use of document sources for the study of population in the later seventeenth century*, Local Population Studies, supplement, Oxford, 1992, p. 171.

31 D. V. Glass, *London inhabitants within the walls 1695*, London Record Society Publications, 2, 1966, pp. xiii–xiv. For a fuller discussion see C. Brooks, 'Projecting, political arithmetic and the act of 1695', *English Historical Review*, XCVII, 1982, pp. 31–53.

32 Arkell, 'Examination of the poll taxes', pp. 171–7; Glass, *London inhabitants*, pp. xiv–xv.

33 On the latter point, Glass, *London inhabitants*, p. xiv.

34 R. W. Hoyle (ed.), *The military survey of Gloucestershire, 1522*, The Bristol and Gloucestershire Archaeological Society, Gloucestershire Record Series, 6, 1993, pp. ix–xvii, ix, xi.

35 *Ibid.*, p. xvii.

36 H. Hope Lockwood, 'Those greedy hunters after concealed lands' in K. Neale (ed.), *An Essex tribute. Essays presented to Frederick G. Emmison* ..., London, 1987, pp. 153–70; p. 155.

37 Chandaman, *English public revenue*, p. 40.

38 Brewer, *Sinews*, pp. 96–8.

39 P. K. O'Brien, 'The political economy of British taxation, 1660–1815', *Economic History Review*, 2nd series, XLI, 1988, pp. 1–32; p. 26. See also J. V. Beckett, 'Land tax or excise: the levying of taxation in seventeenth- and eighteenth-century England', *English Historical Review*, C, 1985, pp. 285–308. For the shorter-term perspective, M. J.Braddick, 'Popular politics and public policy: the excise riot at Smithfield in February 1647 and its aftermath', *Historical Journal*, XXXIV, 1991, pp. 597–626. The blue-water defence strategy, among other things, depended on the maintenance of a powerful navy to put economic pressure on enemy trading interests and to protect Britain's. On land the emphasis was on the provision of subsidies to foreign allies rather than the commitment of troops. In both senses it was clearly dependent on the command of large revenues. See Brewer, *Sinews*, p. 257.

7

The politics of taxation: legality, legitimacy and liberty

There is always a temptation to assume that political objections to the payment of taxation derive from financial self interest rather than principled concerns. This may be justified in many cases and it is certainly convenient if following one's conscience leaves one better off. Nonetheless, the taking of taxation does raise questions about property rights and there are issues of principle at stake. Whatever the motives of some complaints about taxation, it is plain that there are serious questions arising from its payment. In this chapter we consider questions of legality raised by taxation. By this is meant the legality of kinds of taxation, rather than the details of their assessment and collection, which are considered in the next chapter.

Law and politics were in many ways inseparable in this period. The most fundamental political questions were expressed in terms of rights, liberties and precedent.

To seventeenth-century Englishmen politics was a branch of the law. Perhaps their deepest political feeling was a sense of law as a 'bulwark' protecting their property and their personal liberty alike against the 'inundations' of arbitrary power. The law protected them because it was fixed and certain; tyranny robbed their lives of this comforting certainty by forcing them to 'live by one man's will'. Law was, in its entirety, the 'inheritance' of a 'free-born Englishman', and every right guaranteed by law was one of the sacred 'liberties' of the English. Thus no clear distinction was made between rights to life and liberty and trivial pieces of property. A minor infringement of the latter was the thin end of a wedge that would force open all the defences against popery and absolutism.[1]

As with the arguments discussed in the previous chapter these views might have simply been an expression of tightfistedness. But even if we accept this initial assumption we have to admit that, once expressed in terms of general legal principle, the issues at stake in the argument become more important than the sum of money being raised. In some cases these issues might be more fundamental than the legality of a tax: they might, for example, touch on the legitimacy of the regime that was demanding tax or the authority of its agents.

We have seen, through previous chapters, how the administration of taxation required participation. The degree of participation forthcoming could be related to influential opinion about the propriety of a particular tax – opinion mattered since the national government lacked the bureaucratic power to override or ignore it. In this and the next chapter we see how the need to mobilise consent shaped the kind of taxes that were raised, and how they were raised. In part this was related to the fairness or propriety of the non-revenue effects of taxation discussed in the last chapter. In part also, though, it could be related to legal or constitutional concerns. This chapter concentrates on the expression of these views in parliament, the courts, the localities and in the pamphlet literature. The following chapter then examines the reactions of taxpayers faced with a demand for payment. These reactions ranged from the unwillingness of an individual to pay up to more clearly 'political' reactions. All these reactions, however, were potentially influenced by the issues explored in this and the previous chapter.

Legal concerns about national revenues

We have seen how, in the case of the monopolies and purveyance, grumbles about the fairness of the distribution of taxation shaded into more fundamental complaints (see documents 4–7). Other disputes, particularly in the early seventeenth century, tackled these issues more directly. We consider here some famous legal cases: those of John Bate, the 'Five Knights' and John Hampden, as well as some less well-known cases brought in the 1620s and 1650s.

John Bate, a London merchant, was brought to court as a result of his opposition to the imposition on imported Venetian currants. This case was significant in that it was subsequently interpreted as proof of the legality of impositions and, after the judges found for the king, the range of impositions expanded very quickly. For this reason, perhaps, the constitutional aspects of the hearing have traditionally received considerable attention. In fact, though, the case was heard on more restricted legal grounds. It has been suggested, as we will see, that there was fundamental agreement about the 'dual view of the prerogative'. This held that part of it was restrained by common law, but that part of it was transcendent. For example that relating to truces, shippings, declaring of war and making of peace could not be constrained. The difference was not about the nature of the prerogative, nor about the relationship between the prerogative and the rights of the subject. The difference centred on whether or not the right to levy impositions lay within the transcendent prerogative.

Bate was not the first merchant to challenge impositions. In fact, over the previous fifty years there had been five exchequer cases which might have offered precedents. However, the use made of them in the course of the case was limited because they were technical and ambiguous, or because records of the decisions were not available. One, in particular, illustrates this complexity: the case brought by London merchants in 1558 relating to woollen duties. The crown was entitled to a duty on wool that was heavier than the duty on woollen cloth: a sack of wool paid 40s, a short cloth 1s 2d. For the rates to be equal, in terms of the wool content, the short cloth would have to have paid more – 10s each. In 1558, by authority of the privy seal, this gap was closed, the duty being increased to 6s 8d. This left a gap of 3s 4d, which was narrowed by further impositions in 1584 and 1618. These duties were known as the praetermitted custom. The 1558 duty was challenged, however, by London merchants complaining that it 'was not granted by Parliament but assessed by Queen Mary of her absolute power'. No decision is recorded, though the silence has subsequently been interpreted as a sign of a decision hostile to the crown. Fleming, in Bate's case, argued that it was not relevant for three reasons: no judicial decision had been reached, only a conference at the request of the queen; the commodity in Bate's case was foreign not domestic; and London merchants had continued to pay, unlike Bate. Clearly such precedents were difficult to interpret. Nonetheless, they underline the fact that an important source of crown revenue was of questionable legality.[2]

Bate's case started with simple tax refusal. It was noted in chapter 3 that a single commodity might pay several duties and this was the case here. Bate was a Levant Company member who loaded currants at London. He paid the subsidy of 8d per hundredweight, but refused to pay the imposition of 5s 6d. It became something of a *cause célèbre* because it coincided with parliamentary discussion of the issue. Bate's refusal took place on 2 April, and on 7 and 9 April a House of Commons debate about grievances to be brought before the king mentioned the issue. By 11 April, when he was summoned to the council and committed to Marshalsea prison, parliament was hearing speakers on behalf of the merchants and the customs farmers. Bate's name was mentioned by Hitchcock, who spoke on behalf of the merchants. When Bate's case came to trial, Hitchcock was one of the judges who found in his favour. In this way, then, Bate's refusal to pay quickly became a national issue. When James dissolved parliament on 27 May it was with the intention that the courts should decide on Bate. The case cannot be understood, however, without understanding the more restricted issue that lay behind it.[3]

One practical issue that lay behind the case was that the imposition that Bate refused to pay had originally been levied not by the crown but by his company of merchants. He had belonged to the Levant Company, a group of merchants who had been granted a trading monopoly with the Eastern Mediterranean. In return for this privilege they paid rent to the crown. In order to protect their trading interests the company supported an ambassador at the court of the sultan of Ottoman Turkey. It was to support this ambassador that the company imposed a rate on currants imported by its members. This charge was, perhaps, a dubious proceeding. It had been challenged as an infringement on the royal prerogative by a customs officer. When the company folded, unable to pay its rent to the crown, the need for an ambassador remained. He was important for both commercial and foreign policy reasons and as a result the crown continued to collect the duty on currants to support him.

This was an irritation to the merchants involved in the trade, however. They were still paying for the maintenance of the ambassador, but they no longer enjoyed a monopoly on the trade. At the same time, it seemed that James I was not protecting the interests of the trade very effectively. Eventually a new charter was negotiated but by this time the imposition on currants had become an important part of royal revenues. It had also been farmed out and some people in crown circles thought it might be an important part of a solution to the revenue problems of the crown. Thus, when a new charter was granted, the imposition remained a royal levy. In this respect the Levant merchants had clearly lost out. Bate had opposed this resolution of the wrangle and was also involved in opposition to purveyance. Like most importers of luxury goods he was a member of the Grocers' Company, which was in conflict with the Board of the Greencloth over purveyance. Bate was already a figure of some prominence when he refused to pay the duty on the quayside in April 1606.[4]

The grievance that resulted in the legal case has a complicated context and the terms in which the argument was conducted in court were also complicated. It was once commonplace to suggest that at stake was resistance to non-parliamentary taxation, the defence of private property from the prerogative authority of the monarch. In this sense the case was thought to constitute an important step on the 'highroad to civil war', part of an escalating conflict between a crown with absolutist ambitions and parliament. More recently it has been suggested that this case and others revealed fundamental differences of principle. On one hand were those who believed in an absolute right of property which could not be taken away without consent. On the other were those who believed in the absolute power of the monarch, which could not be constrained by common law defences of private property.[5]

Plainly, however, it would be possible to argue differently. Recent commentators have pointed to the substantial agreement on both sides.

> Everyone agreed that the common law protected property, within England at least, and that the king could not infringe upon property rights without his subjects' consent. Most agreed also that the king had both an ordinary and an extraordinary (or absolute) prerogative, the latter properly used not to *contravene* the common law (through which the king exercised his ordinary prerogative) but to

supplement it. It provided a basis for royal action in areas where the common law had no force, whether geographical (possibly the high seas) or institutional (possibly the church).

In short, the 'dispute was not primarily theoretical at all, but more about whether impositions were in fact properly a matter for the absolute prerogative and thus of no concern to the common law'.[6] The crucial question is how seriously to take the disagreement. Was it a relatively minor question which was contained within a consensual view of how the constitution worked in general? Or did it reflect an important rift? Consensus here is clearly a matter of degree and our answer to this question might depend on why we are interested in the case. It might not be obvious that this disagreement could generate a civil war, but it was still sufficiently serious to disrupt the revenue potential of the state. It was also, as we have seen, part of a longer series of disputes about the impositions, an increasingly important component of the revenues.

Bate's case, then, has to be understood in the context of sectional interests in the merchant community and the technicality of the issues being heard. It was not, in any straightforward sense, a defence of property against the prerogative power of the monarch. Nonetheless, contemporaries and historians have discerned the presence of this more fundamental question. Again there has been a tendency recently to downplay the importance of this more general argument. It has been suggested, for example, that the campaign against purveyance, with which Bate was associated, was really a process of negotiation. The House of Commons promoted bills against purveyance which were clearly too restrictive for the crown to accept. There was little hope of seeing them through the whole process of legislation therefore. Instead, they were intended by the Commons to satisfy local constituencies that their grievances were being represented. In doing so, it was hoped to apply pressure to the king to accept a national composition in place of the power to take goods by purveyance. Unfortunately this negotiation failed, leaving the House of Commons with an uncomfortable choice of upsetting their local constituencies by dropping their opposition or upsetting the king by sustaining it. In the end a futile gesture was made: a bill taking strong measures against purveyance was passed by the House of Commons only once it was clear that the House of Lords would reject it. Face was saved by a proclamation from the king promising reform.[7]

Clearly, here, we should be wary of believing the rhetoric of politicians. This point has been further elaborated: people use different 'languages' for particular audiences. Language here means more than rhetoric referring to 'specialized sets of words and concepts designed for dealing with special areas of debate'.[8] Apparently fundamental disagreements might, in this view, result from the application of different or inapplicable languages to a particular problem. Bate's case is an example of how difficult it is to interpret such arguments. So, for example, it was politically acceptable to use the language of the transcendent or absolute prerogative in relation to the high seas but not in relation to private property, which was protected by common law. The peculiarity of the impositions was that they might have been interpreted as a matter of property or of the high seas (document 21).

There is still another level of complexity, too. During the hearing considerable pressure was brought to bear on the judges on behalf of the crown. Moreover, the decision, although based on fairly narrow legal questions, was subsequently interpreted more broadly. In this sense, it has been suggested, the case helped to create a growing distrust of the judiciary. This distrust, a belief that the judiciary was prey to political pressure and manipulation has been seen by others as a product of the 1620s, but it may have existed considerably earlier.[9] Contemporaries may not have been any more sensitive to the legal niceties of the issues than historians have traditionally been.

Discussion of the other cases being considered here is similarly fraught. The famous legal case associated with the 1626 forced loan was, like the challenges to impositions, conducted on a more restricted issue than is frequently appreciated. However, a recent major study of the forced loan makes it clear that responses to it cannot be understood simply in the context of the peculiarities of the loan and the circumstances of its demand. Reactions were also affected by hopes and fears regarding foreign policy and parliament, the characters and aspirations of politicians in court and council, and the expanding access to political news in the localities. Within this complex of issues the loan assumed a political significance and symbolic importance out of proportion with its fiscal impact. 'It would seem, from the experience of both the 1590s and the 1640s, that most shires were capable of sustaining the burdens of war for at least as long as they had to during the 1620s. The real issue was whether or not they had the will to do so; and this was largely related to political considerations.'[10] This will was lacking and led some opponents of the loan to develop a 'drastic' means of expressing dissent. 'What was needed [they argued] to deter the king from his tyrannical intentions was nothing less than an aggressive demonstration of opposition.'[11]

This fed, and fed upon, opposition. However, the issue that was tested was not the right to demand such a loan but the measures taken to enforce it. The council had to face this issue as large numbers of gentlemen refused to subscribe. In late 1627 refusers had been summoned to London and imprisoned. Eventually seventy-six people were arrested and, as the prisons filled up, an alternative means of enforcement had to be found. Initially refusers were summoned before the council every three days, a tedious and expensive process, and this continued for three months. Rumours began to circulate that the refusers would be let off, or that a crack-down was imminent. Division emerged in the council between those unwilling to run the risk of a legal hearing and those eager to put the issue to a legal test in order to secure firm legal backing for their proceedings. The issue was brought to a head by a suit from five gentlemen to the lord chief justice 'that counsel might be assigned them to plead for their relief out of prison'.

The king was consulted, and the matter was allowed to proceed to a hearing. The hearing did not deal with the legality of the loan, however, but with the propriety of the confinement. This, it was argued, was 'by his majesty's special commandment' and therefore legal. The public outcry at this decision seemed to vindicate the view of those counsellors who thought that such a hearing should have been avoided. The decision on discretionary imprisonment fed into the Petition of Right, picking up other issues as the debate continued. Since Charles had not filed substantive charges against the Five Knights, the issue was merely whether or not they could be released from discretionary imprisonment: the judges could not legally consider the causes of the imprisonment. The decision did not provide a strong precedent, therefore. This might explain why the attorney-general, Sir Robert Heath, sought to alter the record in King's Bench to provide a stronger precedent: 'a precedent cannot be stronger than it appears on paper'.[12] The thought of the attorney-general tampering with legal process was clearly frightening. He had attempted to turn the decision into a much stronger claim – that no subject could be freed from imprisonment if that imprisonment was at his majesty's absolute command. It raised broader fears for liberty, and connected the issue to the Petition of Right. As it was, if Heath's precedent had not been enrolled, the refusers could continue to sue out a writ of habeas corpus *ad infinitum*. Heath's attempt failed, but not before the issues had been raised. The Petition of Right debates sought safeguards against such actions in the future, ultimately denying the right of the crown to imprison for reasons of state. The fault for this lay with the attempt to pervert the course of the King's Bench. The precedent provided by the judgement was weak: as some of those involved in the debate acknowledged, it could not provide the precedent that the House of Commons ultimately sought to resist. As with impositions though, the political effect of judgements could be far greater than their legal meaning, raising fundamental questions about political authority. It has also been pointed out that, at root, the issue related to property.[13]

A series of legal questions arose from Charles I's collection of tonnage and poundage without parliamentary sanction (document 22). In 1625 a bill had been proposed which would have given him the right to collect tonnage and poundage for twelve months. This would have allowed time to consider a reform of import duties as a whole. The Lords rejected this proposal, under official pressure driven by a fear that such a bill would force the king to call parliament in a year's time. Despite the lack of a settlement, collection continued and when parliament next met a bill was prepared to indemnify him for having collected the duties without sanction. This parliament was also dissolved early, however, in order to forestall attacks on the king's favourite, the duke of Buckingham. As a result the duties were not granted and the matter of indemnity for the king was unresolved. In 1628 some merchants refused to pay and were imprisoned. They were released having given bonds to pay what was found to be due. Once again, however, negotiation in parliament broke down and the issue was taken up in more ringing terms. on 25 June 1628 the House of Commons declared 'that the taking tunnage and poundage "and other impositions not granted by Parliament" was in breach of fundamental liberties of the kingdom and contrary to the Petition of Right'. This, in effect, confused two kinds of custom duty by suggesting that tonnage and poundage levied without parliamentary sanction was a kind of imposition.[14]

In this context, of continuing negotiation, tax refusal was clearly a politically charged action. Early in 1629 Richard Chambers sought to rescue goods seized from him for non-payment of tonnage and poundage. He was summoned before the privy council where he suggested that English merchants were more oppressed than their Turkish counterparts. He was imprisoned for scandalous words, an action which, incidentally, hardly disproved his argument. Meanwhile he had been trying to recover his goods by legal process, by suing a writ of *replevin* (see p. 215, below). This legal process was stopped by the exchequer, which could call all revenue matters before its own judges. All this put the crown in a very tricky legal position, however. The House of Commons was still seeking to grant tonnage and poundage. If the exchequer could enforce the seizure of goods for non-payment, however, it suggested that the duties could be legally collected anyway. In short, parliament had nothing to grant. Eventually Chambers had to pay the duty to receive back his goods and was fined £2,000 for his insolent words.[15] Not surprisingly, perhaps, the number of merchants refusing to pay was falling and parliament's bargaining position became weaker. In particular, the king clearly possessed tonnage and poundage now, and that implied some kind of legal right to it.[16]

A further example of the way that these legal challenges could raise fundamental questions is provided by the legal disputes about ship money. This duty also raised, or was thought by some to raise, fundamental issues. The significance of the legal queries raised against ship money is particularly hotly contested (document 15). The interpretation placed on these issues is usually taken to be central to our verdict on the viability of personal rule in the 1630s and, ultimately, the causes of the English civil war. No one has denied that for some people, at least, ship money was a significant issue, however, and that the legal challenges against the levy were more fundamental than any raised against parliamentary taxation. There are two separate legal hearings to be discussed in this context – the referral of his constitutional position for consideration by the common law judges by Charles I in February 1637, and the case brought by John Hampden.[17]

The levies faced a number of legal queries in 1635 and 1636. These often took the form of a tax refusal which was followed by a legal challenge to the distraint (see below, chapter 8). Some of these doubts were raised by substantial figures: Viscount Saye and Sele challenged the distraint of oxen from his lands in Lincolnshire, and the earl of Warwick sought an audience with Charles in order to express his misgivings about the tax. In February 1637 Charles wrote to the twelve common law judges seeking clarification of his legal position, particularly in relation to two legal questions. Firstly, could he, when 'the good and safety of the kingdom in general is concerned', command all subjects, under writ of the Great Seal, 'at their charge to provide and furnish ... ships with men, victual and munition' and compel this contribution by law? Secondly, was he not 'the sole judge' of the danger? Although justices Croke and Hutton expressed doubts they fell in with the unanimous decision of the judges in affirming the king's right in both respects.[18]

These doubts were not the only reason to regard this unanimous decision as less than satisfactory for the king. Much attention has been paid to notes made by a Kentish gentleman, Sir Roger Twysden, of reactions in Kent to the judges' decision.[19] When the decision was read at the assizes, Twysden thought, there was an air of disappointment among the auditors. In subsequent discussion, some welcomed the willingness of the king to hazard such a central policy to legal test. On the other hand, others felt that any 'just king would take counsel of his judges' and, further, that 'in a case of this weight, the greatest was ever heard at a common bar in England, that in a judgement that not only may but doth touch every man in so high a point, every man ought to be heard and the reasons of every one weighed, which could not be but in parliament'.[20] Misgivings were expressed on more limited issues, too – whether the decision gave power to raise ships, not money, and whether the affirmation of an emergency meant that there really was one. Both issues were pursued subsequently.

Clearly it is wrong to assume that the opposition to ship money represented a challenge to the prerogative – the issues were more complex than this and uneasiness about the levy might proceed from much more restricted issues of legal principle. This is manifest, too, in Hampden's case, where the issues were heard in both broad and narrow senses. St John, representing Hampden, did not question the power of the monarch to raise money from subjects in an emergency, merely whether such an emergency existed. Edward Littleton, representing the king, argued on this issue, too. Robert Holborne, Hampden's other counsel, raised the more fundamental question of the king's power to declare an emergency in this context, which affected the property of the subject, and this was opposed by Sir John Bankes. The presiding judges were not confronted with a decision about common law or prerogative but by a variety of relatively narrow and relatively broad legal questions. Thus Bramston and Davenport, for example, decided against the king because the ship money writ demanded a service (the provision of ships), not money. Hampden was being prosecuted for a debt, however, a cash sum to be paid into the king's general funds. If the prosecution for debt was appropriate then the ship money must be a tax because it demanded money not a service. If the demand really was for a service not money then Hampden could not be prosecuted for debt. The crown could not have it both ways.[21] Their judgement is based on a technicality but there is at least a suggestion that they shared the broader concerns being expressed about taxation without consent.

The end result was a decision in favour of the king which was difficult for contemporaries to interpret. It is usual to give the verdict as 7 : 5 in favour of the king but contemporaries seem to have interpreted the decision differently, finding arguments on each 'side' in many of the judgements.[22] Perhaps because of this complexity, the reactions to the judgement were ambivalent. Collection speeded up in many localities whose payers had hoped for release, but there is plenty of evidence of continuing doubt on both narrow and broad issues. It is surely correct, however, to question how far the case provides evidence of an opposition to personal rule, as many earlier historians seemed to suggest.

The discussion of these cases, and of Hampden's case in particular, is, in a sense, distorted by the centrality that they have assumed in the discussion of the causes of the English civil war. In practice, people were likely to have been motivated by a number of things. They might have been reluctant to pay tax, or concerned by relatively narrow legal queries about the power of the sheriffs to collect. Others, clearly, argued about the existence of the emergency and the king's power to levy money rather than ships. Behind these latter arguments might have lain concerns about constitutional principle. The precise nature of this mix of motives affects our view of the extent and nature of opposition to the personal rule and this has obvious implications for our view of the plausibility of attempts to rule without parliaments. The fact that the case was 'the constitutional *cause célèbre* of the personal rule'[23] requires that contributors to the debate about the causes of the civil war give the case some prominence. As a result, the interpretation of resistance to ship money is controversial. Recent commentators, however, have tended to emphasise the complexity of the issues at stake. Sharpe has pointed out that the hearing of these issues at law did not drive anyone to challenge the legal system or to pursue opposition to the levy outside the usual channels of 'appeal, protest and counsel'.[24] In short it was not obviously a prelude to a civil war. However, ship money tested the limits of political acceptability far more than parliamentary levies. If a government could secure sufficient parliamentary revenue, it risked far less in terms of political cost and potential revenue loss than it did by raising money by these other means. It was by no means obvious that this was an option in the period before the civil war because parliamentary revenues had frequently proved disappointing in their yield. In the 1630s the king may not have faced this choice. But the contrast does explain why the regimes after 1640 were (largely) able to avoid these legal entanglements.

We can read all these cases in a variety of ways, then. On the face of it, they seem to present a challenge to central aspects of the legal authority of the crown, but in fact, frequently, they were really testing quite detailed points of law. There is a danger of overstating their significance, in this sense. However, that they were interpreted broadly after the fact suggests that we should not push that argument too far. Clearly a government would rather not risk challenges of this kind – the potential loss of revenue was much greater from legal challenges to the principle of a tax than from the more restricted legal challenges we explore in the next chapter. In this sense, parliamentary grants had a clear advantage because their provenance was unimpeachable. Since the government won these cases, however, the long-term significance is open to doubt – the victory in Bate's case, however equivocal and limited, provided the basis for a lucrative revenue in the 1630s which was not challenged. Perhaps, here, the reactions of some people to Hampden, recorded by Twysden, are significant in that they were suspicious of the meaning of the decision. Certainly the opportunity was seized to overturn these decisions when it arose in 1641. It was not inevitable that prerogative taxation should fail, but, on the other hand, the parliamentary taxes that replaced it were free of this legal doubt and political cost.

Many of the prerogative taxes were subject to legal challenge, on points of detail but also on the legality of the exaction. Additionally the negotiations around compositions for purveyance raised questions about the powers of purveyors and the legal restraint of their activities. On the whole, taxes granted by parliament were not open to such objections, with some notable exceptions to be considered below, arising from the questionable legitimacy of the protectoral regime. Concerns were expressed about all the parliamentary taxes we have considered here, but the legality of the particular taxes was not questioned. For example, the hearth tax was abolished as a badge of slavery on the people, and taxpayers were encouraged in their resistance in the 1660s by parliamentary reservations about the tax. However, the tax enjoyed parliamentary sanction and there was no great test case. On the whole, then, these cases tested the legality of particular powers rather than the legitimacy of the regime but such questions may have been implicit for some observers.

The legality of the revenues after 1649

As we have seen, these legal queries could raise issues (and may have proceeded from issues) of fundamental importance – including the legitimacy of particular sources of political power. The regimes in place after 1649 were vulnerable to such challenge, and there are two examples of this – the legal case brought by George Cony, a London merchant, and a strike by taxpayers in 1659. In November 1654 a London merchant, of independent religious views, refused to pay customs duties on imported silk. When officials tried to distrain goods from his house they were violently expelled. He was then called before a committee of the council of state for the preservation of the customs and fined £500, a sum he refused to pay. He was then imprisoned. In response he sued a writ of habeas corpus and his case, after some hearings related to technicalities, was heard before the Upper Bench (the protector's equivalent of the King's Bench). There were several issues on which his treatment was questionable. The government rested on the Instrument of Government, the legal status of which was unclear. It had been drawn up by John Lambert and effected after the ejection of the Nominated Assembly in December 1653. It provided for government by protector, council of state and parliament, but parliament was not immediately called. In order to cope with this interim period the Instrument had given the protector power to legislate by ordinance with the council, but this power should have lapsed once the first protectoral parliament met in September 1654. When parliament did meet it did not meekly accept the Instrument, setting about some revisions which were not completed before its dissolution. In fact, it had only accepted the 'fundamentals of the constitution' under extreme pressure from the army. The status of the Instrument, then, was unclear, and the power of the protector to rule by ordinance even more so. Cony challenged a customs duty raised under the authority of an ordinance and was arrested, fined and imprisoned by a 'court' established by ordinance. His case, then, was of great political significance, seeming to challenge the powers of the protector to rule without parliament.

There was a counter-case, however, since the Instrument had called for the maintenance of standing armed forces by means of the customs duties and other revenues. The Instrument empowered the protector and council to make 'laws and ordinances for the peace and welfare of these nations' which were to be binding until order was taken in parliament on the issues. Since no countermanding order had been taken, the ordinances made prior to parliament were still in force. Moreover, the Instrument gave the customs to the protector in order to support the military. They could not be taken away without the consent of the protector and parliament. Clearly, then, the customs were given to the protector by the Instrument itself. The challenge to these duties has been interpreted by some historians as a challenge to the authority of the Instrument itself, since it effectively challenged an article of the Instrument.[25] It has recently been suggested that there 'was provision for the imposition of the custom under the Instrument of Government, though perhaps not for the erection of a court'.[26]

The case put the protectoral regime in an uncomfortable position. The duty was justified by necessity, an argument uncomfortably close to that used to justify ship money. Furthermore, in attacking the authority of the committee of the protector's council, Cony's representatives urged the statute passed against Star Chamber. The attack on the authority of ordinances raised central questions about the authority of the Instrument. They were imprisoned for refusing to retract an argument seemingly challenging protectoral prerogative, an action many have seen as symptomatic of Cromwell's authoritarian style. Worse still, however, Lord Chief Justice Rolle (whose brother had been among those who refused to pay tonnage and poundage in 1628) seemed to share some of these scruples, being inclined to bail Cony on the 'grand exception that he should be fined and imprisoned upon an ordinance never published, nor of which he had notice'.[27] While this argument did not threaten the authority of ordinances directly, it did suggest that it was not equal to statute. Statutes could be presumed to be known and so ignorance was no defence. By the end of the Easter term, 1655, this threatened to be a serious defeat for the protectorate. Even if the decision favoured the argument of necessity and declared the duty legal this would have retrospectively legalised ship money, too. The alternative was to create a new legal doctrine distinguishing the power of the protector from that of the king and parliament.[28] In the event the difficulty was avoided. Over the summer Rolle resigned (historians differ in their assessment of how voluntary this decision was). He was replaced by the more pliable Glyn; and Cony was persuaded to drop the case. Once again, however, central questions about the limits on the power of the executive to interfere with private property were raised by questions regarding taxation.

Later in the year similar issues were raised by the actions of Sir Peter Wentworth in Warwickshire, who refused to pay his assessment. When a distraint was taken he had two constables arrested for illegal entry, declaring the tax to be contrary to law and to the Instrument. He was summoned before the protector and council and persuaded to withdraw the action by the direct command of the protector. Significantly, he, too, is described as a republican, and like Cony he may have had a political purpose in challenging the relatively conservative settlement represented by the Instrument of Government. His case was less damaging, though, since the Instrument had not mentioned the assessment.[29]

In December 1659 a fairly well-orchestrated threat to boycott taxation helped to persuade Charles Fleetwood that army rule could not continue. Fearing an imminent army coup, in October 1659 parliament had passed a bill declaring it treason to raise taxes without consent. Clearly this was intended to make rule without parliament very difficult for the army. Following the coup there were organised attempts to withhold taxes, which helped to put pressure on Fleetwood and the Committee of Safety, the body that had taken over government. In a sense, then, an argument that tax could only legitimately be raised by consent contributed to constitutional change. On the other hand, reactions such as those of Robert Bocking, a Norwich brewer, may have been motivated by self-interest. Bocking refused to collect excise from his customers for the seven weeks between the passage of the bill and the assembly of the Rump on 25 December 1659.[30]

The legitimacy of agencies of collection

A more mundane expression of the same concern about the legitimacy of political authority was the suspicion expressed of the activities of professional tax collectors, or agents of collection who made a personal profit from their activities. In the ports this was less of a problem – the links between the customs service and the merchant community were close to the point where this closeness was a source of concern (document 18). In the excises, however, there was a demonstrable hostility to professional collectors and there was hostility to all forms of direct taxation which involved such people. Weighing up the relative advantages of land rates and the excise in meeting the urgent need for supply in 1667, John Milward noted that the land rate was preferable for a number of reasons. For example, 'we know the track thereof'. It was more than familiar though. A major advantage was 'that it is neither chargeable to the King nor extreme troublesome to the people, it being assessed and collected by their neighbours'. This was a clear contrast with the excise which was not only 'a stranger to us' but was collected 'with exceeding great charge both to the King and trouble to his people, it being to be collected by such a sort of people as must necessarily be employed in the collection of it'.[31] This sense, that magistrates were to be preferred to professionals in tax collection, was common throughout this period. It is particularly clearly expressed in the vilification of excise men in pamphlets published during the 1650s.[32]

We have already noted the hostility to the 'general excise' in the context of the discussion of the distributive principles of the duties. Another issue tied up in that opposition was a constitutional one – a fear that the executive might become over-funded. From the point of view of the executive, as we have seen, the excise was predictable in its yield, came in gradually and was fairly insensible to the taxpayer. For these very reasons the excises became viewed as a threat to the constitutional position of parliament after 1660 (documents 23–4). There is an irony here that 'the Excise, originally suspect because of its revolutionary origins, came to be associated with an imagined threat of royal absolutism'.[33] These misgivings, along with resentment of the powers of excisemen and the numerous industrial or commercial objections, fuelled a powerful and persistent hostility to the general excise throughout the restoration period and into the eighteenth century.

It has been noted that between 1660 and 1688 the 'legislature ... was to be almost as consistently suspicious or hostile' to the idea of a general excise as the executive was attracted by the proposal. The most common objection was that it was ' "un-English" and subtly degrading, with a threat to the privacy of the individual implicit in the inquisitorial activities of the exciseman'. Thus, the history of political debate about the excise in the restoration period is one of executive eagerness opposed by the Commons. In 1666, with sources of direct taxation apparently exhausted and large sums of money required for the Dutch War, a determined attempt to extend the excise was made, with a view to raising 'a general excise of all inland goods'. However, 'prejudice against a General Excise was much too strong to be overcome even in conditions of emergency'. The proposal coincided with a crescendo of opposition to the hearth tax and this, too, was seen as a possible persuasion to the adoption of a general excise. However, there was further resort to direct taxation instead, itself a measure of the unpopularity of the excise, and despite some extensions of the excise duties in general 'the attempt to expand the Excise failed. It was not until well after the Revolution [of 1688] ... that parliamentary antipathy to the Excise somewhat diminished, allowing some broadening of the limited basis upon which the tax had been settled in 1660.'[34] As we have seen, though, the objection was not the one that we might have expected, that the tax was regressive. Instead, it was connected with broad fears about liberty and the legitimacy of executive authority.

Just as the second Dutch War had produced a proposal for a general excise, so did the Nine Years War during the 1690s. A government scheme for an excise on staples failed in parliamentary committee in 1689 and further proposals were prepared in 1691 and 1693. Even a more limited proposal for excises on leather and soap became the focus for protracted debate in the Commons.[35] The attractions to the government were the familiar ones, reinforced by the fact that James II's successor inherited a remarkably efficient excise administration marked by considerable professionalism. The counter-case also contained familiar elements: that the yield of the tax was unpredictable and might free the executive; and that the tax entailed the sanctioning of the activities of 'an army of officers'. The fear of a general excise informed the reaction to a proposal to any particular duty, too: 'A single excise presaged a general one; a general excise promised fiscal independence to the crown; fiscal independence threatened the revolutionary settlement; excises therefore jeopardised the Glorious revolution.' It was, additionally, argued that the tax burdened the middling sort, whereas wardship revenues that it had replaced had penalised the rich. Members of parliament feared the attractions of the tax to a parliament of landowners. The chief concern, though, was the suspicion of executive power. This explains the preference for land tax, which was more easily revoked and administered by local officeholders. The same suspicion led to the introduction of various taxes designed to pre-empt the introduction of a general excise – poll taxes, the marriage duty act, a proposed capitation in 1696 and the duty placed on wine retailers in 1693. The variety of opposing arguments, combined with the difficulty of managing parliament in the 1690s and early 1700s, ensured that the government plan, of a low land tax and a general excise, proved unachievable.[36]

In the case of direct taxation and the inland excises, as well as the household taxes, this hostility to administration by non-officeholders was a manifestation of a particular claim to liberty – freedom from assessment by the chief magistrate (documents 9, 30, 39). Petty noted the objection 'against this so exact computation of the Rents and works of lands. &c.' in 1662. It consisted, he said, of the fear 'that the Sovereign would know, too, exactly every mans Estate'. He sought to reassure readers that the king would not misuse this information since 'it would be a great discommodity to the Prince to take more than he needs ... where is the evil of this so exact knowledge?'. The hopes may have been rather naive, though. He also suggested that taxpayers could not be sure of consistently benefiting from inaccurate valuations. It was, he hinted, rational self-interest for taxpayers to be assessed accurately.[37] Here he was clearly in a minority.

This claim of freedom from assessment was made so frequently and in relation to so many taxes that it is difficult not to take it seriously as a point of principle. It was in this sense that the hearth tax was a badge of slavery on the people. We have seen how strict valuation for direct taxation was used as a threat by the early Stuart privy council.[38] An alternative was assessment on oath, but this too met with principled resistance: 'even the idea of placing assessors [of direct taxation], let alone the taxpayers, on oath was strenuously resisted'.[39] The removal of the oath from subsidy valuations in 1566 led to a serious fall in receipts from that tax, but that should not be taken as proof that escape from oaths was simply a ruse for evading taxation. In fact it suggests, in itself, how important oath-taking was to early modern society.[40] On the other hand, it should be noted that when oaths were introduced into the assessment of the land tax during the 1690s the yield actually declined (see above, chapter 5).

These concerns, which in a later age we would refer to as concerns about the powers of government, brought argument about the politics of taxation to the issue of liberty. The insistence on administration by the magistracy, the suspicion of professional or specialised agents, the claim to freedom from assessment and the hostility to any direct assessment of wealth in any form, all point to a particular claim about individual rights. As Bacon said in the sixteenth century, the Englishman was 'most master of his valuation and the least bitten in purse' of all his European contemporaries. One achievement of the seventeenth century English state was to overcome the lack of bite without affecting the English-man's mastery of his own valuation. Strikingly, none of the revenue strategies of long-term significance after 1640 involved direct valuation (except the window tax, and that was done by the land tax administration without entering houses). Similarly, whatever else was unsettled by the restoration settlement, the legal basis of the revenues was clear. There was no legal test case which raised the fundamental issues touched upon by Bate, Hampden and Cony. There was a continuity in concerns about threats to liberty arising from the attentions of the agents of revenue collection, but there was a change in the constitutional significance of arguments about the revenue. Before 1640 a number of important revenues were of questionable legality, and were justified on narrow technical grounds. None of the revenues after 1660 were subject to this questioning, but there was a new concern that parliament might grant away its power by ceding financial independence to the crown.

In the last two chapters we have examined public debate under the headings of the burden of taxation, its political economy, legality, legitimacy and liberty. Parliamentary debate in any particular part of our period proceeded on all these fronts but there was a chronological change. Attitudes towards the political economy of taxation became increasingly sophisticated and the constitutional status of the revenues became much less contentious. In the early part of the period covered by this book constitutional argument ranged over the relative claims of the crown to powers in cases of necessity and the rights of the subject to property. Discussion of the economic effects of taxation was restricted largely to the burden of taxation on the poor. There were not clearly opposed constitutional arguments, in fact 'King and Commons both insisted upon their sedulous respect for the inchoate conventions that had previously governed their fiscal relations; but they asserted, intermittently and perhaps reluctantly, polar theoretical positions.'[41] In the later seventeenth century public debate about the political economy of taxation was more elaborate whereas constitutional discussion was in some ways less so. The *de facto* dependence on parliamentary taxation meant that discussion and parliamentary action centred on fears that parliament might grant away its independence by giving inappropriate forms of taxation.[42] In these discussions of taxation and its implications parliament seems to provide a microcosm of the broader arena of public debate (documents 5–9, 17, 23–4, 36–9).

Notes

1   A. D. T. Cromartie, 'The rule of law' in J. Morrill (ed.), *Revolution and restoration. England in the 1650s*, London, 1992, pp. 55–69; p. 55.

2   G. D. G. Hall, 'Impositions and the courts 1554–1606', *Law Quarterly Review*, LXIX, 1958, pp. 200–18.

3   P. Croft, 'Fresh light on Bate's case', *Historical Journal*, XXX, 1987, pp. 523–39.

4   *Ibid.*

5   J. P. Sommerville, *Politics and ideology in England 1603–1640*, Harlow, 1986, esp. pp. 145–63.

6   G. Burgess, *The politics of the ancient constitution. An introduction to English political thought, 1603–1642*, Basingstoke and London, 1992, p. 142.

7   E. N. Lindquist 'The king, the people and the House of Commons: the problem of early Jacobean purveyance', *Historical Journal*, XXXI, 1988, pp. 549–70. On purveyance see also P. Croft, 'Parliament, purveyance and the city of London 1589–1608', *Parliamentary History*, IV, 1985, pp. 9–34; and Lindquist, 'Supplement: the bills against purveyors', *ibid.*, pp. 35–43.

8   Burgess, *Politics of the ancient constitution*, p. 116.

9   Croft, 'Fresh light', pp. 538–9.

10   R. Cust, *The forced loan and English politics 1626–8*, Oxford, 1987, pp. 322–3.

11   *Ibid.*, p. 185.

12   J. A. Guy, 'The origins of the Petition of Right reconsidered', *Historical Journal*, XXV, 1982, pp. 289–312; p. 294.

13   Sommerville, *Politics and ideology*, p. 145.

14   W. J. Jones, *Politics and the bench. The judges and the origins of the English civil war*, London, 1971, pp. 74–5.

15   *Ibid.*, pp. 76–7.

16   C. Russell, *Parliaments and English politics 1621–1629*, Oxford, 1979, pp. 400–02.

17   For a summary of these legal hearings see Sharpe, *The personal rule of Charles I*, New Haven and London, 1992, pp. 719–30.

18   Jones, *Politics and the bench*, pp. 125, 202; W. Prest, 'Ship money and Mr Justice Hutton', *History Today*, XLI, 1991, pp. 42–7.

19   See the varying interpretations of K. Fincham, 'The judges decision on ship money in February 1637: the reaction of Kent', *Bulletin of the Institute of Historical Research*, LVII, 1984, pp. 230–7; B. Quintrell, *Charles I*

1625–1640, Harlow, 1993, pp. 64–5; Sharpe, *Personal rule*, pp. 719–21.

20 Quoted in Sharpe, *Personal rule*, p. 720.

21 C. Russell, 'The ship money judgements of Bramston and Davenport', *English Historical Review*, LXXVII, 1962, pp. 312–8.

22 Sharpe, *Personal rule*, p. 725.

23 *Ibid.*, p. 717.

24 *Ibid.*, p. 730.

25 S. R. Gardiner, *History of the commonwealth and protectorate, 1649–56*, 4 vols., London, 1903 edition, III, p. 300n.; I. Roots, 'Cromwell's ordinances: the early legislation of the protectorate', in G. E. Aylmer (ed.), *The interregnum. The quest for settlement, 1646–1660*, London, 1972, pp. 143–64; p. 160.

26 A. D. T. Cromartie, 'Sir Matthew Hale (1609–76)', Cambridge PhD thesis, 1991, p. 65. I was unable to consult the revised version of this thesis, published as *Sir Matthew Hale, 1609–1676. Law, religion and natural philosophy*, Cambridge, 1995, which appeared after this book had gone to press.

27 Quoted in Cromartie, 'Sir Matthew Hale', pp. 66–7.

28 *Ibid.*, p. 66.

29 Gardiner, *Commonwealth and protectorate*, pp. 301–2. For Wentworth see A. Hughes, *Politics, society and civil war in Warwickshire, 1620–1660*, Cambridge, 1987, *passim*.

30 R. Hutton, *The restoration. A political and religious history of England and Wales 1658–1667*, Oxford, 1985, p. 65. For problems of tax collection in this period see *ibid.*, 77, 78, 79. Public Record Office, E.134/15 Charles II/E.8, interrogatories for Robert Bocking and depositions. See also G. Davies, *The restoration of Charles II 1658–1660*, San Marino, 1955, pp. 150–1, 181.

31 Upon the proposal for raising the £1,800,000 by a land rate, in C. Robbins (ed.), *The diary of John Milward, Esq., 1666–8*, London, 1938, pp. 310–12.

32 M. J. Braddick, *Parliamentary taxation in seventeenth-century England. Local administration and response*, Royal Historical Society Studies in History, 70, Woodbridge, 1994, esp. pp. 197–9.

33 C. D. Chandaman, *The English public revenue 1660–1688*, Oxford, 1975, p. 40.

34 *Ibid.*, pp. 40, 44, 86–7, 49.

35 J. Brewer, *The sinews of power. War, money and the English state, 1688–1783*, London, 1989, p. 146.

36 *Ibid.*, 145–51.

37 *A treatise of taxes and contributions* (1662), reprinted in Charles Henry Hull (ed.), *The economic writings of Sir William Petty*, New Jersey, 1986 edition, pp. 53–4.

38 Above, p. 86. For resistance to assessment on oath see also W. Kennedy, *English taxation 1640–1799. An essay on policy and opinion*, London, 1913, p. 42.

39 Chandaman, *English public revenue*, p. 141.

40 Braddick, *Parliamentary taxation*, pp. 83, 105 and *passim*. For the importance of oaths more generally see C. Hill, *Society and puritanism in pre-revolutionary England*, London, 1969, chapter 11.

41 C. Holmes, 'Parliament, liberty, taxation, and property' in J. H. Hexter (ed.), *Parliament and liberty from the reign of Elizabeth to the English civil war*, Stanford, 1992, pp. 122–54; p. 122.

42 Compare, for example, the accounts of parliamentary debate in: Russell, *Parliaments and English politics*; Holmes, 'Parliament, liberty, taxation and property'; Chandaman, *English public revenue*; Brewer, *Sinews*; E. A. Reitan, 'From revenue to civil list, 1689–1702: The revolution settlement and the "Mixed and Balanced" constitution', *Historical Journal*, XIII, 1970, pp. 571–88; and E. A. Reitan, 'The civil list in eighteenth-century British politics: parliamentary supremacy versus the independence of the crown', *Historical Journal*, IX, 1996, pp. 318–37.

8

Tax collection and the taxpayer

When confronted by a tax demand the reluctant taxpayer had a number of options in seeking to limit or avoid payment. There is in this sense another level of politics to be considered, once a tax had been granted by parliament or levied by the king. Taxpayers might attempt to avoid the burden of taxation within the law or to evade the taxation illegally. They might obstruct collection in the law courts or by physical resistance. Such physical resistance might range from personal assault to riot. These distinctions are difficult to draw very clearly, but we might discern a sliding scale of seriousness. At least it seems fair to say that a tax easily evaded or avoided was unlikely to provoke a riot. The availability of these various strategies of non- or partial payment depended on the nature of the administration and also, as we will see, on the attitude of local courts. In this chapter we first examine local responses to taxation thematically, in the light of the administrative structure of each tax. Having done this we review the material in order to examine the effect of the attitude the magistracy on responses to taxation.

Tax evasion and tax avoidance

The line between tax avoidance and tax evasion is notoriously difficult to draw, because the seeking-out of legal loopholes through which to avoid taxation can lead the taxpayer into very murky areas. There is, though, a clear difference between, say, avoiding liability to the customs as a result of legal exemption, and organised smuggling. We will start this account with some examples of strategies for limiting payment that were clearly legal, that is, strategies of avoidance as distinct from evasion.

All quota taxes were subject to attempts at avoidance, in the sense that all were subject to attempts by taxpayers to shift the liability elsewhere. As the fifteenth and tenth neared the end of its life, it was granted more frequently. As the value of the subsidy declined the fifteenth and tenth seemed to be, by comparison, increasingly heavy. The inequities in the distribution were thus more galling, and legal challenges to the distribution of the burden are fairly frequent in exchequer records from 1590 onwards. These legal queries could be complex, because the means by which the fifteenth and tenth was rated could be very complicated. In Southwell, Nottinghamshire, a market town, the goods of visiting traders were liable if they were in Southwell on the day of the rating of the tax. In Binham, Norfolk, only copy-holders were liable. Other inhabitants could become liable, how-ever, because there was also a rate raised on cattle that were depastured on copyhold lands. But in order to be liable the cattle had to be kept there permanently ('levant and couchant'), not just for part of the day. The possibilities of avoiding this rate are obvi-ous. Some of these disputes were bewilderingly complex, but there were some characteristic sorts of disagreement. The exemp-tion of former monastic lands or of the lands of cathedral chapters were disputed in several parts of the country. Newly enclosed or drained lands might also escape the tax because they were not customarily taxed, and this, too, caused problems in a number of places. For example, there were substantial disputes in areas of Lincolnshire where there had been enclosure, and both Salisbury and Norwich saw protracted disputes over the liability of lay inhabitants of the cathedral closes.[1] There might be other ways of avoiding quota taxes, too: a Cambridge brewer worth £4,000 a year sought to avoid paying ship money by buying a place as a servant in the university. In this way he hoped to secure exemp-tion.[2]

These legal challenges, or attempts at legal avoidance, make clear how difficult it is to draw clear distinctions between strate-gies of non-payment. In some cases a local complaint about the distribution of the quota was well-known, and could not be agreed. In such circumstances the tax, enforced as it was by legal process, was collected anyway, to the chagrin of the party who felt the distribution unfair. This would lead to obstruction, physical assault or legal cases. Tax collectors faced with non-payment were usually empowered to distrain goods to the value of the tax due. Frequently, when trying to distrain, collectors were assaulted, or the distrained goods were seized back. Alternatively, tax collectors seeking to collect taxes or officers seeking to distrain goods were maliciously prosecuted for assault or trespass. In some cases this was tax resistance, but in many instances what lay behind the case was an attempt to avoid the tax, to shift the burden elsewhere (document 16). Sometimes, it seems, this was done by agreement, in order to secure a legal hearing. During the interregnum Robert Walker and John Philpotts were sued, having distrained goods in Herefordshire, for non-payment of the assessment. They petitioned the indemnity committee in London for protection against the suit but the committee refused to intervene. This was because the refusal had, apparently, been a way of precipitating a legal test of rival claims in a boundary dispute.[3] Evidence relating to resistance to distraint is, therefore, very difficult to interpret (document 15).

These forms of avoidance were, perhaps, the characteristic response of those seeking to limit their payment of inland taxation in this period. They could involve physical violence, and even riot as we will see. At root, however, they sought redress for a grievance through the law and so they were not a vehicle by which to question the legality of the tax as a whole, nor the legitimacy of the regime that raised them. Of course, avoidance might be motivated by such considerations, as was probably the case in Cony's tax refusal described in the previous chapter. On the whole, though, avoidance did not convey this threat.

Attempts at avoidance dogged all quota taxation. We can trace this in the response of the city of Chester to quota taxation from the ship money of the 1630s to the later seventeenth-century assessments. During the 1630s the city sought to bring a number of resources within the remit of the payments made by the city. Jurisdictional objections were also raised such as, for example, the claim to be exempt from the authority of the sheriff of the county. The city tried to include the ward of Gloverstone in the areas contributing towards its payments; to tax the profits of a customs farm in the city held by Sir Thomas Aston; and to tax the bishop, dean and chapter. In these instances tax avoidance may be a reasonable description, but it was not perhaps the main business. The sums at stake were insignificant by comparison with the total tax due so that 'these disputes could drag on indefinitely and the main business of the collection of ship money could proceed more or less unimpaired'.[4] The heart of the matter may have been local pride and local rivalries. Complaints about the quotas imposed continued in response to quota taxation during the 1640s and afterwards. Appeals were made for a reduction of the share of taxation borne by the city in the late 1640s and again in the mid-1660s (see pp. 113–14). During the latter dispute it was claimed that the quota imposed in the 1640s had been deliberately heavy in order to punish the city for loyalty to Charles I. The city, though, consistently sought to prove that it was over-rated, and adduced the pound rate paid in the city as evidence. However, it did not suggest the use of direct valuation in place of quotas. This may reflect again the deep-seated hostility to accurate direct valuation for national taxation. The city also continued to try to pass on the burden – seeking to tax the profits of the excise in the early 1650s – and sought remission following particular misfortunes such as visitations of the plague or the collapse of the spire of St Peter's.[5]

The sums at stake in these disputes were a small proportion of the total and did not threaten the overall success of the taxes. The disputes over ship money actually facilitated collection as parties to the dispute vied to appear assiduous in the collection of other portions.[6] This may also be true of the dispute in the 1660s, in the course of which both sides lobbied a number of institutions of national government seeking help. They sought, for example, protection against the exchequer from the treasury, and from the king, parliament and privy council against both. Successful lobbying required the parties to appear willing to pay taxes. The city was certainly embarrassed when the exciseman complained to the privy council of mistreatment by the magistracy, at a very sensitive point in the in the development of the dispute.[7]

Any form of taxation that offers legal exemptions is, inevitably, open to avoidance. This is the intention of the exemptions after all. The hearth tax and the window taxes were also fruitful sources of attempts at avoidance for this reason. The records of the tax provide one of the fullest forms of population listing for

late seventeenth century England and have been much used by
economic and social historians. There is a temptation, given the
fullness of the listing, to assume that those listed as exempt were
the poorest local inhabitants, but in fact the categories of exemp-
tion were more complex. There were four kinds of exemption:
those exempt from paying poor rates; those in houses worth less
than 20s per annum; hearths that were industrial; and houses
with only one chimney. These categories overlapped, and certainly did not correspond straightforwardly to a measure of
poverty. There were genuine legal queries as a result. For example, Smith's forges and baker's ovens were not mentioned in the
statute but were claimed by many to fall into the category of
industrial hearths. This avoidance, though, shaded into evasion.
Local officeholders were widely believed to have been over-
indulgent in their interpretation of these exemptions, and this
was blamed for the disappointing yield of the tax under the
administration of the sheriffs (see above pp. 102–3). Under other
forms of administration, however, there was friction between the
interest of collectors or farmers and those local officeholders
inclined to generous interpretation of exemptions. There were
also, particularly in the early years of the tax, more obvious evasions. For example, chimneys were bricked up on the assumption
that the first valuation would stand for some time. In Southwark,
tenants-at-will (people on very insecure leases requiring little
notice to quit on either side) were said to have moved, giving a
day's notice, in order to be away when the tax was being
assessed.[8]

The window tax statutes and orders in treasury grew more and
more complex in order to clarify legal liability. Originally the tax
had been the responsibility of the land tax commissioners, but
suspicions that they were partial or complicit in evasion led to the
appointment of surveyors. These officials checked the commissioner's assessments and represented the national government
interest in appeals and restricted evasions. Some of the attempts
at avoidance were sophisticated, however, as the legislation of
1747 shows. This stipulated that no window that had been
blocked up could be unblocked without informing the surveyor
and that windows lighting more than one room were to be
charged per room, for example. There was sustained friction
between commissioners, seeking to avoid strict interpretations of

the legislation, and the surveyors (documents 31–2). The trend of the legislation was towards increasing the pay and importance of the surveyors and to bypass the commissioners. A measure of the discretion being exercised is that in Cumberland the tax was raised by a customary rate called the purvey – essentially it had been transformed into a land tax.[9]

The customs were prey to avoidance to some extent, but here avoidance began to shade into the evasion for which they are more commonly known. Cargoes were landed without registering them, quantities of goods were concealed and officials were bribed to under-record the quantity or quality of particular cargoes. All these strategies were beyond the law but there were other means by which to restrict liability that lay in a greyer area. For example, certain ports claimed freedom from particular duties in the late sixteenth century.[10] Goods carried on board ships for the victualling of the crew were exempt and sustained attempts were made to secure exemption from excise for beer carried on fishermen's boats. There were also allowances for spoiled goods. Finally, duty paid on import could be reclaimed if the goods were re-exported (these payments were known as 'drawbacks'). All these exemptions could be explored and extensions sought, in order to limit liability legally. In the case of allowances and drawbacks this could shade into evasion if officials were bribed or threatened into extending these allowances beyond the law. Thus, the line between avoidance and evasion in the case of the customs was very hard to draw. Concern about this clearly drove the evolution of the administration, however. The initial division of labour between customer and controller, the introduction of the office of surveyor, the elaboration of checks in the later seventeenth century, and the increase in salary levels, were all attempts to reduce the grey area as well as to combat more obvious frauds.

A document among Burghley's papers illustrates how easily the customs were evaded in late sixteenth-century London. The custom house was not well-enough appointed to insist that merchants should land their goods there. As a result, they had considerable room for deceit. For example, two chests could be tied together under one canvas which was observed by the officer and allowed to be taken ashore to the merchant's house. When the officers arrived to check the contents one of the chests would have been removed. Alternatively, an identical chest containing less valuable goods could be substituted or high value goods concealed in chests of coarser goods. Small packets could be smuggled ashore in the clothes of shippers. Exporters could make up two identical chests, securing papers to export one. They loaded the chest on which custom had not been paid and later claimed to the customers that they had not been able to fit the chest on the ship. They were thus able to put it on their next load. Other evasions were more straightforward – lying about the quality of goods, shipping the goods of foreign merchants as if they were English, securing false cockets and so forth. An accompanying paper makes a number of suggestions to prevent these frauds. Principally this involved forcing merchants to land their goods at the customs house and increasing the powers of the customs men to demand true accounts of what the cargoes contained, which could be tested by searching the cargoes.[11] Fairly simple reforms could make it more difficult to evade the duties, particularly if those responsible for the administration had a personal financial stake in making the collection more rigorous.

Methods of limiting tax liability were not mutually exclusive. In 1594 the customs officers in Ipswich complained to Lord Burghley about the activities of local woodmongers. The woodmongers, it was said, had used a variety of means, from concealment, to lying about the destination or ownership of the goods, to physical intimidation. They bought up 'most part of the wood and charcoals in our counties of Suffolk and Essex, and under colour of loading it for London and elsewhere, convey it by themselves and Flemish hoys into Flanders and Zealand'. More than this 'in their loading [they] do cunningly lay under their lighters of wood sometimes corn, butter and tallow' in order to conceal it. The searcher had found this, but the woodmongers, when challenged by the officers, claimed that the wood was the Queen's and therefore exempt. This was, the officers claimed, untrue. Worse, 'Our Searchers' deputy at Harwich hath of late been cast overboard in performance of his duty. We therefore humbly crave your Honour's letters, authorising us to call those woodmongers into the customhouse and there charge them, upon forfeiture of the wood carried out of port' to submit to the procedures of the customs officers.[12]

Smuggling in the eighteenth century was clearly very big

business. Organised groups with specially constructed boats, armed and with elaborate systems of local support, brought in large amounts of high value commodities on which large amounts of duty were leviable. The rewards obviously outweighed the risks and the risks were reduced in any case by the strength and organisation of the gangs. By contrast, we know very little about evasions and smuggling before the eighteenth century. Any account is no more than plausible, then, and this is clearly a subject on which we need more research.

Two assumptions currently mould our views of evasions of the customs duties. One is that underpaid customs officials in outports with little regular contact with London were unlikely to be vigorous in their activities, and were likely to be complicit in evasions of various kinds. Secondly, higher duties offer a greater incentive to evasion. The general view then, is that evasions were practised throughout the history of the customs and persistent attempts to check on the conduct of officials in the ports reflect that. In the later sixteenth and through the seventeenth centuries some progress was made in this area. This encouraged evasions that did not rely on the collusion of local officers, that is, smuggling. At the same time, high duties on some very lucrative trades (tobacco and liquors in particular) made the competitive advantage of the successful smuggler very considerable. Thus, in the later sixteenth century smuggling grew increasingly attractive and was perhaps less likely to enjoy the cooperation of the customs officials. The economic advantages of smuggling became particularly obvious in the later seventeenth century when more and more duties were added. It has even been suggested that, with tariff policy becoming more sophisticated, some evasions had a political tone. In the 1690s Jacobites disaffected with the Orange regime were involved in breaking prohibitions on trade with France. From the 1690s onwards, it has been argued, illicit trade in tobacco and tea was such big business that it seriously affects the reliability of official trade statistics. For example, in some years Scotland, not noted for its tobacco cultivation, apparently re-exported 1.5 million lb of tobacco more than it had imported.[13]

The excises on inland goods were also evaded, sometimes it seems, with the active collusion of the officers. The desire to restrict this helped, as it did with the customs, to drive the development of the administration. For example, early ordinances made provisions that goods should not be purchased unless proof of payment of the excise was available and goods were to be landed only in the presence of an excise officer. At the level of the national administration, layers of superior officers were added to oversee the assessment and collection. The remarkable process of professionalisation in the excise in the later seventeenth and eighteenth centuries was clearly driven by a desire to police these things. As with the customs, there was a grey area: allowances were made for leakage and spillage of beer and ale, and different rates were applied to different qualities of various commodities. Thus, tasters tested the quality of tobacco, gaugers that of beer. Just as merchants liable to *ad valorem* customs duties could lie about the value of their wares, and bribe officials to accept the under-valuation, so too could merchants of excisable goods. Farming was one way to combat this, improved conditions of service and powers of closer audit another. As the excise developed in the 1650s and 1660s this grey area became institutionalised in the beer excises. Brewers struck deals with gaugers (known as 'compounding for payment') in order to avoid 'going on the gauge'. In other words, they offered to pay a certain amount, less than their legal liability but sufficient to satisfy the excisemen. This was enabled by the adoption of farming, which allowed the farmer to negotiate compositions that would allow a profit to both parties. Some attempts at avoidance were very creative indeed, such as that of Michael Heathcot, an innkeeper of Hathersage, Derbyshire. He claimed that his guests paid for their food, fodder for the horses and lodging and that the beer was served to them free. On these grounds he refused to pay excise on the beer. In Monmouthshire those liable to the tax shut their doors on excisemen, in the knowledge that the officers did not have the legal power to break doors open.[14] Elsewhere magistrates and minor officials looked generously on laws which protected the subject from the attentions of the exciseman.

Quotas for direct taxation were a response to the severe problems of evasion that resulted from attempts to assess personal wealth directly. The most obvious example of such evasion is in the case of the subsidy. The underassessment of wealth in the subsidy rolls is notorious and hardly needs stating here (document 12). It was achieved by vastly under-estimating the wealth of individuals, but also by removing some people from the books altogether. In some places rotas for payment seem to have operated. Elsewhere a practice known as the use of bearers was used, whereby one individual was named in the assessment but the money was paid by him and 'bearers' – people not named in the roll but contributing nonetheless. Evasion reduced the subsidy assessments to the point that not even the greatly increased frequency with which they were granted could secure significant overall increases in yield. This is the only systematic evidence of under-assessment – the fall in the total yield while the wealth of the nation was almost certainly increasing. But there are numerous pieces of anecdotal evidence of radical under-valuation (documents 11–12). This process did not favour everyone equally, however. Magistrates frequently paid relatively high rates. At the same time, assessments were generally settling towards the bottom of the roll. This seems to have favoured the relatively wealthy. This was because, eventually, many people reached a point below which they could not go without disappearing from the roll altogether. However, they may have been unwilling to do this because some statues attached to the ascription 'subsidy-man'. Thus, with the possible exception of the magistracy, the gap between the highest and lowest valuations closed, and this probably made the subsidy more regressive among those who did pay the tax. Of course, many people did not pay the tax at all.[15]

The crucial flaw, then, in the administration of the subsidy was the scope it left for evasion through the concealment of wealth. This evasion was evidently achieved with the active connivance of local officeholders (document 11). In a sense the quota taxes, in restricting the room for evasion, left taxpayers seeking to avoid the tax instead. Characteristically they did this by proving the liability to be that of another person. On the other hand, direct taxation which did not rely on quotas invited evasion rather than avoidance – to test legal liability would invite a test of the accuracy of valuation (document 12). This, in fact, was acknowledged by government and used as a threat by the privy council to persuade commissioners to enforce more accurate valuations (document 10).

Poll taxes were also evaded. Sometimes, it seems, this was done with the cooperation of the magistracy, as, for example, in allowing under-assessment, over-generous interpretation of exemptions or simply under-recording the population. The ever-quotable Samuel Pepys noted that he had expected to pay £10 for the 1660 poll tax but was only rated as 12*s*. His diary records 'I think I am not bound to discover myself.'[16] However, the yield of the taxes was consistent, but also consistently disappointing. One reason for this was that contemporaries were wildly over-optimistic, another that they were ignorant of the total size of the population.[17] This should caution us against an uncritical acceptance of contemporary comment to the effect that these taxes were widely evaded, but local studies suggest that it was not uncommon.[18] Both the poll tax and the marriage duty act could be avoided by a mobile population, and the latter by concealing vital events from assessment. Most notably, clandestine marriage was a temptation, as the legislation recognised.[19] A recent study of London suggests that under-registration, for legitimate as much as illegitimate reasons, of births might have been as much as 17.5 per cent. Magistrates may well have been complicit in evasions of the tax, on occasion (document 33). On the other hand, the acts seem to have had a significant impact in improving the accuracy of the recording of marriages and deaths were also well-recorded.[20]

These assessed taxes were not just prey to evasion in the form of under-reporting. They usually offered provision for those liable under more than one heading to pay only once. Generally, this was to be under the more onerous heading which would allow for legal avoidance of a burden. In practice it is not always clear that this was the case. An important feature of the decline of the yield of an individual subsidy in London during the reign of Elizabeth was a change in the law regarding liability. Taxpayers liable in more than one place were required to pay only once, securing a certificate which would exempt them from payment elsewhere. Initially, liability was for the greater sum, but this was changed in 1559 so that they paid where 'he then shall be most conversant abiding or resident or shall have his most resort or shall be best known at the time'. In 1559 the yield lost in London as a result of these exemptions was 6.5 per cent, by 1596 it was 18.8 per cent.[21] The impact of this was probably most marked in the cities. The residence qualification clearly affected payments towards the marriage duty act, too,[22] and there were complications arising from the fact that, for example, individuals were not always buried in the parish in which they had normally lived.[23]

Poll taxes which taxed status, a difficult thing to specify with precision, were also prey to avoidance. The 1660 act contained a 'deeming' clause, specifying the circumstances under which an individual could be assumed to enjoy a particular status. The logic of this is made clear by Thomas Werden's remark in 1641 that 'it were worth any wise man's laughter to see how these apple esquires that glorified in the title do now assume humility and a lower style'. There were also certificates of residence and other legal difficulties. One example can demonstrate the technicalities involved. A man and his wife paid at least 6d each. Some contemporaries were not sure (or said that they were not) whether this was a joint charge of one shilling or two separate charges. This became relevant if the husband was liable to a higher charge because of his rank. Those who thought that there was a joint charge on husband and wife argued that it was superseded by the higher charge on rank. The less generous view was that there were two charges, the higher one on the husband and the usual 6d on his wife. In Northwich hundred, Cheshire, the former policy was adopted, affording the possibility of avoidance to a number of taxpayers. The point was defensible, apparently, although we might have our suspicions about the motivation behind this particular interpretation.[24]

Later forms of direct taxation which did not have the discipline of a quota were also prey to evasion, as were the poll taxes. In this, local officials were crucial. With no target yield in sight for which collectors were personally bound, there was no restriction, beyond conscience, on the degree to which officeholders could help their neighbours to evade taxation through concealing their wealth.

All taxes are, to some extent, avoided and evaded, but particular forms of taxation are prey to these things in characteristic ways. One of the pressures on the development of the tax system in this period was to find forms of wealth that were difficult to conceal and a form of administration that assured this. The bureaucratic weakness of the seventeenth century state led to a dependence on local officeholders and collusion in evasion was an obvious danger. In the case of direct taxation the preferred solution was not professionalisation but the application of quotas. This left the distribution of the burden in local hands and therefore allowed a degree of flexibility in locating and assessing forms of wealth. This was impossible without local cooperation, given the existing administrative capacity of the national government. In the case of indirect taxes, and household taxes, the problem was tackled by fixing a range of commodities or easily visible indicators of wealth on which assessment would be straightforward. Those framing legislation for the indirect and household taxes, or drawing up the books of rates, had to be aware of the political limits on governmental action outlined in the previous chapter. There were certain commodities that could not be taxed without considerable resentment, for example. Evasions were also tackled by employing farmers, thus harnessing private interest to improve the revenue. After the abandonment of farming in 1671 other administrative checks were applied, and direct collection became a great success by professionalising collection. The relationship between this new bureaucracy and established elites, however, had to be carefully negotiated, as we will see.

Legal obstruction

Evasion and avoidance, then, were characteristic strategies of those seeking to limit their tax liability. They did not, in themselves, raise questions about the legality of a particular exaction or the legitimacy of the regime that demanded it. Nonetheless, they could be preliminaries to legal action and behind them might lie a sense that a particular tax was illegitimate. The best example of this, perhaps, would be the extent to which eighteenth century smuggling was viewed favourably by local communities.[25] As we saw in chapter 7, some of the legal cases which appeared to challenge the right of the government to sources of revenue started with tax refusal and distraint – the cases brought by Bate, Hampden and Cony, for example. Indeed, there were many such cases relating to ship money (document 15). The government seems to have ducked one such challenge posed by the refusal to pay by Lord Saye and Sele, and his subsequent prosecution of a constable who had taken distraint. In June 1636 Richard Chambers, a merchant, brought a case against the mayor of London, who had jailed him for ship money default. This apparently routine chain of events elicited from Justice Berkeley, one of the judges of King's Bench who refused to hear the case, the comment 'that there was a rule of law and a rule of government, and many things which might not be done by the rule of law might be done by the rule of government'.[26] This sort of talk can make people nervous and it is significant that it was prompted by apparently fairly innocuous forms of resistance. The political debates outlined in chapter 7 are not to be regarded as separate from the strategies of individual taxpayers discussed here.

The legality of purveyance was not really questionable, nor was the legality of composition agreements, since they had been freely entered into by the county magistracy. The system of composition did not end the problems associated with it, however (documents 2–3, 5–6). Local people remained suspicious of the activities of its agents, the operation of purveyors raising goods not compounded for produced complaints. Many county benches also appear to have become unhappy with the terms on which they had compounded. In these complaints we can perceive a suspicion of outside interests raising money in the localities, and a struggle between these agents and the magistracy. A similar tension found expression in parliament, too. In a sense, what was at stake was an unwillingness to see property handled by officials outside the magistracy whose only function was to raise purveyance. Obviously such people were ripe for suspicions of corruption.[27]

Excisemen were similarly regarded, and again depended on the goodwill of constables. They were very vulnerable to the authority of magistrates, who could use legal powers to regulate aspects of excise collection. There are numerous examples of what are pretty clearly malicious prosecutions of excise officers from the early years of the tax. On occasions this was quite sophisticated. In September 1668, for example, the privy council was informed that the constable of Ripon, Yorkshire, had not only refused to execute a writ for non-payment of the excise, but had openly discouraged local people from paying. He also publicly refused to help the excisemen, saying that he would spend £100 at law before cooperating. Other local people apparently offered to bear the cost of any legal charges with him.[28] It was not just outsiders who were subject to these indignities, however: much of the evidence that survives regarding local attitudes to taxation in the seventeenth centuries is in the form of legal cases arising from distraint, or prosecutions of tax collectors for assault or trespass.

Such cases were more likely to proceed if there was division of responsibility between the magistracy and revenue officers, but it might also reveal divisions within local society. Evidence arising from this legal obstruction, throughout the seventeenth century, is very difficult to interpret, however.

Physical obstruction

Some of the responses of taxpayers clearly reflect a sense of the illegitimacy of a form of taxation or of its administration. This could result in a conflict between agents of a regime and the localities. Legal challenge, physical assault and riot are all potentially glossed as examples of local resistance to central authority in a way that evasion and avoidance are not. In fact, strategies of avoidance more frequently led to clashes *within* the localities, as we have seen in the case of Chester, for example (above, pp. 113–14). Similarly, evasion (if not open equally to all) could also cause division locally rather than between centre and locality. For example, complaints about partiality in the assessment of the subsidy were reasonably common (document 11). In a sense, taxpayers who suggested this were claiming that their under-assessment was not as generous as that of their more favoured neighbours. In general, the taxes which caused obstruction and violence were those that were perceived unfairly to burden the poor and whose administration was in the hands of professional tax collectors remote from local interests and unamenable to mediation. Quota taxes did not raise these issues, and the customs administration was usually well-connected with the trading community (documents 18–20), to some extent too closely.

Contemporaries sometimes referred to violent words when describing resistance by taxpayers. This abusive language seems to have been modulated according to the relationship of the tax collector to the taxpayer. For example, constables were often referred to as being 'too busy', an accusation that amounted to saying that they were being so good at their job as to be interfering in the business of their neighbours. This kind of sleight must have been a very effective restraint on officeholders in small-scale communities that placed a high premium on honour and status. For taxes collected by these people, cases of physical assault seem to have been comparatively rare, although they were sometimes assaulted when distraining goods or assisting in the distraint of goods. Professional tax collectors, notably of the excise, were the targets of more violent language: they were more likely to be referred to as rogues or knaves than castigated for being too busy, and were sometimes called caterpillars (that is, that they devoured local crops like a biblical plague). Such language was frequently used to describe monopolists, too, (see documents 7–8, 23, 25). Like constables they were sometimes assaulted while taking distraints, but they were also assaulted in the course of their more ordinary business of valuation and collection. This reflects, perhaps, the fact that they were less easily restrained by local disapproval of their actions, because their livelihood depended on the enforcement of excises or monopolies. In general historians have been slow to place tax collection in this social context, but clearly there are points of contact here with a broader history of protest and disorder (see frontispiece).

Two taxes and two periods are particularly noted for these hostile responses, and these examples illustrate the general observations: the excises in the 1640s and the hearth tax in the mid-1660s. The excise was, notoriously, liable to large-scale riotous resistance, but there are a number of qualifications we should add to this. Firstly, other responses (avoidance, evasion, obstruction, abuse or assault) were more usual, and the typical response was to pay up. Secondly, the riots that did occur were restricted to particular times and places and often to particular kinds of excise duty. Many of the riots of which we have records were aimed against the meat or salt duties (Derby, Smithfield, Droitwich, Cheshire, Norfolk) and took place in areas where meat and salt production were of particular importance to the local economy. The abolition of the duty on meat thus removed a substantial source of unrest, as did the temporary abandonment of that on salt. This helps to explain the survival of the excise – these disorders were a product of particular excises, not the excise as a whole. It also explains a lot about the distribution of riots, as we have seen. It does not explain why there were riots rather than other forms of resistance to these duties, however, and for this we must turn to the nature of the administration of the excise.

Excise collectors were not, generally, drawn from the ranks of county and borough officials and they lacked the status of their colleagues responsible for the collection of direct taxes. Some of them were outsiders in the geographical sense too – foreign to the area in which they were working. In this sense they were less amenable to the pressure of local expectation which could limit the actions of other tax collectors. Mediation, then, was more difficult. This made it more likely that discontent could escalate to the point of physical confrontation. Finally, the excise was often collected in market places where large groups of people were gathered, many of whom might share resentment of the excise collector. In other instances, excise collectors visited, set up a temporary centre and were present only to collect the excise (document 26). These circumstances are obviously much more likely to generate riot than, for example, door-to-door calls by a constable collecting assessment money whose burden had been apportioned with reference to a local commission or rating scheme. Similarly, when the excise fell only on beer and was collected directly from brewers, as it was during the 1660s, the likelihood of riot was considerably reduced.

Excise rioting was not, then, simply a response to the total burden of the tax or of its social profile, but was partly a product of the shape of the administration and was targeted on particular duties. The actions of rioters, where they are described, betray a similar sense that they were 'political', a response to the particularities of the tax or the legitimacy of the authority of its agents. For example, at Smithfield in 1647, rioters burned down the excise office, destroyed its papers and spoiled or burned £80–£100. The targets of the violence were quite specific and it is interesting that the rioters were reported as having spoiled, not stolen, money. At Droitwich the salt workers who eventually attacked the excise collector and his men had made prior attempts to negotiate, and their actions were affected by their working hours.[29] A final, intriguing account of riot is that against excise collectors in Derbyshire, which reveals a ritual shaming of an excise collector who was fastened to the bull ring. He was, presumably, collecting the excise on meat (document 26). This may be a very faint echo of the ritualised violence with which some tax collectors were attacked in France in the 1630s.[30]

There is, then, a kind of ritual, political or demonstrative element to these disturbances, as there was to tax disorders elsewhere in Europe. This political aspect of riot explains the sensitivity of governments to disorder, but there were other factors helping to magnify the significance of riots in England in the 1640s. This has perhaps led to an exaggeration of the prevalence and seriousness of excise disorders in this decade. Notably, in the summer of 1647, the embattled presbyterian interest in the city of London and then dominating the Houses of Parliament, responded very belatedly to the riot against the meat excise at Smithfield four months earlier. In this parliament was responding as much to national political circumstance – threatened as it was by the march of the army towards London – as to the 'objective' threat of excise disorder. Similarly, in the last days of the Rump, certain newssheets gave some emphasis to excise resistance which, when analysed more coolly, appears altogether less threatening. Significantly, the response of the government was not only to allow counties to farm their own excise duties, but also to suppress some hostile newssheets.[31] More generally, the potential complicity of influential local people or officeholders made governments more sensitive to these disorders, but this sensitivity should not lead us to exaggerate their frequency or seriousness (document 28).

Another period when taxation seemed to pose a generalised threat to order was the mid-1660s, when a series of hearth tax disturbances worried the farmers of the tax and absorbed the attention of the privy council. Here, again, similar points emerge. As in the 1640s conditions were hard: in the earlier period harvest failure and economic dislocation arising from the civil war, in the later period the disruption of trade by war and plague. These conditions and the regressive nature of the tax help to explain hostility to the tax, but once more it is the nature of the administration that explains why this hostility was expressed in riot. It may also help to explain the geographical distribution of the riots. The disorders occurred during the period of the first farm of the hearth tax, and in this period farmers frequently complained about the obstructiveness or hostility of local officeholders. Virtually all the disturbances recorded in the privy council registers note the active hostility or lack of support forthcoming from local officeholders (document 29). This may be because these were the sorts of disorder in which the privy council was most likely to be interested. Nonetheless, it was the case that this rivalry and friction was a product specifically of farming: when collection was in the hands of constables they (obviously) did not lead resistance, but it also appears that resistance was less marked. The suspicion that constables had connived at evasion had led to the resort to farming in the first place and, if true, would explain the relative lack of violence and resistance that they had experienced.[32] The same point can be made in relation to excise disorders reported to the privy council in the 1660s, which are clustered in places where excise farms had recently passed out of local hands: in Yorkshire and London in 1662 and 1665 and in Bristol, Monmouthshire, North Wales, Somerset and Salisbury in the latter year. The seriousness of these incidents involving both the excise and the hearth tax may be exaggerated by their blanket designation as 'riots', but the complicity of local officeholders makes them worthy of note. This complicity clearly interested the privy council. These disturbances were, however, of their very nature, confined to periods when there was a division of responsibility between local officeholders and tax collectors.

One other feature of the hearth tax disturbances is worthy of note, and that is that they coincided with attempts in parliament to regulate the tax by increasing the supervisory role of local officeholders. This certainly did not help the farmers, who petitioned the king hoping that he could secure a declaration in parliament confirming the grant of the tax. The dual pressures of popular resistance and parliamentary hostility might have been connected in two further ways. Firstly, the farmers succeeded persuading the privy council to make representations to the committee of the House considering the regulatory bill. They may have been exploiting reports of disorder for this purpose. Secondly, officeholders may have been reluctant to act quickly to suppress disorder because it was known that parliamentary commitment was limited. For example, Mr Pinson 'advised' local people against paying the tax in Weymouth, Dorset, and thereby exacerbated the problems faced by the collectors there. He may have offered this advice in the knowledge that reform was being considered. Alternatively, parliament may have been considering closer scrutiny in response to reports of local resistance to the farmers in which local officeholders appeared to sympathise with the protesters. In any case, it is a reminder of the artificiality of dividing the 'response of taxpayers' from a discussion of 'public opinion'.[33]

The more usual explanation for tax riots holds in both cases:

that heavy, regressive and new taxes were being raised in periods of economic hardship. However, this explanation, in the context of an examination of the full range of responses to taxation, is inadequate. There are other periods in which we might have expected disorder if this was all there was to it, for example the 1690s. Similarly, the fifteenth and tenth was undoubtedly regressive, unprecedentedly heavy and falling on an ailing economy in the 1620s, but hostility was not expressed in riot. Ship money levies in the 1630s were innovative and very heavy burdens by comparison with anything that had come before, but here hostility was expressed most notably not through violent words or physical attacks, but through the law. As a final observation on tax rioting, then, we might note that it was not necessarily more damaging to the long-term prospects of a particular levy than legal challenge.

The role of the magistracy

Throughout this chapter we have noted the importance of the attitudes of the local magistracy. The way in which collection could be hampered by reluctant magistrates is clear from the experience of the window tax. In March 1698 the treasury lords wrote to the justices for Herefordshire complaining 'that the books of assessments upon houses and upon marriages &c. are not yet signed and settled by you according to the Act for the same, whereby the collection of those Duties is altogether omitted in your county'.[34] In May they wrote to the justices for Pembroke complaining of more active obstruction. The justices, it was claimed had paid no regard to a survey of houses and ignored 'the opinion of the King's learned Counsel ... on points that may seem doubtful to you in relation to the said assessments though the same has been useful to and observed by the Commissioners acting in the several counties of England'. They were required to 'give all assistance to the officer for the just improvement of that Duty and not give opinions prejudicial to his Majesty's service and directly repugnant to the intention of the Act and to the practices of all other Commissioners thereof'. On the same day the justices in Cumberland were rebuked for delaying the settling of the assessment.[35] Justices might also use their position to pursue personal interests. Subsidy commissioners were frequently accused of penalising enemies or rewarding friends through their control of tax assessments (see document 11).[36] A similar accusation arose in rating disputes over the quota taxes, as we have seen. The financial benefit might be more direct, too. In May 1698 William Middleton complained 'that having paid the Capitation Tax in London and Chelsea besides the tax upon Marriages and Births he is of opinion that the King is cheated of the money paid at Chelsea'. He urged that 'Justice Alstow of Chelsea may be directed to search the collector's books to see if Middleton's name is entered and the money duly answered to the king.'[37] This may, of course, have been a malicious accusation. The financial benefit of commissioners did not derive only from straightforward corruption. The use of tax money between its collection and payment into the exchequer seems to have been one of the attractions of acting in the administration (see below, p. 198).

It was not only in these obvious ways that the fate of tax collection lay in the hands of magistrates. To an extent it was the involvement of local officeholders that determined the extent of the availability of avoidance and evasion. Local courts could also offer a sympathetic hearing to aggrieved taxpayers against specialised agents of revenue collection. The legitimacy conferred on collection and assessment by the involvement of men of social standing, who were not acting so obviously for personal financial gain, was important in making the direct taxes of this period acceptable. Additionally, these taxes were frequently assessed with reference to rating schemes developed locally for such purposes as provision for the poor, the militia or the maintenance of the highways. This sense of legitimacy was also associated with parliamentary sanction. Parliamentary reservations about the hearth tax seem to have acted, in some sense at least, to encourage the disorders in the mid-1660s. To reiterate the point made above, in the 1690s the principal direct taxes enjoyed clear parliamentary sanction and were collected by local officeholders. Even if this did not always lend them positive legitimacy it made the prospects of successful resistance seem remote.

The opposite is clearly true: that collection and assessment by those from outside the ranks of local officeholders was resented. In general the window tax was marked by the kinds of response that we associate with magisterial taxation. The treasury consistently suspected that a fairly easy regime of assessment was being run in many localities. Given the opportunities to mediate the tax by allowing avoidance and evasion, assault and violence were obviously less frequent. Moreover, the men assessing and collecting the money were local officeholders who were more easily restrained or pressured by local censure. The standard account of the administration of the window taxes mentions only one riot.[38] Here, again, the detail is significant (document 32). The man attacked was a surveyor, an outside official employed to check on the accuracy of valuations made by local officeholders. Not all outsiders were attacked, of course, but most of those attacked were outsiders. In Norfolk during the 1660s the only tax collector from outside the ranks of the county magistracy was the hearth tax collector, Christopher Lloyd. He is also the only one of the tax collectors for whom evidence of assault survives. A search of national archives for evidence of tax resistance between 1590 and 1670 revealed two fatalities, that of a soldier arriving in Coventry to assist with the collection of the excise in 1649 and that of Mr Knight, a hearth tax collector, who died from wounds he received having been stoned by a crowd at Bridport in 1668. Knight, a sub-collector to the farmers in Dorset, was not, apparently, a local man.[39] All this might suggest, then, not only that local men were amenable to less drastic forms of pressure than these 'outsiders', but also that their activities enjoyed a greater sense of legitimacy, something reflected in the terms of abuse used of them when they did offend local feeling (documents 2, 23, 25, 27–9, 32).

There were a number of possibilities for reducing tax liability facing the reluctant taxpayer. Avoidance, evasion and legal obstruction were common to all taxes, and there were ways of applying more direct pressure to assessors and collectors, through violent words or physical assault. Riots were unusual, and even for those taxes which provoked riot these other forms of response were more common. The availability to taxpayers of these counter-strategies was determined partly by the personnel of the tax administration. Local officeholders were more amenable to pressure. This reduced the likelihood of disorder and considerably increased the prospect of securing tax revenues by means that were regarded as fair and legitimate in the locality. On the other hand, this kind of mediation might have had revenue consequences, as potential forms of taxable wealth were effectively concealed. In the case of direct taxes the answer was the quota, but for indirect taxes the national government persisted, ultimately successfully, in seeking to bypass local elites with specialised revenue agents. The relationship between these men and local officeholders was fraught, however, and the formal division of responsibility occasionally damaging. The contrast in perception between the two forms of administration is aptly summarised by Brewer, who argues that in the 1690s the excise was perceived as a considerable threat by those suspicious of executive power.

> The land tax, on the other hand, offered no such threat. Voted annually, the tax of a fixed term and, by the end of the Nine Years War, had a fixed yield of *c*. £500,000 for every shilling in the pound levied by the lower house. Controlled in the metropolis not by the crown but by the commons, the tax's administration in the field was in the hands of local dignitaries and not in the power of the royal bureaucracy. Land tax assessors, collectors and receivers were all private citizens rather than state employees. They were appointed by local commissioners and were not answerable to a central board or office in London.[40]

Given the arguments in favour of excises, that they were responsive to consumption not wealth, it was not open to governments to collect them by quotas through the magistracy. Professionalisation was one way of reassuring the treasury that the scope for evasion was being actively restricted. There was, however, a political cost associated with this strategy.

Notes

1 M. J. Braddick, *Parliamentary taxation in seventeenth-century England. Local administration and response*, Royal Historical Society Studies in History, 70, Woodbridge, 1994, pp. 39–54.

2 K. Sharpe, *The personal rule of Charles I*, New Haven and London, 1992, p. 718.

3 Braddick, *Parliamentary taxation*, p. 156.

4 P. Lake, 'The collection of ship money in Cheshire during the sixteen-thirties: a case study of relations between central and local government', *Northern History*, XVII, 1981, pp. 44–71, p. 50.

5 See M. J. Braddick, 'The centre and localities in seventeenth-cen-

tury England: resistance to the royal aid and further supply in Chester, 1664–1672', unpublished paper; *Parliamentary taxation*, p. 144.

6   Lake, 'Collection of ship money'.

7   Braddick, 'Centre and localities'.

8   Braddick, *Parliamentary taxation*, pp. 243–52.

9   W. R. Ward, 'The administration of the window and assessed taxes, 1696–1798', *English Historical Review*, LXVII, pp. 522–42; p. 526. The purvey was also used for the poll tax!

10   These liberties presumably disappeared once all duties were raised under a single authority.

11   British Library, Lansdowne Ms 41/18, 41/19.

12   Officers of the port of Ipswich to Lord Burghley, July 27 1594, *Historical Manuscripts Commission, Calendar of the manuscripts of the … Marquis of Salisbury*, IV, London, 1892, p. 570.

13   N. Williams, *Contraband cargoes. Seven centuries of smuggling*, London, 1959, chapters 1–3. For Scottish tobacco smuggling, *ibid.*, p. 92. See also T. S. Willan (ed.), *A Tudor book of rates*, Manchester, 1962.

14   Braddick, *Parliamentary taxation*, pp. 221–2.

15   *Ibid.*, pp. 72–8.

16   *Ibid.*, p. 236.

17   Arkell, 'An examination of the poll taxes of the later seventeenth century, the marriage duty act and Gregory King' in K. Schurer and T. Arkell (eds.), *Surveying the people. The interpretation and use of document sources for the study of population in the later seventeenth century*, Local Population Studies supplement, Oxford, 1992, pp. 162–3.

18   S. Cooper, 'Household form and composition in King's Lynn: a reconstruction based on the poll taxes of 1689–1702' in Schurer and Arkell (eds.), *Surveying the people*, pp. 201–21, pp. 207–9.

19   Arkell, 'Examination of the poll taxes', p. 170.

20   J. Boulton, 'The marriage duty act and parochial registration in London, 1695–1706', in Schurer and Arkell, *Surveying the people*, pp. 222–52.

21   These are the findings of Dr Ian Archer, quoted in Braddick, *Parliamentary taxation*, p. 83.

22   Arkell, 'Examination of the poll taxes', p. 170.

23   D. V. Glass, *London inhabitants within the walls 1695*, London Record Society Publications, 2, 1966, p. xiii.

24   Braddick, *Parliamentary taxation*, pp. 233–41.

25   C. Winslow, 'Sussex smugglers' in D. Hay *et al.*, (eds.), *Albion's fatal tree. Crime and society in eighteenth century England*, Harmondsworth, 1977 edition, pp. 119–66. The wider inferences drawn by Winslow have since been criticised by a number of authors.

26   Sharpe, *Personal rule*, pp. 718–19.

27 A. H. Smith, *County and court. Government and politics in Norfolk, 1558–1603*, Oxford, 1974; A. Woodworth, *Purveyance for the royal household in the reign of Queen Elizabeth*, Transactions of the American Philosophical Society, 35, Philadelphia, 1945; P. Croft, 'Parliament, purveyance and the city of London 1589–1608', *Parliamentary History*, IV, 1985, pp. 9–34.

28 Braddick, *Parliamentary taxation*, p. 216.

29 *Ibid.*, pp. 177–92.

30 For a brief discussion of French tax resistance see H. Kamen, *The iron century. Social change in Europe 1550–1660*, London, 1976 edition, pp. 391–4, 419.

31 M. J. Braddick, 'Popular politics and public policy: the excise riot at Smithfield in February 1647 and its aftermath', *Historical Journal*, XXXIV, 1991, pp. 597–626; *Parliamentary taxation*, p. 200.

32 In fact this is questionable – nationally the yield under the sheriffs was actually higher than under the first farm.

33 L. M. Marshall, 'The levying of the hearth tax, 1662–1688', *English Historical Review*, LI, 1936, pp. 628–46; Braddick, *Parliamentary taxation*, pp. 252–262.

34 W. A. Shaw (ed.), *Calendar of treasury books*, XIII, London, 1933, 11 March 1697–8, p. 268.

35 *Ibid.*, 17 May 1698, p. 337.

36 Braddick, *Parliamentary taxation*, pp. 118–23.

37 Shaw (ed.), *Calendar of treasury books*, XIII, p. 339.

38 Ward, 'Administration of the window and assessed taxes', p. 525. His account does not emphasise this important detail. See Shaw (ed.), *Calendar of treasury books*, XIII, p. 133.

39 Braddick, *Parliamentary taxation*, pp. 250–1, 256, 276–7.

40 J. Brewer, *The sinews of power. War, money and the English state, 1688–1783*, London, 1989, p. 147.

9

Taxing the people: the limits of the possible in England, 1558–1714

The politics of taxation

The last three chapters have considered the kinds of grievance excited by taxation, both in public debate and in the eyes of tax-payers. These ranged from the equitability of the principles of a particular tax to the fairness of the actual burden within a village; from the constitutional propriety of the tax as a whole to the legal liability of a particular form of wealth in a village or a ship's hold; and from the legal powers of the crown to the powers vested in particular officers to search for and seize property. All these griev-ances could form a cloak for simple tightfistedness, but equally they could be genuinely held convictions. We have been less sys-tematic, so far, about the practical measures available to express such grievances.

Most exactions were open to challenge at three stages before money was received by the government: the initial claim or (in the case of parliamentary taxes) grant; division of the burden or the assessment of liability; and at the point of collection. Success-ful negotiation or mediation at the first two stages reduced the likelihood of confrontation at the third stage. However, con-frontation at this final stage would result in non-payment, at least initially.

The results of non-payment could be very varied. It might result in mediation, for example, through composition. On the other hand, tax collectors might distrain goods, selling them in order to cover the tax demand. Alternatively there might be vio-lent attacks on the collector, either by individuals or groups. Of these responses mediation was most likely where the officer had some room for manoeuvre. This flexibility might result from the fact that he could offer some concession on the amount collected, or because he was a neighbour who could, perhaps, offer a non-tax concession. Violence was most likely where these circumstances did not pertain. Distraint could result in a legal case, if the payer was intent on further resistance. He could accuse the collector of trespass, assault or abuse of his powers, for example. Distraint might also lead to violence, if seizure was resisted. Violence – riot or assault in response to a demand for taxation, or in response to distraint – could also result in legal hearings. Prosecutions for assault could be brought by either side. Collectors who had distrained goods were sometimes prosecuted for trespass. The chances of violence were most restricted where mediation and legal channels were thought to be available, and this was most likely where the magistracy was involved in collection or mediation. Mediation had obvious advantages, therefore, but central government had to measure these advantages against the potential effect on yield: too much room for manoeuvre at this level might produce unacceptable levels of avoidance and evasion.

Figure 9.1 represents the four stages of tax collection graphically. Every tax had to 'pass through' these four stages: there was an initial *demand or grant*; the burden of taxation was *apportioned*, or the rate was assessed; and the sums arrived at had to be *collected* before *payment* arrived at the exchequer. In principle each stage could be passed through very readily, resulting in the receipt of a high proportion of the hoped-for yield, rapid receipt and easy cooperation at all levels. This was the route which governments aspired to. Equally, however, the tax could meet reluctance at each stage, resulting in a political cost to government, the necessity of force or coercion, delayed and possibly partial payment. Obviously, governments were willing to accept this if necessary, but readiness was preferable.

In practice, of course, the choice was not as stark as this. Readiness could be secured by mediation, consultation and collusion at each stage. But, equally, this could fail and the passage of the tax demand to the next stage might still be marked by reluctance (figure 9.2). Mediation in order to secure ready compliance might, of course, result in loss of yield. To this extent there is a balance to be struck between political cost and yield.

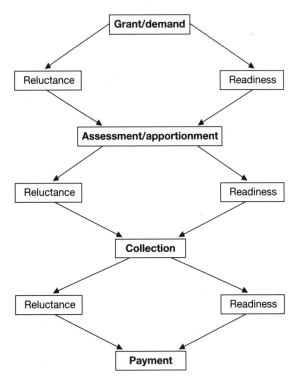

9.1   A schematic view of tax resistance I

If mediation failed, reluctance might lead to legal obstruction of the grant, assessment or collection of the tax, or physical resistance to the collection (figure 9.3). Successful legal resistance would result, ultimately, in avoidance of the burden. This represented a serious financial cost therefore. Resistance of any kind carried a political cost which had to be measured against the value of any particular revenue. At the point of collection, resistance took the form of an initial refusal to pay. This could result in further mediation, distraint of goods or violence. Distraint could be successful in securing payment, but might lead to violence, or to legal obstruction in the form of charges of assault or trespass against the collector. Violent resistance to the collection was likely

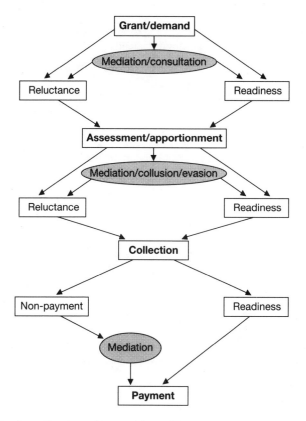

9.2 A schematic view of tax resistance II

to lead to legal hearings. This resort to law might lead either to payment or to avoidance of the burden.

All taxes, then, needed to pass through the four stages represented by the black boxes. Any tax passing through a stage represented by a 'shaded round' risked loss of yield. It also reflected an increase in the political cost of the exaction. Any 'shaded oval' indicates a degree of reluctance to pay and, if there is no discipline over yield, presented the possibility of financial loss. For example, at the level of assessment or collection this might mean collusion in tax evasion in order to secure consent. In general, any exaction whose passage from grant to collection can be imagined to have

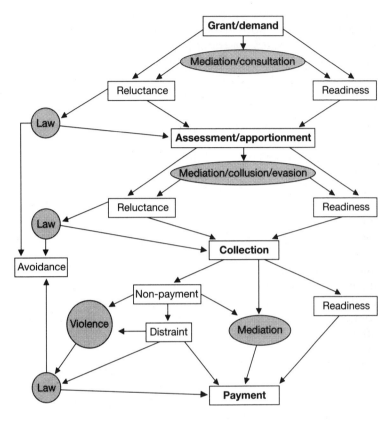

9.3 A schematic view of tax resistance III

been predominantly towards the left hand side of the diagram required enforcement. As such it was vulnerable to delay and loss of yield. More than this, however, enforcement required cooperation in the absence of a bureaucracy. Early modern states were successful in their aims more often by co-opting pre-existing elites than by creating elites of their own in order to by-pass vested local interests. In general co-option was preferable therefore, and an exaction depending on enforcement was relatively less reliable.

The variety of possible responses is striking. Mediation might entail bribery, corruption or political favours. On the other hand, it might consist of informal but legitimate arbitration by tax commissioners or farmers. Distraint might lead directly to payment, or to legal hearing regarding liability or equitability. This in itself might become part of a broader process of conciliation or negotiation. We can compare responses to a number of taxes to illustrate how variations in each of these options helps to explain the degree of open resistance, on one hand, and yield, on the other. For example, the forced loan was negotiable at the point of contact with individual taxpayers, the privy council having empowered deputy lieutenants in the late 1580s to divide the burden of an individual between several local people. On the other hand, the legality of the whole proceeding in 1626 was regarded as questionable by some and the prospects of using this strategy repeatedly were not good. The political cost in these circumstances was high in relation to yield. The excise on meat was not questionable in this way, since it was granted by parliament, and the payer often had no means of negotiation at the point of collection. The result was sometimes violence. The duty on beer, by contrast, was open to negotiation between farmer or minor official and brewer, and violence is not really associated with the excise on beer.

Returning to figure 9.1, we could read reluctance as a counter-pressure to the demand for taxation, a rival interest pressing upwards against the downward pressure of tax demands. The level of tax demands was obviously variable and so too was this counter-pressure. This is clearly the case with the early Tudor subsidies, which secured a remarkable degree of cooperation both in the assessment of national wealth and in the taxation of a proportion of it.[1] It may be possible to make a similar, though less striking, case for the later seventeenth century, too. It is less clear cut, because the taxes of the later seventeenth century were much less vulnerable to legal challenge than those of the early seventeenth century. The greater success of the later period may simply have been the result of the lack of promising means of avoidance. Similarly, the financial loss consequent on mediation of direct taxation, given the discipline of quotas, was significantly reduced. Financial success is not a clear indication of a level of consent beyond acquiescence. Nonetheless, it does seem that the increased downward pressure resulting from military expenditure did not elicit an equal and opposite reaction. Put another way, the early modern state may have been mobilising consent more effectively, not just securing resources through political and administrative reform.

Such an argument is clearly flirting with what is often termed 'whiggery', that is, a sense of the inevitability (and even desirability) of particular historical developments. It is worth emphasising, therefore, that there is no suggestion of inevitability in all this. To take another comparison, ship money experienced hostility at the top, resulting in a legal challenge to the whole exercise. Here the government risked a catastrophic loss of yield. At the level of assessment, there were numerous disputes over the sheriffs' quotas and at the point of collection many constables faced an uncomfortable time (with much consequent foot-dragging). By comparison the land tax was a huge success. There was no legal challenge, mediation was possible through the gentry commissions but the quota ensured that this did not result in loss of yield. Collection became routinised in many areas with the adoption of customary rates. Clearly, as a direct tax drawing predominantly on the landed wealth of the population, this was a substantial improvement. We do not mean thereby that ship money was an inevitable failure, however. Ship money in its turn was an improvement on the subsidy which, although not really vulnerable to legal challenge or prone to violence, was mediated in such a way as to produce a catastrophic loss of yield. Reluctant taxpayers were unlikely to pursue legal resistance to a rating, in part at least, because their rating was likely to have been a vast underestimate of their wealth. This, obviously, was something to avoid revealing in court. The complaint was usually about the relative burden, not the total burden: the degree to which their wealth was under-valued was not as vast as that of their neighbours. It has been argued this evasion made the yield of the subsidy so disappointing as to make the calling a parliament unattractive. Calling a parliament entailed some political discomfort and the money that parliament was able to offer did not compensate the crown for this trouble.[2] This book has been concerned to show why the land tax was a successful solution to the problems faced by national government, not to assess whether it was the only solution.

A successful tax was one that could be negotiated through

these hoops with minimum friction. Broad agreement on excise, customs and land tax had emerged by 1714, but each still required mediation – in parliament over rates and liabilities, in the commissions and between minor officers and taxpayers. These taxes had clear advantages over the congeries of prerogative rights and exactions of the early period, but this does not imply that the shape of the final system was predetermined. The evolution of the system was contingent and uncertain, with numerous failed experiments and apparent setbacks. Within this complex set of relationships, however, what is striking is how rarely individuals confronted a choice that threatened to rob the whole polity of legitimacy – there were almost always avenues of appeal and mediation. Similarly, individuals rarely confronted a choice of whether to pay or not to pay. However, they fairly frequently had the opportunity to pay less or differently, or to lobby in order to achieve those things. Despite the great demands for taxation, which impinged on social structure, economic production and political structures in unprecedented ways, England saw no tax rebellion between 1558 and 1714. Instead it saw piecemeal evolution, as various strategies tested the political and administrative limits of government in order to meet escalating military costs.

Elizabethan and early Stuart taxes were subject to legal challenge and/or mediation with a high financial cost. By comparison with England after 1640 parliamentary grants were infrequent and there were serious problems with many sources of revenue. The subsidy was widely evaded with the collusion of the commissions, and the fifteenth and tenth was of declining real value and increasing unpopularity. Parts of the customs were subject to legal challenge and, of course, to the perennial problem of evasion. The inland taxes in general were collected by officeholders who experienced the counter-pressure of reluctant neighbours. The revenue was composed of a bewildering variety of particular rights and exactions justified with reference to particular items of expenditure, whose yield and burden was unpredictable and even capricious. Many of these were the subject of legal question at the highest point, and this made the revenue rather risky. It also brought with it some political cost.

Looking at the financial system in 1714 we are struck by the paradox noted by Brewer: the bureaucracy usually associated with absolutist regimes was actually more developed in the

British constitutional monarchy.[3] Parliamentary consultation seems to have removed the possibility of legal challenge and to have legitimated the activities of the bureaucracy. The customs were mediated and negotiated at the top, the excise likewise. Both were to a degree professionalised at the bottom, the excise more noticeably so. There were political changes – notably a considerable increase in the sums which parliament was willing to grant – but also important administrative changes which circumvented the bureaucratic weaknesses of the state. The revitalisation of quota taxation enormously increased the effectiveness of direct taxation, while the acceptance of professional tax collection in localities contributed to the great success of indirect taxation. These innovations both had roots in the mid seventeenth century. Problems could still emerge, however, as in the mid-1660s when apparent division in parliament about the future of the hearth tax may have legitimated resistance to it in the localities.

National government sought to sustain its interest by cajoling, threatening and negotiating at the three stages of taxation outlined above. The reluctant taxpayer, likewise, was pushing back. Rarely, however, was there a direct clash – there was plenty of 'give' in the system and flexibility in administration. There was a notable long-term success for the tax raising interest, however, in that much greater sums than before were raised at an acceptable political cost. There was also a much reduced chance of legal challenge and a reduced possibility of financial loss through mediation. The English state had successfully made use of the enabling aspects of its economic and social environment. Clearly the extractive capacity of national government was considerably increased, and this success appears to have been relative, too – it seems to have been superior to other European states operating under similar conditions.

Harnessing resources: the growth of the tax state

It should now be clear how the system of taxation and borrowing that had emerged by 1714 represented a negotiation between the fiscal needs of national government, its limited bureaucratic power and the political limits within which it was exercised. It was not, perhaps, the only solution possible, but we can see why it was a successful one. We can now consider how effective this regime was at harnessing the available resources, looking first at national wealth, and then at political resources.

National wealth

In addressing the extent to which the early modern English state was successful in tapping material resources we are handicapped by the paucity of data and the dearth of research available on the impact of taxation. We cannot, therefore, chart the success of government in tapping new sources of wealth in any great detail. There is, however, sufficient evidence to judge 'success' by two criteria – by comparison with the experience of the English state over a longer period of time and by comparison with contemporary European states. The latter comparison is relevant in other contexts, too. For example, the evolution of the English finances in this period was driven to a significant degree by the rising cost of military survival and successful competition in the European states system. Moreover, all European states faced similar problems of securing information, locating and taxing resources. The administrative repertoire of these states was similar, and a comparison can be instructive as to the best strategies for overcoming these difficulties.

There can be little doubt that government revenue grew more quickly than the economy in our period, that a greater proportion of national wealth was controlled and disposed of by national government. This is clearly suggested by figure 1.1. Raw figures for total revenue comparisons make startling reading and must compensate for deflation by population growth, inflation and increased national wealth. Between 1590 and 1603 ordinary revenue topped £300,000 per annum, supplemented by about £2,568,888 in extra-ordinary revenues. This total of about £450,000–£500,000 per annum would not have cut much ice a hundred years later: between 1688 and 1702 the annual revenue was about £4 million per annum (£58.7 million in total) and long-term borrowing supplemented this considerably.[4]

For a proper comparison these figures would have to be further deflated to take account of differences in the 'costs of collection': the total cost of government probably did not increase as dramatically as did revenues received by central government. The difference between the cost of collection at the beginning and end of our period may have been spectacular. For example, monopolies and excises can be regarded as equivalent in some respects, since some monopolies can be regarded as the equivalent of indirect taxes. Many commodities subject to monopoly grants were later taxed by means of an excise. The proportion of the total yield retained by government in the two cases was very different, however. As we saw above, the monopolies of the 1630s produced £100,000 for the government at a cost of £750,000 to the consumer. The costs of collection for the excises were nothing like this high. In other areas of the revenue this was likely to have been less striking – such as in direct taxation and the customs. The declining gap represented smaller profits for intermediaries and there is likely to have been a political dividend here: we have noted on a number of occasions the hostility that was elicited by the use of private interests in seeking out taxable resources. This hostility is reflected in the woodcut representing the ritual shaming of a monopolist (frontispiece). The punishment places him in the same category as adulterers as a threat to communal values. The narrowing of the gap between cost to the economy and revenues received by central government probably reduced the political costs of collection.

For our purposes though, we are not concerned with the total cost of government but with the revenue received. Thus, we need do no more than note that the difference between the two qualifies statements regarding the changing 'impact of government'. The impact of government must have been more noticeable in the later seventeenth century, however. Again a simple example will suffice. As we saw in chapter 2, between 1688 and 1710 the navy was crewed by between about 40,000 and 50,000 men, and William's army in the low countries reached 100,000. In 1700 the second largest city in England was Norwich, with a population of 30,000, followed by Bristol, 21,000 and Newcastle 16,000. Indeed, only seven cities had a population of 10,000 or more; leaving aside London, their combined population was lower than the number of men in arms.[5]

Much of the pressure to increase revenues derived from the demands of military mobilisation, as we have seen. The last twenty-five years covered by this study were dominated by military spending, either in war-time or as hangover from the massive campaigns then undertaken. The mobilisation of resources in this period was spectacular by both criteria set out above. Figure

1.1 reveals a second historic high in war spending which increased considerably beyond the plateau achieved in the period 1640–80. This peak was not surpassed until the Napoleonic wars. This mobilisation was impressive not just historically, however, but also by comparison with other contemporary European states. The forward commitment of both troops and the navy by the British represented a level of commitment surpassed only by France, a country of 19 million souls compared to the 5.2 million supporting the British effort. British spending was comfortably second and far heavier per capita than anywhere except the United Provinces (table 9.1).

Table 9.1   *War efforts of England and other European powers (various years)*

	Spending (£)			Troops paid for		Navy size (no. of ships)	
	Total (million)	Per head					
England and Wales	8.1	(1.56)	1696–7	75,000		173	(1688)
	10.2	(1.96)	1709–10			323	(1697)
				170,000		247	(1714)
Dutch Republic	4.75	(2.16)	1688	72,714	(1688)	180	(1698)
	6.90	(3.08)	1695	119,014	(1708)		
Austria	2.90	(0.63)	1695	63,800	(1687)		
	3.78	(0.82)	1704	103,000	(1690)		
				116,000	(1695)		
				135,000	(1705–11)		
France	13.79	(0.73)	1698	444,000	(1691–3)	231	(1700)
	15.00	(0.79)	1711	250,000	(1705)	192	(1704)
						164	(1710)
Russia				195,000–210,000	(1700s)	49	(1725)
Sweden	0.51	(0.34)	1630s	45,000	(1630s)		
	1.19	(0.79)	1677	63,000	(1675)		
				100,000	(1705)	46	(1697)

Source: D. W. Jones, *War and economy in the age of William III and Marlborough,* Oxford, 1988, table 2.1, p. 29.

191

British tax burdens remained heavier than those in France throughout the eighteenth century, rising more quickly in the period down to 1812.[6] The problems this posed were economic and not to do with raising or transferring these vast sums. The instruments of taxing and borrowing had improved to the extent that economic activity in general was threatened by the distortion of demand. The English government did not buy supplies at home and then ship them abroad, preferring to transfer funds abroad and where supplies were purchased locally. In effect there was a vast transfer of demand to foreign markets.[7] In this chronological and comparative perspective, then, the tax instruments created in the civil war and the credit instruments created in the 1660s and 1690s were hugely successful in mobilising material resources. This clearly had extremely important political consequences, and it remained a historic and comparative high through the rest of the eighteenth century, too.

The evidence for aggregate revenues suggests very considerable success by our two criteria. What is less clear is how close the government had come to an ideal distribution of this demand through the economy – whether the targets of taxation were well-chosen, and how accurately they were hit. Here we could quickly review the potential sources of taxation as they developed. During our period the value of land rose and this is reflected in rising rents and prices. At the same time the changing patterns of landholding turned an increasing proportion of the population towards non-agricultural production. Trading wealth increased as overseas trade expanded and diversified, and the volume of internal trade also increased. Associated with all these changes was an increase in the range and availability of financial services – insurance, banking and investment. In all these areas there were expanded incomes and a wider range of potentially taxable wealth. There was also a marked expansion and diversification in patterns of consumption. Governments could, therefore, tap these diverse forms of wealth directly through taxes on consumption.

Table 9.2   *The distribution of wealth in late seventeenth-century England*

Group 1 Above £150 per annum
Temporal lords
Baronets
Spiritual lords
Knights
Esquires
Greater merchants
Gentlemen
Persons in office, greater
Lesser merchants
Manufacturing trade
Persons in the law

Group 2 £150–£30 per annum
Persons in office, lesser
Freeholders, greater
Naval officers
Clergymen, greater
Military officers
Persons in sciences and liberal arts
Freeholders, lesser
Clergymen, lesser
Shopkeepers and tradesmen
Farmers
Artisans and handicrafts

Group 3 Below £30 per annum
Building trade
Common seamen
Miners
Labouring people and outservants
Common soldiers
Cottagers and paupers
Vagrants

Source: D. W. Jones, *War and economy in the age of William III and Marlborough*, Oxford, 1988, table 3.3, pp. 74–5.

It is difficult to gauge where the incidence of taxation really falls.[8] In our period this general problem is exacerbated by the paucity of the data, and there has been little research on this issue. The best recent account of these issues is Jones' estimate of the incidence of taxation in the period 1688–1714. He takes Gregory King's account of the distribution of wealth in 1688 and divides the population into three groups: a low income group earning less than £30 per annum; a middle income group of £30–150 per annum; and a high income group earning more than £150 per annum (table 9.2). Groups two and three will have contributed the bulk of direct taxes. They are also likely to have been the groups liable to customs duties since the imported goods on which customs fell were, on the whole, relatively expensive. People in group one would not have had sufficient margin above subsistence to be able to afford most of these goods. This low income group was, however, liable to excise taxation on beer and spirits. Towards the end of our period, then, this was a relatively progressive profile of taxation, although it was to become less so as the proportional contribution of excise to total revenues increased.[9] Indeed, it has been suggested that the increasing use of excise taxation made the English system as regressive as that of France.[10] This preponderance of excise taxation lay in the future, however, and the land tax remained the most productive tax in our period. As a proportion of the available wealth that it was trying to tax, however, the excise was probably already more effective (table 9.3): taxation may have been relatively heavier for the poor than the rich.

It is almost certain that the relatively rich who did not depend on land were lightly taxed. Excises were regressive and direct taxation difficult to achieve except on lands and there was consistent complaint to this effect. These kinds of liquid wealth were harnessed not so much by taxation as by borrowing: 'The middle income group did escape relatively lightly and much of what the wealthiest office and business groups contributed in loans really represented what the government was unable to raise from them as taxes.'[11] From this, of course, they profited and this exacerbated the complaint that they were not bearing their share of the cost of government. Nonetheless, the success of government borrowing in tapping otherwise difficult to reach forms of wealth was considerable: in the period 1707–9 there were about 10,000 public creditors in England, and on the eve of the South Sea Bubble this number may have reached 40,000.[12] The whole subject of the incidence of taxation is fraught with difficulties and we cannot accept uncritically hostile contemporary testimony. Nonetheless, Jones' account seems plausible. Moreover, persistent attempts to shift the burden of direct taxation away from the land and to find forms of indirect taxation that would hit these other seams provide corroboration of his general conclusions.

Table 9.3   *Tax receipts and the bases for taxation, 1670–1720*

	(a)	(b)	(c)
1670	4–5	4	1–2
1680	2–3	11	3–4
1690	7–8	15	7–8
1700	10	24	11
1710	10	24	13
1720	9	31	15

Notes: (a) Revenue from direct taxation as percentage of agricultural income
(b) Revenue from customs as percentage of value of retained imports
(c) Excise revenue as percentage of domestic consumption of industrial goods
Source: P. K. O'Brien, 'The political economy of British taxation, 1660–1815', *Economic History Review*, 2nd series, XLI, 1988, pp. 1–32; p. 15.

The record of the English state in harnessing material resources improved dramatically in the 1640s and then in the 1690s. By the end of our period this performance was not only good by historical standards but by comparison with other European states. The success of tapping the variety of forms of wealth was impressive given the lack of administrative resources and the consequent lack of information available to government. In the end, though, some forms of wealth were tapped by borrowing rather than taxing, and this created potential political problems.

Participation
So much for material resources. How effectively did this regime

harness social and political resources? In our chronology we noted how many of the prerogative taxes were subject to legal question. Clearly the absence of such dispute after 1660 was a significant advantage of that tax regime. This should not be taken as a whiggish point, however, because to some extent the unpopularity of these taxes was jurisdictional, matters of legal or administrative detail. In the case of ship money rating was left to the responsibility of the sheriff and was a fraught issue. It was, perhaps, no less a fraught issue in the case of quota taxation granted by parliament, but here the advantages of the commission could be considerable. Likewise the difficulties of securing purveyance agreements in Norfolk were partly to do with the desire for quarter sessions control, and a suspicion of outsiders. This was an issue in the excise administration, too. By the late seventeenth century there was considerable pressure from local elites to staff the lower reaches of the revenue departments, and part of the process of professionalisation was to pressurise patrons such as Baron Ashburnham to prefer men who would hold office effectively.[13] In the early seventeenth century members of parliament responding to hostility to purveyance and ship money were not necessarily representing a constitutional position, but could be highlighting frictions arising from matters of administration.

Secondly, as we saw in chapter 7, some of the arguments that have been taken to be 'constitutional' in fact revolved around points of considerable legal nicety and tended to assume a degree of constitutional agreement. There was an extent to which, of course, 'they would say that wouldn't they?', and using the same language does not necessarily entail agreement. Similarly, however, there is a sense in which the early Stuart period saw a system of particular rights tested and elaborated to a point of bewildering sophistication, those rights being tested, proven and applied to solve difficulties in particular parts of the revenue system. In this system, too, local rates and national ones blurred into one another. For example, national armies were partly financed from local rates such as coat and conduct money. This, of course, adds to the difficulties of quantifying a total burden of taxation. This intricate system collapsed in 1642, however, and was replaced by one which was, in some respects, much simpler. The heat produced by legal, administrative and political frictions in raising purveyance, wardship, ship money, forest fines and distraint of knighthood was not matched by their replacement – half the excise of liquors – in the 1660s.

To an extent, then, the late seventeenth century revenue system seems to have drawn on 'political' resources more effectively than that of the early Stuarts. We can examine this by briefly looking at the local administration of land and window taxes, the excise and the customs in the early eighteenth century. It has been suggested that the processes of selection for posts in the land tax administration confirmed 'the structure of prestige and status in the local community' rather than building up 'any framework of a paid provincial civil service'.[14] In this sense, the tax drew not only on fiscal but also on social resources within the locality. It seems that the excise did, more so after 1690 than earlier, as patrons such as Ashburnham sought to colonise the administration through their clients. In the case of the customs, of course, the very cosiness of the relationship between officials and merchants in the localities was a cause of concern. This was a more successful recipe than the 'privatisations' of government represented by informers, farmers and their agents, hunters after concealed lands and so forth. The public role of officials was becoming more differentiated, however, as we have seen in the case of Ashburnham: patronage was not exercised without a sense of responsibility for the needs of the state. This provides something of a contrast with the patronage system of the early Stuart period. One way of expressing this contrast is by saying that there was a more differentiated sense of public and private interest. This has also been discerned in the changing ethos of the administration of the ordnance office, the office responsible for procuring military supplies.[15] The English state was peculiar in not employing tax farmers in the later seventeenth century. Instead, it was dependent on local elites for the assessment and collection of direct taxation and was notable for the (by contemporary standards) highly professionalised and bureaucratised administration of the excise in particular.

The tax regime was, then, harnessing social resources effectively. In this the role of the local elites was crucial. Their hostility to the prerogative taxes of the early seventeenth century was often about liberties rather than liberty, that is, they were defending specific legal rights and privileges as much as they were property in general. The success of the later seventeenth century taxes was partly the result of the fact that the tax administration was

197

colonised, to an extent, by their descendants. Revenue places were distinct from the expanding range of local offices, but not necessarily different in kind. In the early seventeenth century English villages had constables and churchwardens. A century later there was a broader range of officials, among them revenue officials. These offices offered other opportunities for local people to secure local status and prestige.[16] There was another way in which the tax regime drew on broader resources, and that was in the dramatic expansion of the sources of public credit. The national debt rapidly drew large numbers of people into investment, as we have seen. So broad, in fact, was its base, that it had political implications. The debt was seen as a guarantor of the revolution settlement because it gave so many people a vested interest in the existing regime.

There were other material benefits offered by the expanding revenue system, of course. Collectors of the land tax could use tax money for personal ends before they remitted them to the exchequer. Indeed, in the eighteenth century, receivers set up as bankers and bankers sought receiverships.[17] In September 1695 the treasury lords complained to receivers in Norfolk that arrears of £17,000 were 'principally occasioned by the extraordinary advantages you insist upon and receive by the return of the moneys'. Similar complaints were not uncommon.[18] By the eighteenth century 'the land tax was ... a locally domesticated tax whose workings were adapted as much to the needs of merchants, gentlemen and the populace in the provinces as to the requirements of the Treasury Board in London'. The heyday of the excise really lies beyond our period, but it too offered opportunities for some. In 1690 there 1,211 full-time excisemen, in 1708 2,247 and by 1716 2,778. The 'overall impression is that officers came from yeomen's and tradesman's backgrounds, although excisemen's ranks were also swelled by the shabby genteel'. In all revenue departments by 1716 there were 5,947 full-time employees.[19] Those in the excise service had the prospect of a decent salary and opportunities for advancement. Thus, once this system of administration alongside the magistracy gained a foothold in the localities the positive advantages became manifest: hence the colonisation of the system by the clients of Ashburnham. In a weaker sense, earlier regimes had tried to encourage this. For example, the crown showed some interest in persuading the magistracy to farm the excise in the 1660s, or at least securing farmers who were acceptable to the local governors. This had also been, though, to some extent, in tension with the desire to maximise profit.[20]

The role of the magistracy raises once again the rather nebulous issue of legitimacy. Hostility to prerogative taxes in the 1630s was not necessarily 'about' legitimacy, or constitutional principle. However, one reason whig historians may have thought so was because contemporaries feared it could be. The late seventeenth century tax regime had high legitimacy in that respect. Tax flows and officeholding tied the revenue administration to the existing social and political order, and after 1689 it quickly became obvious to many people that the national debt relied upon a particular dynastic settlement. Another part of this jigsaw was, undoubtedly, the role of parliament. At the minimal level, parliamentary control of taxation (and borrowing after 1688) removed the possibility that matters of administration or legal detail could receive rhetorical inflation to the status of matters of constitutional propriety. There was also a more positive commitment to the principle of parliamentary grant: manifest for example in the hostility to benevolences. A minimal claim is that, although hostility to impositions did not necessarily entail a statement about parliamentary rule, parliamentary grants of import duties removed the possibility of that kind of objection. Assessment and collection by the magistracy locally was the safest guarantee of political peace locally, grant by parliament was, perhaps, the national corollary of that. The increasing willingness of parliament to grant taxation was associated with increasing powers to supervise the disposal of funds and to audit the accounts. These powers, of 'audit and appropriation', were necessary to increase the security offered by government borrowing. These powers of audit and appropriation may have helped to make parliaments less suspicious of the purposes to which grants might be put. A significant cause of reluctance on the part of early Stuart parliaments to make grants of taxation was the fear that they were 'pouring water into a leaking cistern', that is, paying for royal extravagance and mismanagement rather than for publicly useful ends.

An appropriate metaphor for all these changes is evolution. This is not meant in the 'whig' sense of progress but in the neutral sense of mutation to fill an ecological niche created by a large number of variables. The early modern English state had evolved very successfully in the period 1558–1714. This evolution occurred in the hostile environment of the European states system and in response to domestic imperatives which were not solely financial. This is not necessarily progress, or development to a higher state of being, nor is the final shape of the mutation predetermined. It is, however, change in response to a constantly changing social, political, economic and military environment. This environment made some forms of mutation more successful than others. If this study has sought to demonstrate one thing it is the potential of the study of taxation as a means of exploring this process.

Notes

1   R. S. Schofield, 'Taxation and the political limits of the Tudor state', in C. Cross, D. Loades and J. J. Scarisbrick (eds.), *Law and government under the Tudors. Essays presented to Sir Geoffrey Elton ...*, Cambridge, 1988, pp. 227–55.

2   C. Russell, 'Parliament and the king's finances' in C. Russell (ed.), *Origins of the English civil war*, London, 1973, pp. 91–116.

3   J. Brewer, *The sinews of power. War, money and the English state 1688–1783*, London, 1989, chapter 5.

4   W. R. Scott, *The constitution and finance of English, Scottish and Irish joint-stock companies to 1720*, 3 vols., Cambridge, 1910–12, III, pp. 507–8; C. G. A. Clay, *Economic expansion and social change. England 1500–1700*, 2 vols., Cambridge, 1984, II, 261, 268.

5   Above, tables 2.3, 2.4, pp. 31, 33. For urban population figures see E. A. Wrigley, 'Urban growth and agricultural change: England and the continent in the early modern period', reprinted in his *People, cities and wealth. The transformation of traditional society*, Oxford, 1987, pp. 157–93, table 7.1.

6   P. Mathias and P. K. O'Brien, 'Taxation in Britain and France, 1715–1810: a comparison of the social and economic incidence of taxes collected for the central governments', *Journal of European Economic History*, V, 1976, pp. 601–50, pp. 604–5. See also the subsequent debate in VII, 1978, pp. 209–13.

7   D. W. Jones, *War and economy in the age of William III and Marlborough*, Oxford, 1988, chapter 2.

8   See, for example, the debate in *Journal of European Economic History*, VII, 1978, pp. 209–13.

9 Jones, *War and economy*, pp. 67–8.

10 Mathias and O'Brien, 'Taxation in Britain and France', pp. 611–33.

11 Jones, *War and economy*, p. 68.

12 P. G. M. Dickson, *The financial revolution in England: a study in the development of public credit 1688–1756*, London, 1967, pp. 262, 273.

13 C. Brooks, 'Interest, patronage and professionalism: John, 1st Baron Ashburnham, Hastings and the revenue services', *Southern History*, IX, 1987, pp. 51–70.

14 C. Brooks, 'Public finance and political stability: the administration of the land tax, 1688–1720', *Historical Journal*, XVII, 1974, pp. 28–300; p. 287.

15 Peck, *Court, patronage and corruption*; Brooks, 'Interest, patronage and professionalism'. For the ordnance office see, H. C. Tomlinson, *Guns and government. The ordnance office under the later Stuarts*, London, 1979.

16 Brooks, 'Public finance and political stability'. J. Kent, 'The centre and the localities: state formation and parish government in England, circa 1640–1740', *Historical Journal*, XXXVIII, 1995, pp. 363–404, provides a context for this.

17 L. S. Pressnell, 'Public monies and the development of English banking', *Economic History Review*, 2nd series, V, 1952–3, pp. 378–97; pp. 382, 390. For the use of tax money for private purposes earlier, see M. J. Braddick, *Parliamentary taxation in seventeenth-century England. Local administration and response*, Royal Historical Society Studies in History, 70, Woodbridge, 1994, pp. 34, 162–3, 206–7; C. D. Chandaman, *The English public revenue 1660–1688*, Oxford, 1975, p. 182.

18 W. A. Shaw (ed.), *Calendar of treasury books*, X, pt III, London, 1935, p. 1208. See also, for example, *ibid.*, XIV, London, 1934, p. 177.

19 J. Brewer, 'The English State and fiscal appropriation, 1688–1789', *Politics and Society*, XVI, 1988, pp. 335–85; pp. 349, 156; *Sinews*, p. 66.

20 Braddick, *Parliamentary taxation*, pp. 207–20.

Selected documents

In the following extracts original spelling has been retained, except for i/j and u/v. Some punctuation has been added for ease of comprehension.

Document 1

Purveyance posed a range of problems that are characteristic of the difficulties of raising revenue in this period. One frequent complaint was that the distribution of the burden was uneven. In 1613, Mr Tomson, the vicar of Crondall in Hampshire, complained to the Board of the Greencloth about having to provide two geese for the royal household. The matter was referred to the justices of the peace who were instructed to

> reveiw ... the auncient rate and to yeeld him such releif as thequitie of his cause maie require. Whereuppon wee making search into the said first charge of composicion poultrie Doe find that there are charged within the hundred of Crondall five geese onlie yearelie ... By which it is plaine that his charge of two geese hath wrongfullie growen uppon his viccaridge by the default of some former constables whoe for thease of some others have imposed this charge uppon the said vicaridg.

Sir Henry Whithed's letter book, I, 1601–1614, Hampshire Record Series, I, Hampshire County Council, 1976, p. 107.

Document 2

The collection of purveyance was sometimes hampered by local officeholders, suspicious of the authority and activities of the purveyors. In this case the privy council sought to ensure that the rate was collected but also that the powers of the purveyors were regulated. This tension between the liberties of the tax payer, the authority of the collectors and the interests of local officeholders is common to many of the exactions studied in this book (see pp. 174–6, documents 23, 25, 27–9, 32). The letter opens by instructing justices of the peace of Hampshire to deliver poultry for the royal household to Edward Dickinson, the purveyor, at Odiham by 9.00 am on 27 December.

> And whereas wee are given to understand that there is a great fault by negligence of the high Constables and Tythingmen whoe will nether see the service performed themselves, as they ought to doe, nor make their returnes as they should, but returne whome they list and what they list. [F]or most of them will returne men that are dead xx or xxxti yeares sithence, bycause they did hold land at that tyme and spare them which of right ought to pay. By reason whereof his Majesties servaunt which is appointed to receave the said service cannot have that which is due unto his majestie, wherefore we further praie that you will give the said purveiour a true coppie of your composicion and what is to be paid out of everie devicion and Hundred that he maie be the better able to demaund the poultrie where it is due. [F]or he knoweth not where to demaund the service but onlie by the Constables returne, which is for the most parte false for they doe not returne somuch as is due out of the Countrie by tenn dozen of Henns and three dozen of Geese everie yeare, which is a great hinderance to his majesties service.

Ibid., pp. 109–10.

Document 3

One response to the unpopularity of purveyance was to seek an extension of the role of local officeholders in regulating the rate (see above pp. 80–2). In Hampshire, in 1605, it was complained that unfairness had resulted when large estates were broken up. Rather than splitting the burden of purveyance proportionately between the resulting smaller farms, the whole burden had been

placed on particular farms. This unfairness was to be addressed
by the justices of the peace, who

> shall call before them such of the Inhabitantes of everie parishe as to
> them shall seeme good and uppon consideracion had of the true
> rates of the composicion Wheate & Oates paieable out of the said
> landes to rate the same uppon the severall possessors of the said
> landes indifferently, as in their discretions shalbe thought reason-
> able, with which all parties interested therein shall stand bound and
> charged with, without further denyall or refusall. And where it is
> farther informed that the composicion and rate of wheate and oates
> have not been in some partes of this Sheire heretofore soe indifer-
> rently preporcioned as it ought to be, It is likewise ordered that the
> said Justices of peace in their severall devisions shall also have
> authoritie to examine the same And if they shall find just cause then
> to proporcion the same as to them shalbe thought good. Provided
> allwaies if anie person shall find himself agreeved with this order
> that then he shalbe at libertie to seeke for reformacion thereof at the
> generall Sessions within this countie … And the said Justices of
> peace are hereby required in their severall devisions by Easter Ses-
> sions next to make a booke of their severall rates by them sett downe
> and imposed.

Ibid., pp. 43–4; at p. 44.

Document 4

Attempts to regulate purveyance were said to raise the threat of
attacks on the prerogative rights of the monarch. This was not the
only 'tax' to raise issues of central constitutional significance. In
this extract Sir Francis Knollys explains to Queen Elizabeth the
relationship between the prerogative right of purveyance and the
common law. The arguments he puts forward made the government very reluctant to allow parliamentary discussion of purveyance, fearing that such discussion might lead to attacks on the
royal prerogative (see p. 81).

> Your lawyers and j[udges] of the laws are not acquainted with, nei-
> ther allow of the prerogative royal of your household because,
> before the courts were appointed in Westminster h[all], the lord
> steward of your household was the only j[udge] of your prerogative
> royal of household, and the whitestaves of your household do assist
> his lordship in that behalf; and, therefore, if you will ask your judges

why you pay no more but 12*d* for a lamb and so of other things, they will answer that they know no law for it; neither do they acknowledge any other prerogative royal to be due unto your Majesty but only such as may be subject to the judgement of their law, which is a great prejudice and a great loss to your Majesty's service of household ... The which hitherto I have resisted, although they have taken upon them to judge of your prerogative royal of household to make it subject to their written law.

British Library, Lansdowne MS 73/34, quoted from A. Woodworth, *Purveyance for the royal household in the reign of Queen Elizabeth*, Transactions of the American Philosophical Society, 35, Philadelphia, 1945, p. 21.

Document 5

Because opposition to purveyance could be interpreted this way, those seeking to restrain the activities of purveyors had to tread very carefully. In the late 1580s, and particularly in 1589, there were attempts in parliament to secure legislation to regulate the taking of purveyance. In this extract a speaker in the House of Commons in in 1589 is anxious to avoid appearing to attack the prerogative.

The abuse only of purveyors is restrained by this bill and her Majesty's purveyance or prerogative therein is nothing thereby impeached.

The untrue information of purveyors or their deputies is only restrained by this bill, by which untrue informations and suggestions her Majesty's poor people are many times unjustly molested to their great travail and expenses, and the prerogative of her Majesty greatly abused.

That the authority of the lord steward, the treasurer, the comptroller of her Majesty's most honourable household doth remain in such state as that they and every of them may at their discretions send for any offender as before time.

To swear a purveyor that his information is true, seemed to be agreeable with like former ordinances, whereby it is provided that every purveyor take an oath for the due execution of his office.

British Library, Lansdowne MS 86/55, quoted from Woodworth, *Purveyance*, p. 25.

Document 6

While the crown was anxious about the implications for revenue and the royal prerogative of attempts to regulate purveyance, it was also clear that real abuses had to be redressed. This tension was marked in relation to other taxes, too, notably the excise (see document 28). In the 1590s the commissioners for household causes were given a brief to enquire into the activities of purveyors in the counties, in order to redress grievances. Here is an extract from a letter from them to the justices of the peace of Norfolk, asking them summon the high and petty constables, and 'such other of every parishe as you shall thinke to be most fytt' by

oathes & otherwise by your discretion to ... fynde out all the nomber and quantityes of every kynde of provisions purveyed, & taken up and at what prizes [*sic*] the same were had, as also what sommes of money hath ben paid to the purveyors or others for anie provisions that should have ben delivered unto Her Majestes houshold or stable [for the year ending 1 October 1590 and between that date and the end of their enquiry], setting downe the daie & yeare the same provisions were made & delivered, and by what purveyor & by what person, and what money & contentment hath ben made for the same. And further that you enquire what soommes of money doe remayne dew & to whome and for what provisions in the same tymes or at anie time before. And as wee doubt not of your great care & diligence herin, so wee require you to enquire of all their misdemeanours & abuses comytted & don in anie fayres, markettes or other places by the said purveyors contrary to their commissions, that like reformacion maie be made.

A. H. Smith and G. M. Baker (eds.), *The papers of Nathaniel Bacon of Stiffkey, III, 1585–1595*, Norfolk Record Society, LIII, 1987 and 1988, p. 325.

Document 7

Many of the tensions and ambiguities which we have noted in relation to purveyance also emerged in parliamentary debate about monopolies. These exchanges show hostility to the monopolies, sensitivity to charges of trespassing on the prerogative and some very violent language.

Dr *Bennet* said, He that will go about to debate her Majesties

Prerogative Royal, had need walk warily. In respect of a grievance out of the City for which I come, I think my self bound to speak that now which I had not intended to speak before; I mean a Monopoly of Salt ... Fire and Water are not more necessary. But for other Monopolies of Cards ... Dice, Starch and the like, they are (because Monopolies) I must confess very hurtful, though not all alike hurtful. I know there is a great difference in them; And I think if the abuses in this Monopoly of Salt were particularized, this would walk in the fore rank ...

Mr *Martin* said, I do Speak for a Town that grieves and pines, for a Countrey that groaneth and languisheth under the burthen of monstrous and unconscionable Substitutes to the Monopolitans of Starch, Tinn, Fish, Cloth, Oyl, Vinegar, Salt and I know not what, nay what not? The principallest commodities both of my Town and Country are ingrossed into the hand of those blood-suckers of the Common-Wealth. If a body ... being let blood, be left still languishing without any remedy, how can the good estate of that body long remain? ... If these blood-suckers be still let alone to suck up the best and principallest commodities which the earth there hath given us, what shall become of us, from whom the fruits of our own Soil and the commodities of our own labour, which with the sweat of our brows even up to the knees in the Mire and Dirt, we have laboured for, shall be taken by Warrant of Supream Authority, which the poor Subjects dare not gainsay? ...

Sir *Robert Wroth* ... There have been divers Patents granted since the last Parliament; these are now in being, Viz. The Patents for Currants, Iron, Powder, Cards, Ox-shin Bones, Train Oyl, Transportation of Leather, Lists of Cloth, Ashes, Anniseeds, Vinegar, Sea-Coals, Steel, *Aquavitae*, Brushes, Pots, Salt-Peter, Lead, Accidences, Oyl, Calamint Stone, Oyl of Blubber, Fumathoes or dryed Piltchers in the Smoak and divers others.

Upon the reading of the Patents aforesaid Mr *Hackwell* ... asked thus; Is not Bread there? Bread quoth one, Bread quoth another; this Voice seems strange quoth a third: No quoth Mr *Hackwell*, If Order be not taken for these, Bread will be there before the next Parliament ...

Mr Secretary *Cecill* ... The question was of the most convenient way to reform these grievances of Monopoly: But after disputation, of the labour we have not received the expected fruit ... This dispute draws two great things in question; First the Princes power; Secondly the freedom of Englishmen. I am born an Englishman and am a Fellow-Member of this House; I would desire to live no day, in which I should detract from either. I am servant unto the Queen, and before I would speak or give consent to a Case that should debase her Prerogative or abridge it, I would wish my tongue cut out of my head ...

Mr *Francis Moore* said, I must confess Mr Speaker, I moved the House both the last Parliament and this touching this point, but I never meant ... to set limits and bounds to the Prerogative Royal. But now seeing it hath pleased her Majesty of her self, out of the abundance of her Princely goodness, to set at liberty her Subjects from the thraldom of those Monopolies ... I would be bold in one motion to offer two considerations to this House; The first, that Mr Speaker might go unto her Majesty to yield her most humble and hearty thanks and withal to shew the joy of her Subjects for their delivery, and their thankfulness unto her for the same; The other, that where divers Speeches have been made extravagantly in this House ... I would therefore that Mr Speaker not only should satisfy her Majesty by way of Apology therein, but also humbly crave pardon for the same.

Sir Simonds D'Ewes, *The journals of all the parliaments during the reign of Queen Elizabeth ...*, London, 1682, pp. 644–54.

Document 8

The language used by Mr Martin in the 1601 exchanges regarding monopolists (document 7) was forcefully echoed by Sir John Culpeper in a famous speech to parliament in 1641. They are described in terms of a biblical plague, devouring all in their path. This reflects the fact that they were making a private profit at public expense, unlike the magistrates who acted as collectors of other taxes. This attitude may have been reflected in official punishment of some of these officers too (see frontispiece). He added a more technical complaint that they were allowed their monopolies because they had established bogus corporations. This was an evasion of legislation of 1624 that had made it illegal to grant monopolies to individuals. The speech is more famous, however, for the following description of monopolists. The language later used of excise men was equally violent (see documents 23, 25).

... Neast of Waspes, a swarme of Vermin which have overcrept the land I meane the Monopolers, the Polers of the people, These like the froggs of Egipt have gotten possession of our dwellings, we have scarce a roome free from them, They sipp in our Cupp, they dipp in our dish, they sitt by our fire, We find them in our Dy-fatt, Wash-bowle and Powdring tubb, they share with the Butler in his Box, They have marked and sealed us from head to foote. Mr Speaker, they will not bate us a pynne, We may not buy our owne Cloathes, without theire Broacage, These are the Leeches that have sucked the Comon wealth soe hard, that it is almost become Hecti-call.

John Culpeper, Sheffield University Library, Hartlib Papers, 55/5/1a–4b.

Document 9

The weakness of the subsidy in our period was under-valuation. This was often justified with reference to the poverty of the country, as in this extract from a parliamentary debate in 1593. Thorough-going reform would have required the imposition of strict valuation, but the crown was wary of such innovation. One of the central problems faced by government in seeking to tax was the lack of information. Taxpayers were reluctant to yield up the information for fear that it would be used for other purposes, too. Other issues were also raised in this debate such as the abuse of the exemptions of the cinque ports from payment and way in which richer tax payers were able to evade payment more easily than their poor neighbours.

> Sir *Henry Knivet* affirmed the poverty of our Country ... He made these two Motions; First that the Queen should be helped by a survey taken of all mens Lands and Goods in *England*, and so much to be yearly levyed as to serve the Queen to maintain Wars, the proportion being set a hundred thousand pound yearly; And secondly, if this were misliked, every man upon his word and power to deliver what were the profits of his Lands and worth of his goods, and so a proportion to be had accordingly ...

> Sir *Thomas Heneage* her Majesties Vice-Chamberlan ... advised that the wonted course should be followed. For he heard her Majesty speak of it, that she loved not such fineness of device and novel inventions, but liked rather to have the antient usages offered. It is best so to have it paid as it hath been heretofore...

> Sir *Francis Bacon* ... The *dangers* [of granting three subsidies to be

collected in in less than six years] are these. We shall first breed discontentment in paying these Subsidies, and in the Cause endanger her Majesty's safety, which must consist more in the love of the people than in their wealth ... thus we run into a double peril. In putting two payments into one, we make a double subsidy ... The second is this, that this being granted in this sort, Princes hereafter will look for the like; So we shall put an evil precedent upon our selves, and our Posterity. And in Histories it is to be observed, that of all Nations the English are not to be subject, base or Taxable...

[Another member said] I could very well agree to the Subsidies if they were not prejudicial to the Subject in other services. For Subsidies be in the valuation of every mans Lands and Goods by Records called the Queens Books, and according to mens valuation of Subsidies, are they at all other charges, as to the Wars and in time of Muster with Horse and Armour; and this charge maketh men so unwilling to be raised in the Subsidy; but if these Subsidies brought in no other charge with them, they would be yielded willingly. But the tail and appendage of it being so great, and higher than the Subsidy itself, is the reason that men are so unwilling to yield it. Wherefore if a greater Tax or Assessment than heretofore be desired, I would with a Proviso to be added in the Statute, That by this Subsidy no man should be raised as to the defray of other charges above the rate they were put to before.

Speeches in the House of Commons, 1593, D'Ewes, *Journals of the parliaments of Elizabeth*, pp. 491–4.

Document 10

Those being solicited for loans in the late 1590s were clearly expected to require a considerable degree of encouragement. The privy council wrote to the lord lieutenant of Norfolk and Suffolk on 18 February 1589, instructing him to activate the loan. One of the inducements that the privy council thought could be used to encourage payment draws on the fears expressed by the unnamed speaker in document 9 that being raised in the subsidy book might provide the basis for other payments, too. This was not the first resort, however. The deputy lieutenants who were to call justices 'meet for their credytte and good disposition towardes this service' before them. The justices were to be responsible for delivering the privy seals demanding particular sums to the individuals named. Initially they were to call these individuals before them in order to persuade them to pay willingly. However, if they found

> anie of the parties to whome the privie seales are directed unwilling
> & consequently refusinge to yealde to the soomes required, then
> shall thei be by your Lordship directed to take bondes of them to
> appeare before your deputie lieftenantes, to whome upon their
> apperaunce made accordingly, the said deputies are to be directed
> by your Lordship that, using the like gentle persuasions to induce
> them to yealde thereunto, in case thei shall find them to persist in
> their refusall then to let them understand that it is determyned that
> inquiry shalbe made by comission & by jurie of the true valew of
> their landes & goodes and thereof reterne shalbe made both to the
> Privie Councell and also into the Excheker to remayne ther of
> recorde, by which in tyme to come Her Majestie maie justly cause
> them to be rated both for subsidies & all other ordinary charges for
> musters & otherwise levies of men for service of the realme not by
> such lowe & favorable rates as now are accustomed.

Smith and Baker, *Papers of Nathaniel Bacon*, III, pp. 80–1. See also the later letter in the light of continued reluctance, pp. 88–9 (this is referred to above, p. 86).

Document 11

The requirement that local officeholders assess their neighbours in order to provide the basis for taxation tested the relationship between unpaid officeholders and the crown. Here they faced conflicting loyalties in a particularly acute form. In this extract a former subsidy commissioner, William Tooker, complains about the conduct of his erstwhile colleagues. He distinguishes between commmissioners 'who plainly go to work and walk in sincerity with observation of the law and a good conscience' and those 'who to gather applause of their own friends and the common people affect popularity in all their actions'. This popularity is not proper: 'to talk popularly or pleasingly or to smooth them or to be an humourist of the people, is a vain popularity'. This reveals the potential uses of tax commissions to local people but may not be an accurate account of the commissions on which Tooker had served. It also reveals the pressure that could be applied to tax commissioners who stepped out of line, by violent words or

through the pursuit of grudges by other means. Tax collectors
from outside the locality were less liable to these forms of pressure. According to Tooker the ideal commissioners were

> men endued with a reverend fear of GOD, unpartiall of disposition,
> lovers of the prince, lovers of their country, devoid of all faction,
> truly understandinge th' estate of the commonwealth, wherein they
> breath & live, such as have skil & good will to render to every man
> his due, tribute to whom tribute belongeth, custome to whom cus-
> tome, feare to whom fear and honour to whom honour appertaineth
> … [In practice, however] it is to bee feared some of those who are
> busied in this commission that they know to much, others to litle
> belonginge to the service, some sitte for a shew or ostentation, some
> for protection of their frendes, others utterly remiss and slacke,
> some other againe distast the service which their fellow commis-
> sioners undergo by reason of some peccant or malignant humour of
> popularitie or partialitie, last of all some post and hast away the ser-
> vice thrustinge all uppon one day whereas the businesse requireth
> a longer session & more considerate valuation of the parties pre-
> sented … Many other imperfections there are besides, which
> springe and flow from the erroneous mistakinge, or the malitious
> and crafty operation of the subsidys assessors … by reason of their
> partialitie and favour foster and cherish this inbred inequity and
> sinister opinion …
> To raise any man rich or potent whosoever, is not only a matter of
> unkindnesse but action of injurie and revengeable injury also:
> which I can truly speake of a sensible feelinge, partly by challenge
> of wordes offered unto mee and partly by collaterall and indirect
> practises against mee only for this and no other cause then of protes-
> tation of my zeale for his Majesty's service.

William Tooker, 'A discourse touching the diminution of the subsidy and how it may be simply raised', British Library, Harleian
MSS 188, ff. 4r, 5v–6r, 15r, 17r–17v.

Document 12

With the complicity of local commissioners the subsidy was prey
to very successful evasion as the following document reveals. It is
an estimate of the potential of individuals to lend to the king in
1621. The comparison between this potential and the subsidy
valuations is startling.

John Moore a mercer in very great Tradinge, in lands 120^{li} per annum & still purchaseth and buildethe muche [paid subsidy on £3 lands]

William Rowse bruer: geven over the use therof a hundred pounds per annum in lands & besides lately purchased more lands to the value of 300^{li} Riche besides, keepeth no howse but one childe & he richely married [paid subsidy on £2 lands]

Thomas Weld an attorney at the Common lawe: in great practise: 400^{li} a yere in lands purchased: 300^{li} a yere in lands by his wyfe at this instaunt offerethe 1800^{li} for an other purchase & lyvethe at a meane Rate: he may well lend above 100^{li} yett hee is sett downe butt at a hundred [paid subsidy on £6 lands]

Thomas Hobbs yeoman, a hundred pounds p^r ann: in lands, riche in money, gathereth money very much, never a childe and liveth at a meane Rate [paid subsidy on £5 lands]

George ffynderne yeoman, about a hundred pounds a yere in lands, an usurer, & lyveth at a meane rate and gathereth much wealth [paid subsidy on £2 lands]

Edward Colman yeoman, a hundred in lands p^r ann: Riche besides & butt one childe [paid subsidy on £3 lands]

W. Hudson, 'Assessment of the hundred of Forehoe, Norfolk, in 1621: a sidelight on the difficulties of national taxation', *Norfolk Archaeology*, XXI, 1923, pp. 285–309; pp. 287, 290, 291, 292, 293.

Document 13

Given the difficulty of securing compliance in rating taxes, the imposition of quotas was very tempting but an almost universal complaint was that quotas were unfair. However, in the absence of information, an absence which had in a sense led to the adoption of quotas, it was very difficult to gauge the accuracy of these pleas (see pp. 113–14). After the restoration, quota taxation had bad political connotations, too, and there was consistent debate about the virtues of quotas (assessments) as against assessed taxes (subsidies) as means of raising direct taxation.

[The] monthly assessment, being nothing but a military contribution taken up in the civil war, and proportion to the condition of the kingdom, as it then stood forty years ago; the inequality is so exorbitant, both between county and county, division and division, parish and parish, and impossible to be rectified without a punctual survey of the whole, and lying wholly upon the landlord ... wherein the dignified clergy pay not one groat, nor money nor personal estate come into the aid; and which lies so heavy upon the nobility and gentry above all others, to the weakening and diminishing their estates, who are the chief suport of the monarchy; I take it to be the most impolitic and unreasonable method of raising great sums by, that ever was introduced in any nation and impossible to be long borne and continued.

He went on to consider the subsidy as an alternative, hoping that its shortcomings could be overcome by greater responsibility on the part of commissioners. Marquis of Halifax, *An Essay upon taxes, calculated for the present juncture of affairs in England*, 1693, reprinted in *A Collection of source and valuable tracts ... of the late Lord Somers*, 13 vols., London, 1809–15, XI, 73–81; pp. 75–6, 79–80.

Document 14

In 1642, the adoption of quota taxation in the form of the £400,000 subsidy caused immediate complaint in Cheshire about the distribution of the burden. The inhabitants of Broxton complained that their share of the quota was unfair.

> our township (Compared with others) is infinitely overpressed in so much that within a small sum we pay after the rate of seven mizes (besides our personal estates) whereas we are certainly assured some other towns pay but after three or three and a half at furthest; and besides it is contrary to the usual course of all taxes imposed heretofore upon the country and to some hundreds at this time to our knowledge. We have never hitherto been unwilling to pay what hath been imposed upon us nor deny this according to the mize but as being fearful of future inconveniences.

Cheshire Sheaf, 3rd series, X, 1913, p. 79. For the 'mize' see M. J. Braddick, *Parliamentary taxation in seventeenth-century England. Local administration and response*, Royal Historical Society Studies in History, 70, Woodbridge, 1994, pp. 46, 147–8.

Document 15

Ship money is noted for many varieties of reaction. As was the case for many exactions covered in this book, legal obstruction was one of the options open to disgruntled payers. It is very difficult to interpret such evidence, however. Was the reluctant tax payer tightfisted, genuinely unfairly treated or opposed to the tax on principle? In this case William Cox, former sheriff of Somerset, wrote to Lord Cottington explaining the difficulties of collecting ship money in the county. Among the problems faced were the attitude and example of William Strode, who later claimed to have been opposed only to the details of the rating.

> There is one man in Somersetshire that much retards the service, and that is William Strode, the merchant, who having been distrained by one of his cows for five marks refused to pay, but suffered the constable to sell the cow, who tendering the overplus [i.e. the money raised by the sale beyond what was needed to cover the tax due and the legal costs], Strode refused it, and since hearing where his cow was, fetched her away by replevin, and sues the constable for taking the cow. By his example one Stradling and others have taken the boldness to do the like, by reason whereof the constable will do nothing in the service, unless his Lordship be pleased that exemplary punishment be inflicted upon these malevolent people.

Replevin was a legal writ by which distrained goods could be recovered on pledge that the issue would be tested at law. J. Bruce (ed.), *Calendar of state papers, domestic series, 1636–7*, London, 1867, p. 205. For his later defence of his actions *ibid.*, p. 401. This and similar cases are discussed by Kevin Sharpe in *The personal rule of Charles I*, New Haven and London, 1992, pp. 717–19.

Document 16

Distraint was often the moment when opposition to taxation was expressed most forcefully (pp. 180–1). In the following example the resistance to the tax was more complicated than this account might suggest: it followed a lengthy dispute in which the mayor had been involved (see pp. 113–14). We should be wary of assuming that such resistance is 'apolitical' or simply recalcitrant.

> [Thomas Broster] stood in his entry att his doore and denyed [the constables and collectors] entrance into his said house to distraine, and said hee would dye upon the clodd and hee would kill or bee killed before any mann should distraine upon his goods for the said

assessment. And repeated the same words with great earnestnes and vehemency of spirit. [He was also reported to have said] Let Mr Maior come and distraine.

Chester City Record Office, Mayor's Files 90/83. Letter dated 12 April 1672.

Document 17

John Milward, speaking in the Commons on the proposal to raise £1,800,000 by a land rate, argued that this was preferable to a general excise (for the general excise see pp. 148–9, documents 23–4). He went on to note the advantages of land rates: the certainty of the yield meant that parliament knew what it was giving and the king knew what he was being given; and that it was collected by neighbours who were neither 'troublesome' to the tax payer nor a cost to the king. This extract details objections to which he could find no easy reply.

> The first, Sir, is the inequality of the distribution in the several counties where some county shall pay three times, nay may I say not six times as much as other counties do. [His own county was one such and people there were well aware of this and would have given him an ill welcome if he returned having laid more inequality on them.]
>
> Another objection is what I have never heard answered – that our lands being already so much fallen in their value through the great scarcity of money the cheapness of all commodities and the present payment and burden that lieth upon them ...
>
> Another objection, which likewise I never yet heard answered and which is beyond all with me. That it will not do the work, that it will not be a sufficient foundation of credit for the raising of the present money for the setting forth of the fleet next spring [because of the pressure of time]

He goes on to recommend selling the hearth tax which will raise immediate cash. C. Robbins (ed.), *The diary of John Milward, Esq., 1666–8*, Cambridge, 1938, pp. 310–12.

Document 18

In many cases the crown was anxious to appoint people to assess and collect taxes who had good local connections, as in this case in the customs administration (see pp. 174–6).

> John Taylor, Mayor, and five Aldermen of Gloucester, to Lord
> Burghley. Renard Delabere, comptroller of the port there, is willing
> to yield up his office to Thos. Walkely, a well-disposed and able
> man, born there, and of good parentage, who has always resided
> there and has promised to continue to do so, and to exercise the
> office to the good liking of the magistrates. Request his appoint-
> ment, and an order for his residence and due service there, as Her
> Majesty has hitherto been much deceived, and the city and the
> country much abused, by substitutes and deputies in the Custom-
> house.

M. A. Everett Green (ed.), *Calendar of state papers, domestic series,
1591–4*, London, 1867, 18 November 1593, p. 387.

Document 19

On the other hand, these connections might lead to corruption.
There were frequent complaints about partiality in the customs
administration (see pp. 160–2).

> [As] in al other Duties ... as namely those upon lands & goods ...
> the Assesse once agreed upon, by competent authoritie; doth intitle
> and satisfie the *Prince*, binde and acquite the *Subject*, direct and war-
> rant the *Collector*, and so fulfils the Lawe by giving every one his
> right, so in these duties upon *Merchandise* both inward and out-
> ward, the Assesse or Rate of things once digested, is or ought to be
> a rule generall and inviolable; the *Equitie* whereof, consisting in the
> *Certentie* and *Indifferencie* of Assessment, according to a reasonable
> valuation of things in use, and so expressely set downe ...
>   But by reason of some uneven cariage in the MATTER and present
> FORME; the PERSONS aforesaid in their severall degrees and places,
> have their *Offences, Griefes* and *Complaints* ... First the PRINCE, is two
> waies highly displeased, namely either in that her Duties are by the
> *Merchants* defrauded, or by the collectors ill aunswered into the
> Exchequer: or in that they seeme not so well husbanded for her, as
> private Persons by Leases doe make them for themselves.

Thomas Milles, *The Custumers apology*, 1599 edition, B3b–B4a.

Document 20

Customs officials were also frequently suspected of peculation and of enriching themselves at the expense of the public (see pp. 56–9). Here the merchant strangers of London complain that the customs officials there 'serve not the Queen truly but convert much thereof to their own private lucre'. Contrary to statute, they are active traders themselves and

> If any merchant stranger or other bring any wares of commodity or profit, when they come to the customers to make their entry, then immediately their factors shall have knowledge of such wares before they shall make their entry, and if they will not sell it to their factors they shall be searched.' Bribes and rewards given them must needs be very great. 'It is manifest to all men that not only the customer after he is in office is soon a great rich man, although he came bare to it, but also his clerk that keepeth the custom house. Some there be that be well known that at their coming into office to be the customer's clerk were not able to have (your honours not offended) so much as a pair of hosen to their loins, and within 11 or 12 years worth thousands.'

The solution, they suggested, lay in farming the customs. They also suggested that the rates be publicly displayed. Petition to the Privy Council, December 1558, *Historical Manuscripts Commission, Calendar of the manuscripts of the … marquis of Salisbury*, London, 1883, I, p. 148.

Document 21

The constitutional status of the various customs duties was ambiguous and the legality of particular kinds of duty questionable. At some points the debate about these issues was raised to that of fundamental principle. Here, it is argued that the impositions lie within the absolute prerogative because they relate to the king's power to regulate trade. The counter-case was that they were a matter of ordinary prerogative, regulated by common law, because they touched upon the property rights of the subject (see pp. 133–7).

> To the King is committed the government of the realm and his people; and Bracton saith that for his discharge of his office God has given to him power, the act of government and the power to govern. The King's power is double, ordinary and absolute, and they have several laws and ends. That of the ordinary is for the profit of particular subjects, for the execution of civil justice, the determining of *meum*; and this is exercised by equity and justice in ordinary courts,

and by the Civilians is nominated *jus privatum*, and with us Common law: and these laws cannot be changed without Parliament, and although that their form and course may be changed and interrupted, yet they can never be changed in substance. The absolute power of the King is not that which is converted or executed to private use, to the benefit of any particular person, but is only that which is applied to the general benefit of the people and is *salus populi*; as the people is the body and the King the head; and this power is [not] guided by the rules which direct only at the Common Law, and is most properly named policy and government; and as the constitution of this body varieth with the time, so varieth this absolute law according to the wisdom of the King for the common good; and these being general rules and true as they are, all things done within these rules are lawful. The matter in question [the legality of the impositions] is material matter of State, and ought to be ruled by the rules of policy; and if it be so, the King hath done well to execute his extraordinary power. All customs, be they old or new, are no other but the effects and issues of trade and commerce with foreign nations; but all commerce and affairs with foreigners, all wars and peace, all acceptance and admitting for current, foreign coin, all parties and treaties whatsoever, are made by the absolute power of the King; and he who hath power of causes hath power also of effects. No exportation or importation can be but at the King's ports, they are the gates of the King, and he hath absolute power by them to include or exclude whom he shall please; and ports to merchants are their harbours and repose, and for their better security he is compelled to provide bulwarks and fortresses, and to maintain for the collection of his customs and duties collectors and customers; and for that charge it is reason that he should have this benefit. He is also to defend the merchants from pirates at sea in their passage. Also by the power of the King they are to be relieved if they are oppressed by foreign princes.

Bate's case, 1606, J. P. Kenyon, *The Stuart constitution*, Cambridge, 1966, pp. 62–3.

Document 22

Tonnage and poundage was raised, to an extent, by virtue of parliamentary grant. However, it was successfully raised by authority of the council from 1628 onwards, and the council claimed that the reality of parliamentary control was very limited (see pp. 52–3).

Selected documents

fynding that it hath beene constantly contynewed for many ages and is now a principall parte of the revenew of the Crowne and is of necessity soe to bee contynewed for the supportacion thereof, which in this two last Parliaments hath beene thought upon but could not bee there settled by authority of Parliament, as from tyme to tyme by many ages and descentes past it hath beene by reason of the dissolucion of those Parliaments before those thinges which weare theare treated of could be perfected; itt is therefore ordered ... for the reasons aforesaid and for that it was intended to have beene confirmed by Parliament, as it hath beene in all ages ever since the tyme of King Henry the Sixt, that all those duties upon goodes and merchaundize called by the severall names of customes, subsidy and impostes shalbe leavyed, collected and received for his Majestie's use in such manner and forme as the same were levied, collected and received at the tyme of the decease of his late Majestie King James ... [authority to do so to rest on the Great Seal] untill by Parliament as in former tymes it may receive an absolute setling ... if any person shall refuse or neglect to pay theise duties to his Majestie's farmors ... [the privy council, lord treasurer or chancellor of the exchequer] for the tyme being by the authoritie of this Board shall comitt all such persons to prison who shall disobey this order, there to contynew untill they shall conforme and submitt themselves unto due obedience

Acts of the privy council of England, June–December 1626, London, 1938, 8 July 1626, pp. 63–4.

Document 23

Fears were constantly expressed about the dangers to parliamentary and individual liberty posed by the raising of a general excise (see pp. 148–9, documents 17, 37). John Milward, speaking in response to the proposal that £1,800,000 should be raised by a general excise, admitted that the very term excise was 'ungrateful' to him. He pointed out, though, that monthly assessments had overcome a similar prejudice since they had been originally laid by the commonwealth authorities. Now they were known as the royal aid and further supply, however, such objections had disappeared. He went on to enumerate more serious objections. The language that he uses is reminiscent of that used of monopolists (documents 7–8; see also document 25).

First, Sir, the excessive expense that his Majesty and the whole realm must be put to in the maintenance of such a number of officers ... which will eat up a great part of what must be levied upon the people, who will soon become as so many vermin and caterpillars to devour us who will feed themselves with what should go into the mouths of the people and cloth themselves with what should go on to the people's backs, and who will enrich themselves at the cost of the whole kingdom.

Another thing that sticks with me is that when they are once vested in their offices, well fixed and find themselves warm in their places that through the countenance and encouragement that they must and will receive ... they will become so insolent and oppressive ... that the spirits of the English nation will not bear it with patience so as we shall soon fall into disorders, distempers and tumults, which cannot but be very dangerous in this conjuncture ...

Another thing is this, Sir. That though we may quickly resolve to set up such an excise ... yet if it be once up it will not be brought so safely down again.

Robbins, *Diary of John Milward*, pp. 308–10.

Document 24

Many of these fears were echoed by the marquis of Halifax when the suggestion recurred in the 1690s.

A general excise puts an end to theuse of parliaments, and quite changes the present condition of the government; for having already given duties in all foreign commodities, should they admit of this upon native, there were no more to be given, nor could it be carried on without a military power to second it, and might possibly hazard the government itself, if the people should not swallow it; and if once got up, will never be laid down.

Halifax, *Essay upon taxes*, pp. 77–8.

Document 25

Excise officers more generally were accused of personal profit at the expense of the public (see document 23). In this early attack on the new tax and its officers the language is reminiscent of that used of monopolists (see documents 7–8). The author earlier suggests that the governors responsible for imposing excises were even more worthy of censure.

O what Malignant ill-affected persons, what enemies, Pests, Vipers,

Locusts, and Caterpillars to the Kingdome and Nation are all those, who impose, inforce, collect and continue such unjust, illegall, condemned, disclaimed Excizes on them, contrary to the printed Declaration, the forementioned judgements against them in Parliament, and this Declaration of both Houses of Parliament ...

What infinite intolerable oppressions, corruptions, abuses, are daily exercised by viperous Excizers, the Pollers and Caterpillers of the Nation in all places, would require a large volum to display them, and are so well known to most, that it would be expence of paper to record them, which have exasperated the people in some places to oppose and beat some, and to cut off the ears of others of them, to stone and knock out the brains, and geld and cut out the stones of others of them, that they might have none of this Generation of Vipers, herafter to infest them.

The judiciall arraignment ... of the ... Dutch devil excize, 1653, British Library, Thomason Tracts, E.699 (17). I have found no reference in official records to confirm that this violence had taken place. The symbolism of the castration is interesting. For comparison see H. Kamen, *The iron century. Social change in Europe 1550–1660*, London, 1976 edition, p. 419.

Document 26

The pressure brought to bear on excise officers was frequently more direct than that experienced by subsidy commissioners such as Tooker (see document 11), in some cases it took the form of forceful demonstration and riot. In these instances the attitude of local authorities was often crucial, as in the case of the riot reported here. As in other kinds of popular demonstration there was a complex symbolic language which suggests that these were not spontaneous and 'apolitical' outbursts. In this case we can note the use of drums and the fact that an excise man, probably collecting a duty on cattle among other things, was tied to the bull ring. The role of women in this dispute is also not untypical.

The excise sub-commissioner for Derby, John Flatchett, and his partner were obstructed in their duty by important local people. They visited Sir John Gell to ask for his assistance in collection, but he would not offer them protection, claiming that he could not protect himself. Nonetheless, the commissioners issued warrants to summon the inhabitants to pay the excise and collected the excise money for five or six days, without any problems until 23 May 1645, a market day. On that day

two women of the towne went up and downe the Towne beating drums and making proclamation ... that such of the towne as were not willing to pay Excise should Joyne with them and they wold beat the Commissioners out of Towne Whereupon [the excisemen] did adress themselves to ... Mr Luke Whittington [the mayor] ... and desired him that according to the duty of his place he wold take care to appease the tumult, he Answered them that they brought the trouble on themselves ... and told them that he used not to Act without the advise of others and therefore desired them to goe with him to the Recorder Mr Tho: Gell (being then Lt Col to the said Sir Jo. Gell) ... The maior and the said Recorder Lt Col Gell having privately spoken together, they told [the excisemen] they wold come to the maiors house, and send for two other Justices of the peace in the towne to meete them there and then they wold resolve what to doe ... [about an hour later the excisemen returned to find two other aldermen who they asked] to apease the tumult whereupon the said maior and the said Recorder Lt Col Gell answered that one of the women that did beat up the Drums was wife to a souldier and they durst not meddle with them for fear of putting the souldiers into a Mutinie. The mayor said he would not belive there were any such women beating drums but presently one of them did beat her drum upon the markett cross before the maiors window. Thereupon the maior went forth and told [the excisemen] that he wold use his endeavour to make them cease. Upon his speaking to the woman shee did give over at that tyme but when the major cam againe into his house he tolde [the excisemen] that he hoped they were quietted but that he promised the woman (which he hoped that the [excisemen] wold make good) that the Excise should not be putt in Execucion untill they had an answer of a letter that they had sent up to the Parliament.

[Since no punishment had been inflicted the excisemen decided to leave the matter as it was. About six weeks later, though, hearing that some of the London committee were coming to Derby, they thought they might get more assistance. So they began collecting again. For five or six days there was no problem. However, on 4 July, another market day] Edward Barrow a souldier of Sir Jo Gells Company of foote that had assisted our Officers 3 or 4 dayes in sending out warrants and taking distresses was Chayned to the bullring in the market place about 4 of the Clock in the morning till about 2 in the afternoone (& as the man himselfe said) he was fecthed [fetched ?] of the guard that morning for that business ...

The same day againe the women did beat up the Drum and made proclamation to the same purpose as before. Upon this [excisemen] went to Complaine to Col Sir Jo Gell and they acquainted him that it was the second time that drums had bin beaten up by the Women against the Parliaments Ordinance and Authoritie. We humblie desired him that ... he wold now afford us protection and assistance and that he wold either punish those women or secure theire persons untill the pleasure of the Parliament were knowne he refused either to punish or secure the Women but told us that he did not use to meddle with women unless they were handsom.

This persuaded them to go to the chief commissioners of the excise in London. Other local officers had abandoned their jobs subsequently. Derbyshire Record Office, D258 M/34/10 Chandros–Pole–Gell Papers, ff. 3–5, reproduced by permission of the County Archivist. I am grateful to Martyn Bennett for this reference.

Document 27

Relations between excise men and local officeholders were frequently difficult, and this may have lain behind the inaction of magistrates in the face of excise disorders (for similar tensions between officeholders and specialised revenue agents see pp. 174–6, documents 28–9, 32). Here the mayor and aldermen of Chester complain about the effect of the appointment of an exciseman unfit for the service by dint of his social status and character. They claimed that before and after his tenure of office the excise was collected without problems

but during his farm which continued about three yeares the inhabitantes were frequently troubled with his unreasonable & unlawfull demands whereof many complaints have bine made to the maiors & Justices whoe upon evidence and just grounds according to the laws relating to the Excise with all dew respect to his Majesty's service have had sometymes reason to give there judgement for severall of the plaintiffs whereupon hee hath unjustly & unworthyly asperned & given out unworthy speeches against the severall maiors & justices & slaighted their judgement & athority saing he would be heard elsewhere & he cared not a fart for them for which

224

hee hath bine indicted & fined, but his fine hath bine suspended to countenance his imployment.

They went on to claim that he had frequently been a witness in his own cause and had lied, escaping punishment because of the importance of the excise. In these and more general social terms he and his assistant were unworthy of public office. Chester City Record Office, Mayor's Files, 90/52.

Document 28

Sometimes this antipathy led to more active obstruction. This letter to justices of the peace in the West Riding in February 1663 followed a complaint from the excise farmers there about the attitude of the local magistracy. In particular by an order made in the quarter sessions relating to the duty and the officers was said to have hindered collection. The council was worried by this attitude partly because

The people you well know are usually averse from payement & will from the least shaddowe of countenance though perhapes not so intended take encouragement to grow refractory & much more if they shall apprehend themselves back't by persons of your quality & intereste & In authority wherein his Majesty hath been pleased to place you. [The council enclosed a copy of the offending order, inviting the justices of the peace to consider its implications for the revenue.] It is not intended hereby to give the least Countenance-either to the ffarmors or their Officers in any unwarrantable actings, but it is expected that those whom his Majesty hath been pleased to trust with the Execution of the Laws should in all just cases afford them that Assistance which the Lawe allowes. The denyall whereof, as it may perhapps disable the ffarmors to pay their Rent, which is not an unconsiderable one, soe will it unavoidably terminate in the disturbance of his Majesty's Revenewe As well in other partes as these. It was supposed That his Majesty's late Proclamacion would have prevented things of this Nature, but since it does not it gives his Majesty Just occasion to take notice of that disregard which is put upon it. This business therefore so nearly concerning his Majesty's Service wee doe in this especiall manner recommend it to your best Care & expecting your Speedy answer Wee bid you heartily ffarewell.

Public Record Office, Privy Council Registers, PC2/56 f. 293.

Document 29

When the hearth tax collection was taken out of the hands of local officeholders in the 1660s similar tensions arose. On 28 November 1666 the privy council wrote to two justices in the North Riding. The council had heard that the two justices, having heard that Richard Prickard was in the area collecting the hearth tax, had

> got the Country together in great multitudes, commanded the Constable to fetch the said collector before you and Ordered that if he would not come willingly to bring him by force though you knew the said Collector was then in the middest of his collection. And when the said collector having left all his Busines in Disorder appeared and shewed his Authority for receiving the said Duty, you and the said Mr Wharton denyed it, and in the face and hearing of all the People there, said the Collector was a Cheat and not fit to be trusted with the King's money, a perjured ffellow, for that he had in one House returned Two Chimneys where there was but one and that you wondred he could be so brazen facedly impudent to demand or receive the Countrys Money without Authority. And likewise in the presence of the People demanded Sureties to answer the Perjury at the Sessions at Richmond. Whereupon the rude multitude fell upon the said Collector with rayling & reviling Speeches and forced him to leave his Busines with the safety of his life.

Ibid., PC2/59, ff. 224–5. Crown copyright, reproduced with the permission of the Controller of Her Majesty's Stationery Office.

Document 30

One problem confronting government in securing information was resistance to the use of oaths, something that was manifest in reactions to a number of taxes (see pp. 149–51).

> [Another] grievance is by the frequent burthening of mens consciences, by enforcing of othes impossible to be taken … Neither is the rigour of these inforcements, any whit inferiour to that rack of good mens consciences (the Star Chamber, and high Commission Court) formerly so much condemned, and exclaimed against, as a marke of the highest tyrany; but as if their tyrannicall ambition disdained to come short of their Predecessors, they have so farre exceeded them, in this their oppressive Court, that they not only compell men to sweare against themselves, but also apprentice ser-

vants against their Masters, though absolutely contrary to their oaths, and covenants, which they make at their first entrance into servitude to them.

Excise anatomizd, and trade epitomizd ..., British Library, Thomason Tracts, E.999 (1).

Document 31

Dependence on local officeholders rather than professional tax collectors, and the reluctance to use oaths when assessing taxes, meant that government continued to face the prospect of declining yields. In September 1698 the treasury lords wrote to two justices of the peace in Essex reporting complaints

> that upon appeals made lately at Gosfeild on the Window Duties several persons were there discharged without oath, others were abated upon [ground of] being tenants or friends to some neighbouring gent[lemen] and others for reasons not allowed by the Act of Parliament and contrary to the practice of all Commissioners here [in London] and contrary to the opinion of the King's learned Counsel in several particulars. We hold ourselves obliged to take notice of your proceedings herein and desire you to revise your assessments and to set such rates on all persons concerned as are according to the Act and to the trust reposed in you.

W. A. Shaw (ed.), *Calendar of treasury books*, XIV, London, 1934, 15 September 1698, p. 116.

Document 32

The window tax does not seem to have provoked violent resistance very often. In this case the problem is related to the activities of an officer employed to try to check on the activities of local officeholders: a professional tax collector less indulgent of local reluctance to pay. The treasury lords wrote to the mayor of Newark, reporting the complaint of Thomas Rokeby, a window tax surveyor. He had

> endeavoured to make a survey of ... Newark ... but there met with such treatment and opposition as made it difficult if not impossible to perform the same; but that you had sent to him and promised and undertaken that he should meet with no disturbance in relation to

the said survey of the town; we did then forbear to take any notice to you of the tumultuous proceedings of some of the inhabitants. But it is represented to us that William Wynne, another of the said Surveyors endeavouring to make a survey of the town on Tuesday the 12th inst. [this month] the common people of the town got together in a tumultuous and disorderly manner and with stones, dirt and other things forct the said officer from his duty.

The response of the council reflected a suspicion that local officeholders had been insufficiently active in their support, and sought to galvanise them. W. A. Shaw (ed.), *Calendar of treasury books*, XIII, London, 1933, 25 October 1697, pp. 133–4.

Document 33

The marriage duty act and the land taxes of the 1690s were also vulnerable to local officeholders perhaps too sympathetic to the feelings of their neighbours. In August 1698 the treasury lords wrote to the receivers general in London, Westminster and Middlesex

great neglects have been in Receivers General in not examining the produce and duplicates of the Duties on Marriages &c. and in failing to attend the receipts of the same as directed by the Act for preventing frauds in the Duties on Marriages &c. and on Houses; and that thereby the amount of said Duties has fallen considerably short of what might be reasonably expected. We strictly require you to observe the provisions of said Act and to pay in forthwith all your receipts.

In May 1696 they had written to commissioners for assessments in Lincolnshire complaining

that, contrary to the trust reposed in you, you have given directions to the assessors to abate a fourth part of what the said places paid to the like tax last year ... We recommend you to cause such amendments ... as may repair the loss which his Majesty may otherwise sustain by the said ill practices and prevent ill consequences [to yourselves] that may attend your neglect thereof.

Ibid., 26 August 1698, pp. 449–50, and W. A. Shaw (ed.), *Calendar of treasury books*, XI, London, 1933, 26 May 1696, p. 155.

Document 34

Poll taxes employed criteria for assessment which were, potentially, less easily subverted and administration was in the hands of the local officeholders. To this extent they had attractions to government. Sir William Petty (see above, p. 105) was in favour of this kind of taxation, although he recognised that in practice recent poll taxes had used 'wonderfully confused' administrative provisions. This was a disadvantage in itself but it had also made collection more difficult (see pp. 103–6). In this extract, however, he argued for the advantages of a more simple poll tax, with husbands responsible for their wives and children, parishes for their poor and masters for their apprentices.

> 5. The evil of this way is, that it is very unequal; men of unequal abilities, all paying alike, and those who have greatest charges of Children paying most; that is, that by how much the poorer they are, by so much the harder are they taxed.
> 6. The Conveniencies are; first, that it may be suddenly collected, and with small charge: Secondly, that the number of the people being alwayes known, it may be sufficiently computed with what the same will amount unto. Thirdly, It seems to be a spur unto all men, to set their children to some profitable employment upon their very first capacity, out of the proceed whereof, to pay each childe his own Poll-money.

A treatise of taxes and contributions, reprinted in Charles Henry Hull, *The economic writings of Sir William Petty*, New Jersey, 1986 edition, pp. 62–3.

Document 35

The regressiveness of the poll tax was not, usually, regarded as a fatal disadvantage of this form of taxation by contemporaries (see pp. 103–6, document 34). Here the marquis of Halifax considers it compensation for the weight of taxation on land.

> The poll-tax, as it now stands, is grievous to the meaner sort, as to their children, and deserves to be better considered; and though much exclaimed against, yet is an ancient way of taxing upon extraordinary occasions ... And though it be objected, that all noblemen and gentlemen pay alike, notwithstanding the difference of estates, yet, considering that the lands are all under a double tax, and that

they multiply that tax according to the horses that they find in the militia, I think they are sufficiently charged, and much more equal than in former methods; and that this tax is not wholly to be laid aside, but may be easily rectified and made useful.

Halifax, *Essay upon taxes*, p. 76.

Document 36

Later seventeenth century debate about taxation was often more sophisticated than in the earlier period. Elaborate arguments were made about the fundamental economic principles of taxation and about the virtues of different forms of taxation in administrative, financial and political terms (see pp. 119–28). What is often striking is the extent to which the necessity of heavy taxation was accepted.

Here Petty considers how to make taxation more politically acceptable. In other passages he argues that there are compensations to the economy of government spending, by increasing demand for particular commodities or services. Payments to favourites or for extravagant displays find their way back into useful consumption. He also suggests that accepting taxes in kind would reduce frictions, because payers would not have to sell goods at inappropriate times merely to meet tax demands. It would also ease currency problems and save the king buying goods at moments when the market might not be right. The treatise is, therefore, an interesting mixture of economic and political discussion. For example, he also argues that we can all hope to be a royal favourite some day!

> That the people think, the Sovereign askes more than he needs. To which we answer, 1. That if the Sovereign were sure to have what he wanted in due time, it were his own great dammage to draw away the money out of his Subjects hands, who by trade increase it, and to hoard it up in his own Coffers, where 'tis of no use even to himself, but lyable to be begged or vainly expended.
>
> ... Let the Tax be never so great, if it be proportionable unto all, then no man suffers the loss of any Riches by it. For men ... if the Estates of them all were either halfed or doubled, would in both cases remain equally rich ...
>
> ... that which angers men most, is to be taxed above their Neighbours ...

... All these imaginations (whereunto the vulgar heads are subject) do cause a backwardness to pay, and that necessitates the Prince to severity. Now this lighting upon some poor, though stubborn, stiffnecked Refuser, charged with Wife and Children, gives the credulous great occasion to complain of Oppression, and breeds ill blood as to all other matters; feeding the ill humours already in being.

... Ignorance of the Number, Trade, and Wealth of the people, is often the reason why the said people are needlessly troubled ...

... Besides for not knowing the Wealth of the people, the Prince knows not what they can bear; and for not knowing the Trade, he can make no Judgement of the proper season when to demand his Exhibitions.

... Obscurities and doubts, about the right of imposing, hath been the cause of great and ugly Reluctancies in the people, and of Involuntary Severities in the Prince; an eminent Example whereof was the Ship-money, no small cause of twenty years calamity to the whole Kingdom ...

... Taxes if they be presently expended upon our own Domestick Commodities, seem to me, to do little harm to the whole Body of the people, onely they work a change in the Riches and Fortunes of particular men; and particularly by transferring the same from the Landed and Lazy, to the Crafty and Industrious.

Treatise of taxes and contributions, pp. 32–7.

Document 37

The marquis of Halifax tried to outline general principles by which to distinguish the virtues of various forms of taxation. Here he is discussing the home excises and 'how far they are consistent or inconsistent with the government, ease, and liberty of the people' (for this debate see pp. 148–9, documents 17, 23–4). The following are the general rules governing their use.

First, They must not consist of things of common necessity or livelihood, but rather superfluity

Secondly, They must not burthen our native commodities and manufactures, materials or other things relating thereunto.

Thirdly, They have always avoided to impose upon things wherein the people had no benefit or advantage, but rather land, trade and other gainful professions.

Fourthly, They have always avoided new and foreign taxes ...

Fifthly, They have had always great regard to the condition of the several ranks of men among us, to support them in the condition they are in, and consequently to preserve the monarchy.

Sixthly, To charge money and personal estate not employed in trade, double to land and trade.

Seventhly, Above all, that equality should be observed in the imposition.

Halifax, *Essay upon taxes*, p. 74.

Document 38

The impact of taxation on the distribution of wealth, and hence on the social order, was of concern to both Petty and the marquis of Halifax in considering rival forms of taxation (on this issue see pp. 124–8, documents 36–7). According to Halifax, the nobility, the natural basis of monarchy, should be protected.

> ... As to the rich usurer, or tradesman, whose family and expence was small, and gains great, and escaped most burthens, as not being so visible as lands; and the considerable free-holder, whose estate is generally held in his own hands, and managed by himself, and consequently was less discovered than the nobleman and gentleman's that were rented ... and none of all these being obliged by their quality or custom to any port, and are the proper basis of a democracy, or commonwealth; these were generally rated more strictly without any allowance, to prevent the increase of their number and growth

Ibid., pp. 74–5.

Document 39

These more sophisticated arguments appear alongside more familiar ones as the following extract demonstrates. In a sense, the constraints on the freedom of action of the government were not altogether different in the later seventeenth century. Halifax considers here the quantity of taxation, the means of collection and the fairness of the burden.

First, That it did not exceed, by any means the common necessity ...

And 'tis observable, that all those princes who have not stretched prerogative to levy taxes not warrantable by law, or to levy them with too much rigour and exactness, or to impoverish the people, and have expressed a care and regard to their ease, wealth, and welfare, have ever been the most fortunate, great, and prosperous ...

As to the manner of collection, they have taken great care that there should be as much ease, and as little charge to the king or people in collection as may be, by the multiplication of officers, penalties, or subjecting their houses or estates to the enquiries or informations of officers, &c.

As to the equality of imposition, this has been strictly observed, being always the same rate in the pound. Nevertheless, with such qualifications and exceptions, as made it rather a moral equality, than a mathematical one, having respect to the condition of the persons, as I have before shewed ...

Lastly, In all cases the king appointed commissioners generally of persons unconcerned in the places where they acted, and at his own charge, that it might be done with the more indifference and equality ... and once at least in every age ... the parliament had granted that the commissioners and assessors should be sworn, and have liberty to examine all persons ... upon oath, for the better discovery of their real and personal estates, that length of time might not produce too great an inequality, and that the aids might be improved in some proportion to the value of things.

Ibid., p. 75.

Bibliographical essay

The following is by no means comprehensive and works cited are those that provide a good starting point. There are further references in the notes above and many of the following offer valuable guides to particular parts of the historiography of public finances.

There is no overview of English public finances between 1558 and 1714, but there are some fine studies of particular periods. F. C. Dietz, *English public finance 1485–1641*, vol. II, *1558–1641*, London, 1964 is still a valuable introduction. There is a very illuminating discussion of public finances (and of other issues covered by this study) in W. R. Scott, *The constitution and finance of English, Scottish and Irish joint-stock companies to 1720*, 3 vols., Cambridge, 1910–12. Much light is thrown on early Stuart finances by R. Ashton, 'Deficit finance in the reign of James I', *Economic History Review*, 2nd series, X, 1957, pp. 15–29. M. P. Ashley, *Financial and commercial policy under the Cromwellian protectorate*, London, 1934, is the standard account of finances during the 1650s. C. D. Chandaman's magisterial study, *The English public revenue 1660–1688*, Oxford, 1975, contains important insights into the finances as a whole after the restoration. J. Brewer, *The sinews of power. War, money and the English state, 1688–1783*, London, 1989, brings together much technical material and elucidates the political significance of financial change. The account of these issues presented in this book is heavily influenced by J. A. Schumpeter, 'The crisis of the tax state', *International Economic Papers*, IV, 1954, pp. 5–38, and by a case study of Denmark in this period by E. L. Petersen: 'From domain state to tax state. Synthesis and interpretation', *Scandinavian Economic History Review*, XXIII, 1975, pp. 116–48. R. Bonney (ed.), *Economic systems and state finance*, Oxford, 1995, was, unfortunately, published after this book went to press. It contains much important comparative material covering Europe between the thirteenth and eighteenth centuries.

It is difficult to study the economics of public revenue raising before 1688 and the best studies of these issues cover the period after that date. The quantitative data that are available are authoritatively presented and analysed in P. K. O'Brien and P. A. Hunt, 'The rise of a fiscal state in England, 1485–1815', *Historical Research*, LXVI, 1993, pp. 129–76. For the later period the issues are admirably covered by D. W. Jones, *War and economy in the age of William III and Marlborough*, Oxford, 1988, and P. Mathias and P. K. O'Brien, 'Taxation in Britain and France, 1715–1810: a comparison of the social and economic incidence of taxes collected for the central governments', *Journal of European Economic History*, V, 1976, pp. 601–50 (see also the ensuing debate in VII, 1978, pp. 209–13).

Public borrowing is another topic well-served for particular periods but lacking a general survey. Elizabethan borrowing is covered by two articles by R. B. Outhwaite: 'The trials of foreign borrowing: the English crown and the Antwerp money market in the mid-sixteenth century', *Economic History Review*, 2nd series, XIX, 1966, pp. 289–305 and 'Royal borrowing in the reign of Elizabeth I: the aftermath of Antwerp', *English Historical Review*, LXXXVI, 1971, pp. 251–263. The early Stuart period is well-served by two books by R. Ashton, *The crown and the money market 1603–1640*, Oxford, 1960 and *The city and the court 1603–1643*, Cambridge, 1979. For forced loans see G. L. Harriss, 'Aids, loans and benevolences', *Historical Journal*, VI, 1963, pp. 1–19. The peculiar circumstances and consequences of the 1626 loan are dealt with by R. Cust, *The forced loan and English politics 1626–8*, Oxford, 1987. Our understanding of the importance of changes in borrowing during the 1650s is being changed by the work of J. S. Wheeler, in particular 'English financial operations during the first Dutch war, 1652–54', *Journal of European Economic History*, XXIII, 1994, pp. 329–43, and 'Navy finance, 1649–1660', *Historical Journal* (forthcoming). Further developments during the 1660s have been explored by G. O. Nicholls. See, in particular, 'English government borrowing, 1660–1688', *Journal of British Studies*, X, 1971, pp. 83–104. The work of H. G. Roseveare in this area is very important. For a brief introduction see *The financial revolution 1660–1760*, Harlow, 1991, which also contains an excellent bibliography. Fundamental to the period after 1688 is P. G. M. Dickson, *The financial revolution in England: a study in the development of public credit 1688–1756*, London, 1967.

There are excellent accounts of most of the sources of revenue examined here. For the crown lands and forests see R. W. Hoyle (ed.), *The estates of the English crown 1558–1640*, Cambridge, 1992; P. A. J. Pettit, *The Royal forests of Northamptonshire. A study in their economy 1558–1714*, Northamptonshire Record Society, 23, for two years ending 1963, Gateshead, 1968; and G. Hammersley, 'The revival of the forest laws under Charles I', *History*, XLV, 1960, pp. 85–102. For fiscal feudalism and the rights on which it was based see J. M. W. Bean, *The decline of English feudalism 1215–1540*, Manchester, 1968; H. E. Bell, *An introduction to the history and records of the court of wards and liveries*, Cambridge, 1953; and J. Hurstfield, 'The profits of fiscal feudalism, 1541–1602', *Economic History Review*, 2nd series, VIII, 1955, pp. 53–61. Purveyance has been admirably covered by A. Woodworth, *Purveyance for the royal household in the reign of Queen Elizabeth*, Transactions of the American Philosophical Society, 35, Philadelphia, 1945 and G. E. Aylmer, 'The last years of purveyance 1610–1660', *Economic History Review*, 2nd series, X, 1957–8, pp. 81–93. For ship money we must await the publication of the findings of A. A. M. Gill, 'Ship money during the personal rule of Charles I: politics, ideology and the law 1634 to 1640', unpubl. PhD, Sheffield, 1990. In the meantime, an introduction is provided by M. D. Gordon, 'The collection of ship money in the reign of Charles I', *Transactions of the Royal Historical Society*, 3rd series, IV, 1910, pp. 141–162, while K. Sharpe, *The personal rule of Charles I*, New Haven and London, 1992, reviews the present state of play and also deals with other aspects of the finances of the 1630s including monopolies, distraint of knighthood and forest fines.

We lack a modern study of the customs although there are a number of valuable older works. H. Atton and H. H. Holland, *The King's customs*, 2 vols., London, 1908–10 is rather venerable but still useful. N. S. B. Gras, *The early English customs system. A documentary study of the institutional and economic history of the customs from the thirteenth to the sixteenth century*, Cambridge, Mass., 1918 and Dietz, *English public finance*, are also important for the earlier period. T. S. Willan (ed.), *A Tudor book of rates*, Manchester, 1962, deals with important issues. The mid seventeenth-century customs are discussed in Chandaman, *English public revenue*, and Ashley, *Financial and commmercial policy*. E. E. Hoon, *The organization of the English customs system 1696–1786*, New York, 1938, gives a good guide to the administration at the end of our period.

Parliamentary taxation has also been well-covered. Our understanding of Tudor taxation is dominated by the work of R. S. Schofield, in particular 'Parliamentary lay taxation 1485–1547', unpubl. PhD, Cambridge, 1963, and 'Taxation and the political limits of the Tudor state', in C. Cross, D. Loades and J. J. Scarisbrick (eds.), *Law and government under the Tudors*, Cambridge, 1988, pp. 227–55. M. J. Braddick, *Parliamentary taxation in seventeenth-century England. Local administration and response*, Royal Historical Society Studies in History, 70, Woodbridge, 1994, deals with the principal sources of taxation in the period 1590–1670. For the excise see also Chandaman, *English public revenue* and E. Hughes, *Studies in administration and finance 1558–1825 with special reference to the history of salt taxation in England*, Manchester, 1934. For the hearth tax during and after the 1660s, see also Chandaman, *English public revenue*, and

Bibliographical essay

N. Alldridge (ed.), *The hearth tax. Problems and possibilities*, Conference of teachers in regional and local history in tertiary education, London, 1983. L. M. Marshall, 'The levying of the hearth tax, 1662–1688', *English Historical Review*, LI, 1936, pp. 628–46 is also useful. There are valuable studies of the later seventeenth century, too. K. Schurer and T. Arkell (eds.), *Surveying the people. The interpretation and use of document sources for the study of population in the later seventeenth century*, Local Population studies supplement, Oxford, 1992, is a useful introduction. For the window and land taxes see W. R. Ward, 'The administration of the window and assessed taxes, 1696–1798', *English Historical Review*, LXVII, 1952, pp. 522–42; *idem, The English land tax in the eighteenth century*, Oxford, 1953, and C. Brooks, 'Public finance and political stability: the administration of the land tax, 1688–1720', *Historical Journal*, XVII, 1974, pp. 281–300. For the marriage duty act see also D. V. Glass, *London inhabitants within the walls 1695*, London Record Society Publications, II, 1966. Important for this but also suggestive of the possible significance of taxation in general is C. Brooks, 'Projecting, political arithmetic and the act of 1695', *English Historical Review*, XCVII, 1982, pp. 31–53.

Much of the local history of reactions to revenue raising has to be put together from these accounts. The kind of reactions examined in chapters 6 and 7 are often examined more explicitly. W. Kennedy, *English taxation 1640–1799. An essay on policy and opinion*, London, 1913, gives an interesting overview. J. V. Beckett, 'Land tax or excise: the levying of taxation in seventeenth- and eighteenth-century England', *English Historical Review*, C, 1985, pp. 285–308 and P. K. O'Brien, 'The political economy of British taxation, 1660–1815', *Economic History Review*, 2nd series, XLI, 1988, pp. 1–32, give stimulating accounts of parts of the period.

The controversy over the constitutional position of parliamentary taxation under the Tudors has not been summarised here for reasons of space. It can be followed, however, in G. R. Elton, 'Taxation for war and peace in early-Tudor England' in J. M. Winter (ed.), *War and economic development. Essays in memory of David John*, Cambridge, 1975, pp. 33–48; G. L. Harriss, 'Thomas Cromwell's "new principle" of taxation', *English Historical Review*, XCIII, 1978, pp. 721–38; J. D. Alsop, 'The theory and practice of Tudor taxation', *English Historical Review*, XCVII, 1982, pp. 1–30, and 'Innovation in Tudor taxation', *English Historical Review*, XCIX, 1984, pp. 83–93; and R. W. Hoyle, 'Crown, parliament and taxation in sixteenth-century England', *English Historical Review*, CIX, 1994, pp. 1174–96. There is a valuable series of articles by P. Croft on the politics of particular revenues in the early seventeenth century: 'Fresh light on Bate's case', *Historical Journal*, XXX, 1987, pp. 523–39; 'Wardship in the parliament of 1604', *Parliamentary History*, II, 1983, pp. 39–48; 'Parliament, purveyance and the city of London 1589–1608', *Parliamentary His-*

tory, IV, 1985, pp. 9–34; and 'Parliamentary preparations, September 1605: Robert Cecil, earl of Salisbury on free trade and monopolies', *Parliamentary History*, VI, 1987, pp. 127–32. See also G. D. G. Hall, 'Impositions and the courts 1554–1606', *Law Quarterly Review*, LXIX, 1953, pp. 200–18 and two articles by E. N. Lindquist: 'Supplement: The bills against purveyors', *Parliamentary History*, IV, 1985, pp. 35–43 and 'The king, the people and the House of Commons: the problem of early Jacobean purveyance', *Historical Journal*, XXXI, 1988, pp. 549–70. The political implications of reactions to many of these revenues, and of parliamentary taxation, are given some prominence in the works of C. Russell on early Stuart politics. See, in particular, 'Parliament and the king's finances' in C. Russell (ed.), *The origins of the English civil war*, London, 1973; *Parliaments and English Politics 1621–1629*, Oxford, 1979; and *The causes of the English civil war*, Oxford, 1990.

However, the constitutional importance of arguments about taxation in the earlier part of the period remains a bone of contention. For contrasting accounts see the discussion of the issues in J. P. Sommerville, *Politics and ideology in England 1603–1640*, Harlow, 1986 and G. Burgess, *The politics of the ancient constitution. An introduction to English political thought, 1603–1642*, Basingstoke and London, 1992. C. Holmes, 'Parliament, liberty, taxation, and property' in J. H. Hexter (ed.), *Parliament and liberty from the reign of Elizabeth to the English civil war*, Stanford, 1992, pp. 122–54, gives an admirable and subtle account. There is less controversy about the later part of the period. The key works here are Chandaman, *English public revenue*, Brewer, *Sinews of power* and two articles by E. A. Reitan: 'The civil list in eighteenth-century British politics: parliamentary supremacy versus the independence of the crown', *Historical Journal*, IX, 1966, pp. 318–37; and 'From revenue to civil list, 1689–1702: The revolution settlement and the "Mixed and Balanced" constitution', *Historical Journal*, XIII, 1970, pp. 571–88.

Index

239

Index

Norfolk and Suffolk, 86
hunters after concealed lands, 61,
125–6, 197
Hutton, Sir Richard, Justice, and
ship money, 141

impositions, 50, 53–4, 55, 79, 87–8,
133–7. *See also* Bate, John; customs
indemnity committee, 157
index vectigalium, 60, 124
indirect taxation: defined, 2–3; yield,
10–12, 28. *See also* excise; customs
Instrument of Government (1653),
27, 31, 124, 144–5
Ipswich, customs in, 161

Jacobites and smuggling, 162
justices of the peace, 80, 81, 87, 105,
174, 203–4, 210–11, 222, 224–6,
227. *See also* magistracy and tax
collection

Kent, assessment in, 96
King, Gregory, 125, 194
King's Bench, 138–9, 145, 167–8
Kirke, Robert, monopolist, 78
knighthood, distraint of, 15–16, 76,
87–8, 196–7
Knollys, Sir Francis, and
purveyance, 204

Lambert, John, 145
land tax, 97–9, 126, 149, 177, 186,
187, 197, 198, 216: administration,
98; yield, 98–9
Levant Company, 134
lieutenancy, 86–7, 210–11. *See also*
benevolences; forced loans
Lincolnshire: assessment in, 228;
fifteenth and tenth in, 92, 111–12,
156
Littleton, Sir Edward, and
Hampden's case, 142
Lloyd, Christopher, hearth tax
collector in Norfolk, 176
London, 190: customs in, 160–1,
217–8; excise in, 173; marriage
duty in, 175, 228; subsidy in, 94,
113, 165
magistracy and tax collection, 17,

96–7, 98, 100, 104, 118–19, 126,
168–9, 174–6, 222–8. *See also*
justices of the peace
magna carta, 73, 80
marriage duty, 101, 104–5, 125, 126,
149, 165, 175, 228: yield 105
Marshalsea prison, 134
Mayden Bradley, Wilts, fifteenth
and tenth in, 112
mercantilism, 122–3
Meynell, Francis, and government
finance, 107
Middlesex, fifteenth and tenth in,
112; marriage duty in, 228
Middleton, William, and marriage
duty in London, 175
military expenditure, 27–34, 87, 191.
See also army; navy
military surveys, 1522, 125
Milles, Thomas, author of *The
Custumers apology*, 217
Milward, John, MP, 147–9, 216,
220–1
Monmouthshire, excise in, 163, 173
monopolies, 14, 15–16, 53, 87–8,
206–8: parliamentary attacks on,
78–9, 206–9; yield of, 78
Montagu, Edward, Lord, and
distraint of knighthood, 76
Moulton, Lincolnshire, 92
musters, 210

national debt, 19, 42–5, 198
navy, 39, 190–1: cost of, 30–1
Newark, Nottinghamshire, 227–8
Newcastle, 190: host-men, 78
Nine Years War (1688–97), 30, 33,
149
Noell, Sir Martin, and government
finance, 37–8, 41, 63
Nominated assembly (1653), 145
Norfolk, 196, 198: assessment in, 96;
excise in, 170; fifteenth and tenth
in, 93, 112, 156; forced loan in, 86,
210–11; hearth tax in, 176;
purveyance in, 118, 206; subsidy
in, 94, 113, 212–13
Northamptonshire: distraint of
knighthood, 76; royal forests in,
71

242